국제토셀위원회

HIGH JUNIOR
JUNIOR
BASIC
STARTER
PRE-STARTER

KB056786

TOSEL

실전문제집 2

JUNIOR

최신 기출 경향반영 실전모의고사 수록
국제토셀위원회 공식교재

CONTENTS

Actual Test 1 page 12

Actual Test 2 page 36

Actual Test 3 page 60

Actual Test 4 page 84

Actual Test 5 page 108

Appendix (Vocabulary) page 132

OMR 카드

정답과 해설

About this book

토셀 최신 유형을 반영하여
실전 모의고사를 5회 실었습니다.
수험자들의 토셀 시험 대비 및
적응력 향상에 도움이 됩니다.

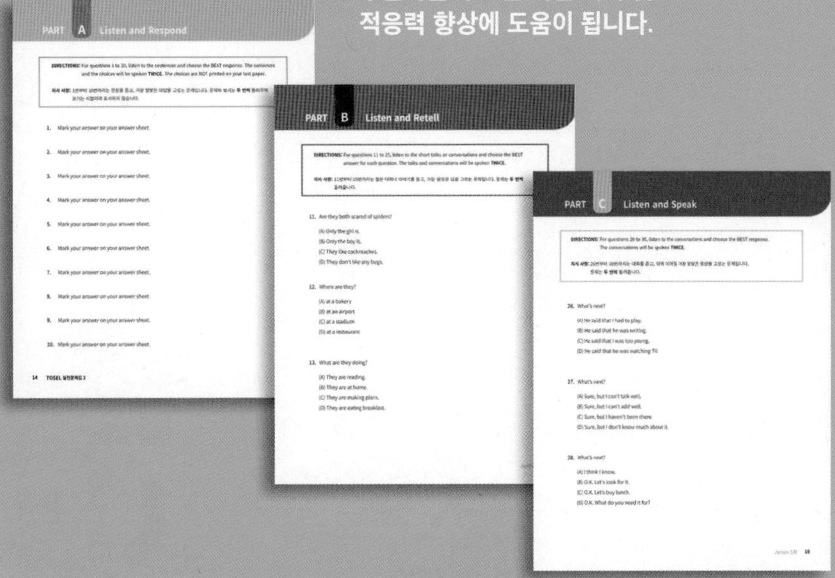

2 Appendix

필수 어휘를 포함해 모의고사
빈출 어휘 목록을 수록했습니다.
평소 어휘 정리뿐만 아니라
시험 직전 대비용으로 활용 가능합니다.

3 Answer

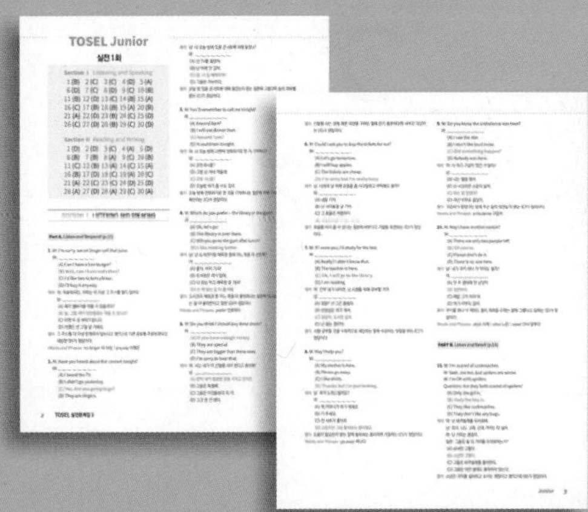

자세한 해설과 문제 풀이로
오답 확인 및 시험 대비를 위한 정리가 가능합니다.

1

영어를 시작하는 단계

2

영어의 밑바탕을 다지는 단계

3

영어의 도약단계

TOSEL

TOSEL
Cocoon

유치원생

TOSEL

TOSEL
Pre Starter

초등 1,2학년

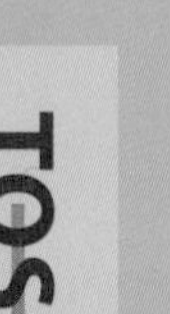

TOSEL

TOSEL
Starter

초등 3,4학년

TOSEL

TOSEL
Basic

초등 5,6학년

4

영어의 실전단계

TOSEL

TOSEL Junior

중학생

5

영어의 고급화 단계

TOSEL

TOSEL High Junior

고등학생

6

영어의 완성단계

TOSEL

TOSEL Advanced

대학생, 직장인

About TOSEL® — TOSEL에 대하여

TOSEL은 각급 학교 교과과정과 연령별 인지단계를 고려하여 단계별 난이도와 문항으로
영어 숙달 정도를 측정하는 영어 사용자 중심의 맞춤식 영어능력인증 시험제도입니다.
평가유형에 따른 개인별 장점과 단점을 파악하고, 개인별 영어학습 방향을 제시하는 성적분석자료를 제공하여
영어능력 종합검진 서비스를 제공함으로써 영어 사용자인 소비자와
영어능력 평가를 토대로 영어교육을 담당하는 교사 및 기관 인사관리자인 공급자를
모두 만족시키는 영어능력인증 평가입니다.

TOSEL은 인지적-학문적 언어 사용의 유창성 (Cognitive-Academic Language Proficiency, CALP)과
기본적-개인적 의사소통능력 (Basic Interpersonal Communication Skill, BICS)을
엄밀히 구분하여 수험자의 언어능력을 가장 친밀하게 평가하는 시험입니다.

대상	목적	용도
유아, 초, 중, 고등학생, 대학생 및 직장인 등 성인	한국인의 영어구사능력 증진과 비영어권 국가의 영어 사용자의 영어구사능력 증진	실질적인 영어구사능력 평가 + 입학전형 및 인재선발 등에 활용 및 직무역량별 인재 배치

연혁

2002.02 국제토셀위원회 창설 (수능출제위원역임 전국대학 영어전공교수진 중심)
2004.09 TOSEL 고려대학교 국제어학원 공동인증시험 실시
2006.04 EBS 한국교육방송공사 주관기관 참여
2006.05 민족사관고등학교 입학전형에 반영
2008.12 고려대학교 편입학시험 TOSEL 유형으로 대체
2009.01 서울시 공무원 근무평정에 TOSEL 점수 가산점 부여
2009.01 전국 대부분 외고, 자사고 입학전형에 TOSEL 반영
(한영외국어고등학교, 한일고등학교, 고양외국어고등학교, 과천외국어고등학교, 김포외국어고등학교,
명지외국어고등학교, 부산국제외국어고등학교, 부일외국어 고등학교, 성남외국어고등학교, 인천외국어고등학교,
전북외국어고등학교, 대전외국어고등학교, 청주외국어고등학교, 강원외국어고등학교, 전남외국어고등학교)
2009.12 청심국제중 • 고등학교 입학전형 TOSEL 반영
2009.12 한국외국어교육학회, 팬코리아영어교육학회, 한국음성학회, 한국응용언어학회 TOSEL 인증
2010.03 고려대학교, TOSEL 출제기관 및 공동 인증기관으로 참여
2010.07 경찰청 공무원 임용 TOSEL 성적 가산점 부여
2014.04 전국 200개 초등학교 단체 응시 실시
2017.03 중앙일보 주관기관 참여
2018.11 관공서, 대기업 등 100여 개 기관에서 TOSEL 반영
2019.06 미얀마 TOSEL 도입 발족식
베트남 TOSEL 도입 협약식
2019.11 고려대학교 편입학전형 반영
2020.06 국토교통부 국가자격시험 TOSEL 반영
2021.07 소방청 간부후보생 선발시험 TOSEL 반영
2021.11 고려대학교 공과대학 기계학습 • 빅데이터 연구원 AI 연구 협약
2022.05 AI 영어학습 플랫폼 TOSEL Lab 공개
2023.11 고려대학교 경영대학 전국 고등학생 대상 정기캠퍼스 투어 프로그램 후원기관 참여
2024.01 제1회 TOSEL VOCA 올림피아드 실시
2024.03 고려대학교 미래교육원 TOSEL 전문가과정 개설

About TOSEL®

TOSEL에 대하여

What's TOSEL?

"Test of Skills in the English Language"

TOSEL은 비영어권 국가의 영어 사용자를 대상으로 영어구사능력을 측정하여 그 결과를 공식 인증하는 영어능력인증 시험제도입니다.

영어 사용자 중심의 맞춤식 영어능력 인증 시험제도

맞춤식 평가

획일적인 평가에서 세분화된 평가로의 전환

TOSEL은 응시자의 연령별 인지단계에 따라 별도의 문항과 난이도를 적용하여 평가함으로써 평가의 목적과 용도에 적합한 평가 시스템을 구축하였습니다.

공정성과 신뢰성 확보

국제토셀위원회의 역할

TOSEL은 고려대학교가 출제 및 인증기관으로 참여하였고 대학입학수학능력시험 출제위원 교수들이 중심이 된 국제토셀위원회가 주관하여 사회적 공정성과 신뢰성을 확보한 평가 제도입니다.

수입대체 효과

외화유출 차단 및 국위선양

TOSEL은 해외시험응시로 인한 외화의 유출을 막는 수입대체의 효과를 기대할 수 있습니다. TOSEL의 문항과 시험제도는 비영어권 국가에 수출하여 국위선양에 기여하고 있습니다.

Why TOSEL® — 왜 TOSEL인가

01 학교 시험 폐지

일선 학교에서 중간, 기말고사 폐지로 인해 객관적인 영어 평가 제도의 부재가 우려됩니다. 그러나 전국단위로 연간 4번 시행되는 TOSEL 평가시험을 통해 학생들은 정확한 역량과 체계적인 학습방향을 꾸준히 진단받을 수 있습니다.

02 연령별/단계별 대비로 영어학습 점검

TOSEL은 응시자의 연령별 인지단계 및 영어 학습 단계에 따라 총 7단계로 구성되었습니다. 각 단계에 알맞은 문항유형과 난이도를 적용해 모든 연령 및 학습 과정에 맞추어 가장 효율적으로 영어실력을 평가할 수 있도록 개발된 영어시험입니다.

03 학교내신성적 향상

TOSEL은 학년별 교과과정과 연계하여 학교에서 배우는 내용을 학습하고 평가할 수 있도록 문항 및 주제를 구성하여 내신영어 향상을 위한 최적의 솔루션을 제공합니다.

04 수능대비 직결

유아, 초, 중등시절 어렵지 않고 즐겁게 학습해 온 영어이지만, 수능시험준비를 위해 접하는 영어의 문항 및 유형 난이도에 주춤하게 됩니다. 이를 대비하기 위해 TOSEL은 유아부터 성인까지 점진적인 학습을 통해 수능대비를 자연적으로 해나갈 수 있습니다.

05 진학과 취업에 대비한 필수 스펙관리

개인별 '학업성취기록부' 발급을 통해 영어학업성취이력을 꾸준히 기록한 영어학습 포트폴리오를 제공하여 영어학습 이력을 관리할 수 있습니다.

06 자기소개서에 토셀 기재

개별적인 진로 적성 Report를 제공하여 진로를 파악하고 자기소개서 작성시 적극적으로 활용할 수 있는 객관적인 자료를 제공합니다.

07 영어학습 동기부여

시험실시 후 응시자 모두에게 수여되는 인증서는 영어학습에 대한 자신감과 성취감을 고취시키고 동기를 부여합니다.

08 AI 분석 영어학습 솔루션

국내외 15,000여 개 학교.학원 단체 응시인원 중 엄선한 100만 명 이상의 실제 TOSEL 성적 데이터를 기반으로 영어인증시험 제도 중 세계 최초로 인공지능이 분석한 개인별 AI 정밀 진단 성적표를 제공합니다. 최첨단 AI 정밀진단 성적표는 최적의 영어 학습 솔루션을 제시하여 영어 학습에 소요되는 시간과 노력을 획기적으로 절감해줍니다

09 명예의 전당, 우수협력기관 지정

우수교육기관은 'TOSEL 우수 협력 기관'에 지정되고, 각 시/도별, 최고득점자를 명예의 전당에 등재합니다.

Evaluation —— 평가

평가의 기본원칙

TOSEL은 PBT(Paper Based Test)를 통하여 간접평가와 직접평가를 모두 시행합니다.

TOSEL은 언어의 네 가지 요소인 읽기, 듣기, 말하기, 쓰기 영역을 모두 평가합니다.

Reading 읽기	모든 레벨의 읽기 영역은 직접 평가 방식으로 측정합니다.
Listening 듣기	모든 레벨의 듣기 영역은 직접 평가 방식으로 측정합니다.
Speaking 말하기	모든 레벨의 말하기 영역은 간접 평가 방식으로 측정합니다.
Writing 쓰기	모든 레벨의 쓰기 영역은 간접 평가 방식으로 측정합니다.

TOSEL은 연령별 인지단계를 고려하여 아래와 같이 7단계로 나누어 평가합니다.

단계	시험	대상
1 단계	TOSEL® COCOON	5~7세의 미취학 아동
2 단계	TOSEL® Pre-STARTER	초등학교 1~2학년
3 단계	TOSEL® STARTER	초등학교 3~4학년
4 단계	TOSEL® BASIC	초등학교 5~6학년
5 단계	TOSEL® JUNIOR	중학생
6 단계	TOSEL® HIGH JUNIOR	고등학생
7 단계	TOSEL® ADVANCED	대학생 및 성인

Grade Report — 성적표 및 인증서

고도화 성적표: 응시자 개인별 최적화 AI 정밀진단

20여년간 축적된 약 100만명 이상의 엄선된 응시자 빅데이터를 TOSEL AI로 분석・진단한 개인별 성적자료

전국 단위 연령, 레벨 통계자료를 활용하여 보다 정밀한 성취 수준 판별
파트별 강/약점, 영역별 역량, 8가지 지능, 단어 수준 등을 비교 및 분석하여 폭넓은 학습 진단
오답 문항 유형별 심층 분석 자료 및 솔루션으로 학습 방향 제시, TOSEL과 수능 및 교과학습 성취기준과의 연계
모바일 기기 지원 - UX/UI 개선, 반응형 웹페이지로 구현되어 태블릿, 휴대폰, PC 등 다양한 기기 환경에서 접근 가능

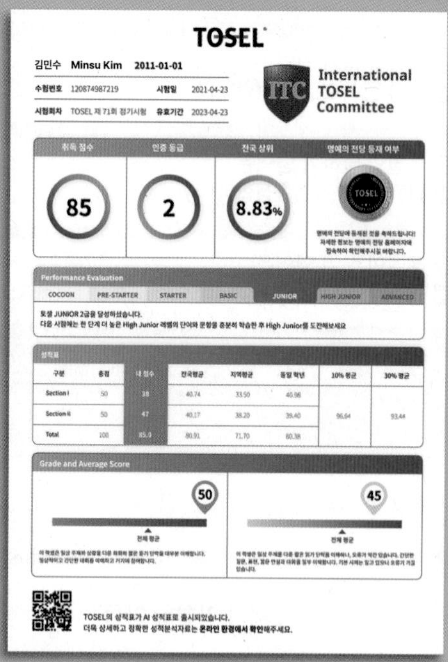

기본 제공 성적표

고도화 성적표 (일부 유료)

단체 성적 분석 자료

단체 및 기관 대상

- 레벨별 평균성적추이, 학생분포
  섹션 및 영역별 평균 점수, 표준편차

TOSEL Lab 지정교육기관 대상 추가 제공

- 원생 별 취약영역 분석 및 보강방안 제시
- TOSEL수험심리척도를 바탕으로 학생의 응답 특이성을 파악하여 코칭 방안 제시
- 전국 및 지역 단위 종합적 비교분석
  (레벨/유형별 응시자 연령 및 규모, 최고득점 등)

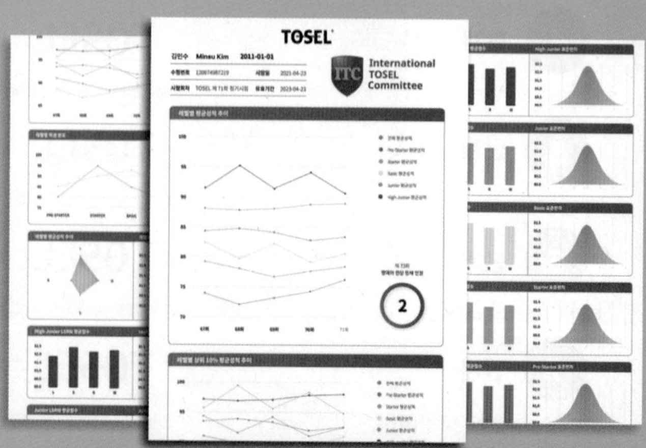

'토셀 명예의 전당' 등재

특별시, 광역시, 도 별 **1등 선발**
(7개시 9개도 **1등 선발**)

*홈페이지 로그인 - 시험결과 - 명예의 전당에서
해당자 등재 증명서 출력 가능

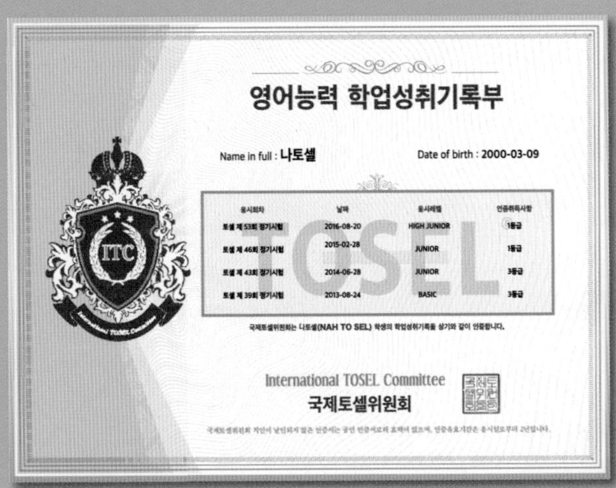

'학업성취기록부'에 토셀 인증등급 기재

개인별 **'학업성취기록부' 평생 발급**
진학과 취업을 대비한 **필수 스펙관리**

인증서

대한민국 초,중,고등학생의 영어숙달능력 평가 결과 공식인증

고려대학교 인증획득 (2010. 03)

한국외국어교육학회 인증획득 (2009. 12)

한국음성학회 인증획득 (2009. 12)

한국응용언어학회 인증획득 (2009. 11)

팬코리아영어교육학회 인증획득 (2009. 10)

Actual Test 1

Section I

Listening and Speaking

Part **A** Listen and Respond
10 Questions

Part **B** Listen and Retell
15 Questions

Part **C** Listen and Speak
5 Questions

PART A Listen and Respond

DIRECTIONS: For questions 1 to 10, listen to the sentences and choose the BEST response. The sentences and the choices will be spoken **TWICE**. The choices are NOT printed on your test paper.

지시 사항: 1번부터 10번까지는 문장을 듣고, 가장 알맞은 대답을 고르는 문제입니다. 문제와 보기는 **두 번씩** 들려주며 보기는 시험지에 표시되지 않습니다.

1. Mark your answer on your answer sheet.

2. Mark your answer on your answer sheet.

3. Mark your answer on your answer sheet.

4. Mark your answer on your answer sheet.

5. Mark your answer on your answer sheet.

6. Mark your answer on your answer sheet.

7. Mark your answer on your answer sheet.

8. Mark your answer on your answer sheet.

9. Mark your answer on your answer sheet.

10. Mark your answer on your answer sheet.

PART B Listen and Retell

DIRECTIONS: For questions 11 to 25, listen to the short talks or conversations and choose the BEST answer for each question. The talks and conversations will be spoken **TWICE**.

지시 사항: 11번부터 25번까지는 짧은 대화나 이야기를 듣고, 가장 알맞은 답을 고르는 문제입니다. 문제는 **두 번씩** 들려줍니다.

11. Are they both scared of spiders?

(A) Only the girl is.
(B) Only the boy is.
(C) They like cockroaches.
(D) They don't like any bugs.

12. Where are they?

(A) at a bakery
(B) at an airport
(C) at a stadium
(D) at a restaurant

13. What are they doing?

(A) They are reading.
(B) They are at home.
(C) They are making plans.
(D) They are eating breakfast.

14. What will the boy do?

(A) He will catch a bus at 3 p.m.

(B) He will meet the friend at 3 p.m.

(C) He will look for the friend at 3 p.m.

(D) He will buy dinner for the friend at 3 p.m.

15. How was the boy's mother?

(A) She was sick.

(B) She was healthy.

(C) She was doing great.

(D) She was at the party.

16. How is the book?

(A) It is old.

(B) It is lost.

(C) It is wet.

(D) It is clean.

17. What does the boy like to do?

(A) He likes to be on TV.

(B) He likes to interview people.

(C) He likes to ask the girl questions.

(D) He likes to write letters to friends.

[18-19]

18. When were the first games held?

(A) less than 600 years ago
(B) more than 2,000 years ago
(C) more than 3,000 years ago
(D) from August 8th until the 24th

19. What is NOT a new Olympic sport?

(A) wrestling
(B) baseball
(C) mountain biking
(D) beach volleyball

[20-21]

20. Where is this?

(A) at a hospital
(B) at an airport
(C) at a train station
(D) at a bus station

21. Why do the flights to Sydney have to be delayed?

(A) because of the weather
(B) because of the gate change
(C) because of a stop in Hong Kong
(D) because of too many passengers

[22-23]

22. What is the advice for?

(A) to help people eat better

(B) to help people eat yoghurt

(C) to help supermarkets sell garlic

(D) to help people from getting colds

23. What is NOT the advice for staying healthy in winter?

(A) eating garlic

(B) taking a bath

(C) washing hands

(D) eating yoghurt

[24-25]

24. Where does she live?

(A) on the path

(B) near the lake

(C) near the beach

(D) next to the store

25. Where does the duck walk?

(A) in the park

(B) in the water

(C) near her farm

(D) after the woman

PART C Listen and Speak

DIRECTIONS: For questions 26 to 30, listen to the conversations and choose the BEST response. The conversations will be spoken **TWICE**.

지시 사항: 26번부터 30번까지는 대화를 듣고, 뒤에 이어질 가장 알맞은 응답을 고르는 문제입니다. 문제는 **두 번씩** 들려줍니다.

26. What's next?

(A) He said that I had to play.
(B) He said that he was writing.
(C) He said that I was too young.
(D) He said that he was watching TV.

27. What's next?

(A) Sure, but I can't talk well.
(B) Sure, but I can't add well.
(C) Sure, but I haven't been there.
(D) Sure, but I don't know much about it.

28. What's next?

(A) I think I know.
(B) O.K. Let's look for it.
(C) O.K. Let's buy lunch.
(D) O.K. What do you need it for?

29. What's next?

(A) Thanks. It must be yours.

(B) Thanks. It must be stuck.

(C) Thanks. It must be from lunch.

(D) Thanks. It must be the teachers.

30. What's next?

(A) No, it's not clean.

(B) Everyone knows that.

(C) Don't think about him.

(D) That would be wonderful.

Section II

Reading and Writing

Part **A** Sentence Completion
5 Questions

Part **B** Situational Writing
5 Questions

Part **C** Practical Reading and Retelling
10 Questions

Part **D** General Reading and Retelling
10 Questions

PART A Sentence Completion

DIRECTIONS: For questions 1 to 5, fill in the blanks to finish the sentences. Choose the option that BEST completes each blank.

지시 사항: 1번부터 5번까지는 빈칸을 알맞게 채워 대화를 완성하는 문제입니다. 가장 알맞은 답을 고르세요.

1. A: Did you get the CD?

B: I got a CD. __________, it is the wrong one.

(A) Since
(B) So that
(C) Instead
(D) However

2. A: You were here last night,________?

B: Yeah.

(A) can't you
(B) didn't you
(C) wasn't you
(D) weren't you

3. A: Pencils are made __________ wood.

B: That's right.

(A) in
(B) at
(C) of
(D) to

4. A: __________ you have any questions, drop by my office.

B: Okay, I will.

(A) If
(B) As
(C) Since
(D) Because

5. A: Taking the bus is __________ than the subway.

B: Then, I'll take a bus.

(A) greet
(B) good
(C) best
(D) better

PART B Situational Writing

DIRECTIONS: For questions 6 to 10, look at the pictures and complete the sentences. Choose the option that BEST completes each sentence.

지시 사항: 6번부터 10번까지는 그림을 보고 문장을 완성하는 문제입니다. 가장 알맞은 답을 고르세요.

6.

The boy at the front is about to _______________.

(A) cry out

(B) fall down

(C) run away

(D) clap his hands

7. 

The man is holding ________________.

(A) a couch

(B) a popcorn

(C) a remote control

(D) an air conditioner

8. 

The box is ________________.

(A) wet

(B) torn

(C) opened

(D) crumpled

9. 

My father is using ________.

(A) a mop
(B) a wipe
(C) a watering can
(D) a vacuum cleaner

10. 

Let's play ____________.

(A) baseball
(B) volleyball
(C) badminton
(D) table tennis

PART C Practical Reading and Retelling

DIRECTIONS: For questions 11 to 20, read the practical materials and choose the BEST answer for each question about the materials.

지시 사항: 11번부터 20번까지는 실용적 읽기 자료를 읽고, 자료와 관련된 질문에 답하는 문제입니다. 각 질문에 가장 알맞은 답을 고르세요.

QUESTIONS 11-12. Refer to the following information.

How to iron a shirt?

Step1) Plug in the iron.

Step2) Fill the iron with water.

Step3) Iron the back of the collar first, then the front.

Step4) Iron the sleeves, then the back from shoulders to bottom. Tada! You have a well-ironed shirt. Unplug the iron.

11. What happens before filling the iron with water?

(A) Iron the collar.

(B) Unplug the iron.

(C) Plug in the iron.

(D) Iron the shoulders.

12. Which happens last?

(A) Iron the collar.

(B) Unplug the iron.

(C) Iron the sleeves.

(D) Fill the iron with water.

QUESTIONS 13-14. Refer to the following map.

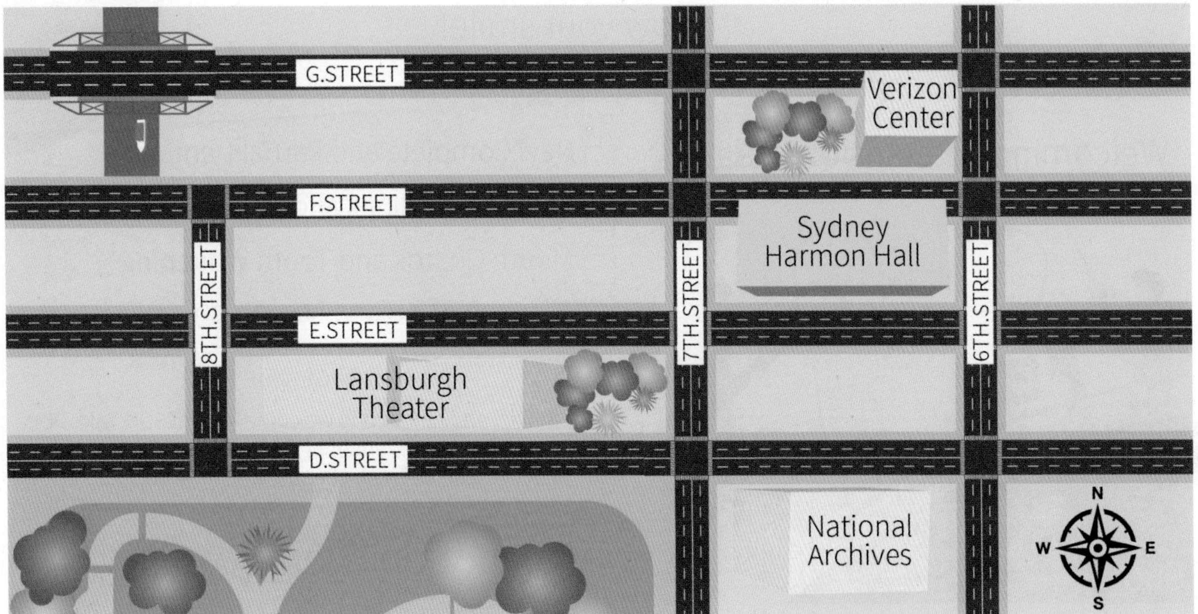

13. At least how many crossroads do you pass from the National Archives to Sydney Harman Hall?

(A) 2
(B) 4
(C) 6
(D) 8

14. In what direction does F.STREET take?

(A) D.STREET
(B) to the right
(C) East - West
(D) North - South

QUESTIONS 15-16. Refer to the following brochure.

Show your smile!

DENTAL CLINIC

Welcoming Veterans of All Ages!

- New Complete and Partial Dentures
- Same Day Relines and Repairs
- Mouth Guards and Tooth Whitening
- All Insurance Plans Accepted

- Announcement -

We are thrilled and honored to welcome MR. WILSON TAM, DD to Show Your Smile. Mr. Tam brings years of experience and is highly respected by customers. Welcome, Wilson!

8763 Bayview Ave. #7
Richmond hill
905-764-7222

WILSON TAM, DD / MONA GALLIERA, DD

15. Who is the new dentist?

(A) Wilson Tam

(B) Veteran Ages

(C) Richmond Hill

(D) Mona Galliera

16. What information does this brochure NOT have?

(A) address

(B) office hours

(C) dentists' name

(D) dental services

QUESTIONS 17-18. Refer to the following chart.

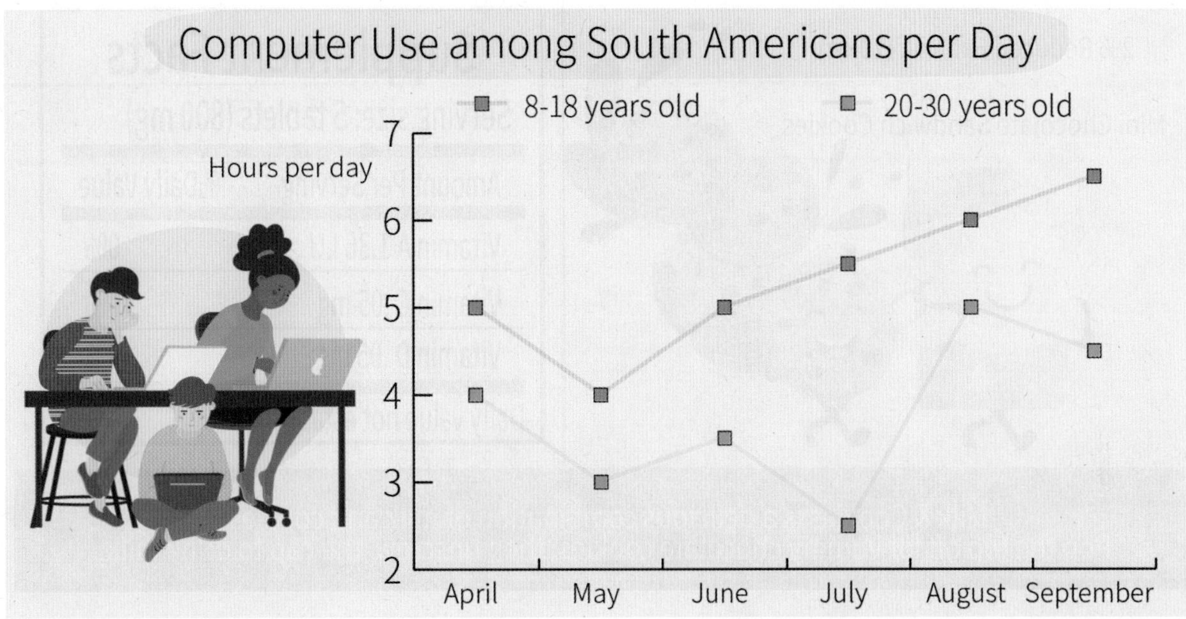

17. Which month did 20 – 30 year olds use the computer the least?

(A) April

(B) May

(C) June

(D) July

18. About how many hours did the younger group use the computer in August?

(A) 2

(B) 5

(C) 6

(D) 8

QUESTIONS 19-20. Refer to the following information.

Supplement Facts

Serving size: 5 tablets (800 mg)

Amount Per Serving	%Daily Value
Vitamin A 1.36 I.U	0%
Vitamin C .05 mg	0%
Vitamin D .05 mg	0%

-Daily value not established

Milk & Cookies is a delicious combination of milk and cookies.
Pop the top off for yummy chocolate cookies, then unscrew the cap to drink milk.

19. Where are the cookies?

(A) in the cap

(B) in the milk

(C) under the milk

(D) next to the milk

20. What is NOT true about this product?

(A) It has two tastes.

(B) It has less fat in milk.

(C) It serves plenty of protein.

(D) It is a mixture of milk and cookies.

PART D General Reading and Retelling

DIRECTIONS: For questions 21 to 30, read the passages and choose the BEST answer for each question about the passages.

지시 사항: 21번부터 30번까지는 글을 읽고, 글과 관련된 질문에 답하는 문제입니다. 질문에 가장 알맞은 답을 고르세요.

QUESTIONS 21-22. Refer to the following passage.

I got chosen for the basketball team! It's one of the happiest days of my life. Every morning I wake up and I practice basketball before school. I play one on one with another friend. We run around the track for 30 minutes and we do other exercises to make us stronger. Then we shoot hoops for 30 minutes. The one with fewer goals has to buy the other one a drink. I usually lost. I didn't think I would make the basketball team but I did. All that practice paid off.

21. If he gets fewer goals than his friend, what does he have to do?

(A) He has to buy a drink.
(B) He has to shoot hoops.
(C) He has to do exercises.
(D) He has to run around the track.

22. When does he practice?

(A) at night
(B) in the evening
(C) in the morning
(D) in the afternoon

QUESTIONS 23-24. Refer to the following passage.

Until a few years ago, all animals entering the UK had to spend six months in quarantine- away from people and other animals. This was because of the threat of a disease called rabies. Rabies or 'mad dog disease' comes from fox or dog bites. Quarantine was very difficult for pet owners. They didn't want to be away from their pets for six months. Now, there is a pet passport that owners can get from a vet to say that their pet doesn’t have rabies. Animals no longer need to wait in quarantine.

23. A few years ago, what did pet owners have to do when coming to the UK?

(A) They had to get a vet.

(B) They had to use a passport.

(C) They had to keep their pet away from people.

(D) They had to buy special medicine so they didn’t bite.

24. Why is it easier to bring your pet to the UK now?

(A) You don’t need a vet.

(B) You can have a holiday.

(C) Your pet doesn’t have rabies.

(D) You can get a pet passport from a vet.

QUESTIONS 25-26. Refer to the following passage.

The Beatles was a British pop and rock group from Liverpool. They are the most famous band in the world. There were four male members to the Beatles. Many girls around the world were crazy about them. The group broke many sales records and charted more than 50 top 40 hit singles, including 20 #1's in USA alone. The band has sold over a billion records worldwide. The band broke up in 1970.

25. How do you know the Beatles were popular?

(A) They were British.
(B) They were handsome.
(C) They are a rock group.
(D) They sold many records.

26. Which sentence means the same as 'The band broke up in 1970'?

(A) The band separated in 1970.
(B) The band went to Liverpool in 1970.
(C) The band broke record sales in 1970.
(D) The band was famous in USA alone in 1970.

QUESTIONS 27-28. Refer to the following passage.

Birds are warm-blooded animals that have wings, feathers, a beak, no teeth, a skeleton in which many bones are joined together. Most birds can fly. Birds have a very strong heart and a good way of breathing—these are necessary for birds to fly. Birds use a lot of energy while flying and need to eat a lot of food so they can fly.

Birds do not have any teeth. Birds have a tongue, but a bird's tongue is hard. Birds build nests in trees, on cliffs, or on the ground. Birds bear their young in hard-shelled eggs which hatch after some time. Some birds, like chickens, lay eggs each day, others only once every few years.

27. Why do birds need to eat often?

(A) because they are hungry
(B) because they lay big eggs
(C) because they have a good heart
(D) because they need strength to fly

28. Where can birds lay their eggs?

(A) on cliffs
(B) in the ocean
(C) in hard shells
(D) under the ground

QUESTIONS 29-30. Refer to the following passage.

A man was walking along the street when he found a penguin. He picked it up and took it to the police station. He said to the policeman "I found this penguin on the street. What should I do with it?" The policeman looked at the man and said "Take the penguin to the zoo."

The man said "Of course, I'll take it to the zoo." and he left the police station with the penguin under his arm. The next day the policeman saw the man walking along the street with the penguin next to him. The policeman stopped the man and said "I thought I told you to take the penguin to the zoo?" The man replied "Yes, I took it to the zoo yesterday. Today I'm taking it to see a movie."

29. Why was the policeman surprised?

(A) He didn't know what to do.
(B) He saw a penguin in the city.
(C) The man didn't leave the penguin at the zoo.
(D) The man was going to take the penguin to the zoo.

30. Where should the penguin be now?

(A) at the zoo
(B) on the street
(C) at the movies
(D) at the police station

Actual Test 2

Section I

Listening and Speaking

Part **A** Listen and Respond
10 Questions

Part **B** Listen and Retell
15 Questions

Part **C** Listen and Speak
5 Questions

PART A Listen and Respond

DIRECTIONS: For questions 1 to 10, listen to the sentences and choose the BEST response. The sentences and the choices will be spoken **TWICE**. The choices are NOT printed on your test paper.

지시 사항: 1번부터 10번까지는 문장을 듣고, 가장 알맞은 대답을 고르는 문제입니다. 문제와 보기는 **두 번씩** 들려주며 보기는 시험지에 표시되지 않습니다.

1. Mark your answer on your answer sheet.

2. Mark your answer on your answer sheet.

3. Mark your answer on your answer sheet.

4. Mark your answer on your answer sheet.

5. Mark your answer on your answer sheet.

6. Mark your answer on your answer sheet.

7. Mark your answer on your answer sheet.

8. Mark your answer on your answer sheet.

9. Mark your answer on your answer sheet.

10. Mark your answer on your answer sheet.

PART B Listen and Retell

DIRECTIONS: For questions 11 to 25, listen to the short talks or conversations and choose the BEST answer for each question. The talks and conversations will be spoken **TWICE**.

지시 사항: 11번부터 25번까지는 짧은 대화나 이야기를 듣고, 가장 알맞은 답을 고르는 문제입니다. 문제는 **두 번씩** 들려줍니다.

11. Where are the girl and the boy?

(A) at a ski slope
(B) in a shopping mall
(C) at a swimming pool
(D) in an amusement park

12. What kind of gift will the boy buy?

(A) a birthday gift
(B) a Christmas gift
(C) a friendship gift
(D) a graduation gift

13. What are they doing now?

(A) They're eating cookies.
(B) They're baking cookies.
(C) They're cleaning the oven.
(D) They're getting ready to go out.

14. Why are they going back home?

(A) Because it is early.

(B) Because it is getting dark.

(C) Because the library is closing.

(D) Because they want to take a bus.

15. Who will the boy visit?

(A) his parents

(B) another friend

(C) his grandparents

(D) a basketball player

16. When did the boy come back?

(A) an hour ago

(B) half an hour ago

(C) fifty minutes ago

(D) fifteen minutes ago

17. How does the boy want to get there?

(A) He wants to take a bus.

(B) He wants to take a taxi.

(C) He wants to walk faster.

(D) He wants to take the subway.

[18-19]

18. What is the girl talking about?

(A) shy people
(B) her pet snake
(C) her pet worm
(D) dangerous snakes

19. What is true about the girl's snake?

(A) It is lazy.
(B) It's not shy.
(C) It bites humans.
(D) It is dangerous.

[20-21]

20. What kind of message is this?

(A) a radio message
(B) a phone message
(C) a computer message
(D) a television message

21. What does Billy want?

(A) He wants to go home.
(B) He wants to call Jin again.
(C) He wants to go to the park.
(D) He wants to answer a question.

[22-23]

22. Where is this announcement made?

(A) in a school
(B) on television
(C) in a supermarket
(D) in a clothing store

23. Which statement is true?

(A) You can get 3 apples for $2.
(B) You can get 5 apples for $1.
(C) You can get 3 oranges for $1.
(D) You can get 5 oranges for $2.

[24-25]

24. Who is speaking?

(A) a school teacher
(B) the gym teacher
(C) the photographer
(D) the school principal

25. What should the 6th grade students do tomorrow?

(A) They should go to the gym at 2:00 AM.
(B) They should go to the gym at 2:00 PM.
(C) They should go to the gym at 9:00 AM.
(D) They should go to the gym at 9:00 PM.

PART C Listen and Speak

DIRECTIONS: For questions 26 to 30, listen to the conversations and choose the BEST response.
The conversations will be spoken **TWICE**.

지시 사항: 26번부터 30번까지는 대화를 듣고, 뒤에 이어질 가장 알맞은 응답을 고르는 문제입니다.
문제는 **두 번씩** 들려줍니다.

26. What's next?

(A) Okay, I'll finish soon.
(B) Sure, I'll take it with me.
(C) Okay, I'll lower my voice.
(D) Okay, I'll speak a little louder.

27. What's next?

(A) Wow! I have more than you.
(B) Wow! You have less than me.
(C) Wow! You have more than me.
(D) Wow! We have the same number.

28. What's next?

(A) You can wear it now.
(B) Your hat looks good.
(C) Don't take it with you.
(D) Don't forget it next time.

29. What's next?

(A) I don't think so.

(B) How about you?

(C) I'm glad we agree.

(D) You don't agree with me?

30. What's next?

(A) Let's look for a park.

(B) I washed mine already.

(C) Okay, let's look for one.

(D) Okay, you can have some water.

Section II

Reading and Writing

Part **A** Sentence Completion
5 Questions

Part **B** Situational Writing
5 Questions

Part **C** Practical Reading and Retelling
10 Questions

Part **D** General Reading and Retelling
10 Questions

PART A Sentence Completion

DIRECTIONS: For questions 1 to 5, fill in the blanks to finish the sentences. Choose the option that BEST completes each blank.

지시 사항: 1번부터 5번까지는 빈칸을 알맞게 채워 대화를 완성하는 문제입니다. 가장 알맞은 답을 고르세요.

1. A: ________ can I fix it?

B: You have to use some glue.

(A) How

(B) Who

(C) What

(D) When

2. A: Your phone is ringing.

B: Thanks, I should ________ it.

(A) answer

(B) answered

(C) answering

(D) have answer

3. A: It's raining very ________.

B: We'd better take an umbrella.

(A) hard

(B) hardly

(C) harden

(D) was hard

4. A: What does a chef ________?

B: He cooks food.

(A) do

(B) did

(C) does

(D) doing

5. A: Do you want to buy it?

B: Yes, I do. ________ I don't have any money.

(A) If

(B) Or

(C) But

(D) And

PART B Situational Writing

DIRECTIONS: For questions 6 to 10, look at the pictures and complete the sentences. Choose the option that BEST completes each sentence.

지시 사항: 6번부터 10번까지는 그림을 보고 문장을 완성하는 문제입니다. 가장 알맞은 답을 고르세요.

6.

The boy is using a ________________ .

(A) mop to melt the snow

(B) rake to move the snow

(C) shovel to clear the snow

(D) broom to sweep the snow

7. 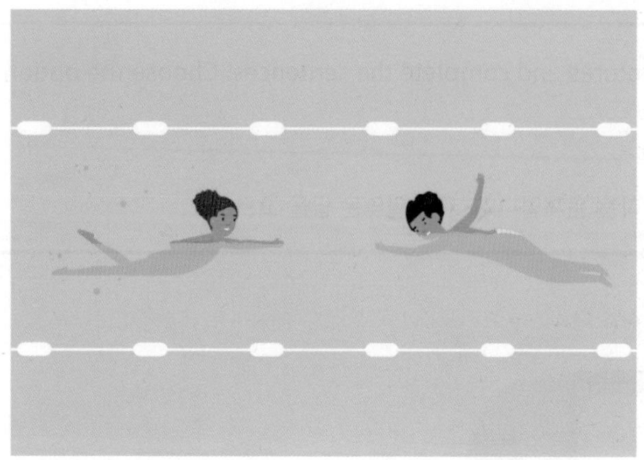

The girl and boy are swimming ________________ .

(A) side by side

(B) next to each other

(C) towards each other

(D) away from each other

8. 

The boy is pulling the girl ______________ .

(A) on her bicycle

(B) with his bicycle

(C) on his rollerblades

(D) with his rollerblades

9.

The boy is ______________________.

(A) waiting in line

(B) watching a movie

(C) walking to the office

(D) waiting to buy popcorn

10.

The piano teacher is ______________________.

(A) playing the piano

(B) learning to play the piano

(C) helping the girl play the piano

(D) helping the girl move the piano

PART C Practical Reading and Retelling

DIRECTIONS: For questions 11 to 20, read the practical materials and choose the BEST answer for each question about the materials.

지시 사항: 11번부터 20번까지는 실용적 읽기 자료를 읽고, 자료와 관련된 질문에 답하는 문제입니다. 각 질문에 가장 알맞은 답을 고르세요.

QUESTIONS 11-12. Refer to the following schedule.

11. Which day is not on the schedule?

(A) Monday

(B) Tuesday

(C) Wednesday

(D) Thursday

12. What day must Peter clean the classroom?

(A) Monday

(B) Tuesday

(C) Thursday

(D) Friday

QUESTIONS 13-14. Refer to the following sign.

13. Who do you think made this sign?

    (A) the owner of the lost dog
    (B) a person who wants to sell a dog
    (C) a person who wants to buy a dog
    (D) the person who found the lost dog

14. Where was the dog last seen?

    (A) a small, brown dog
    (B) wearing a red collar
    (C) on Thursday, April 3rd
    (D) in front of Rainbow Apartment

QUESTIONS 15-16. Refer to the following information.

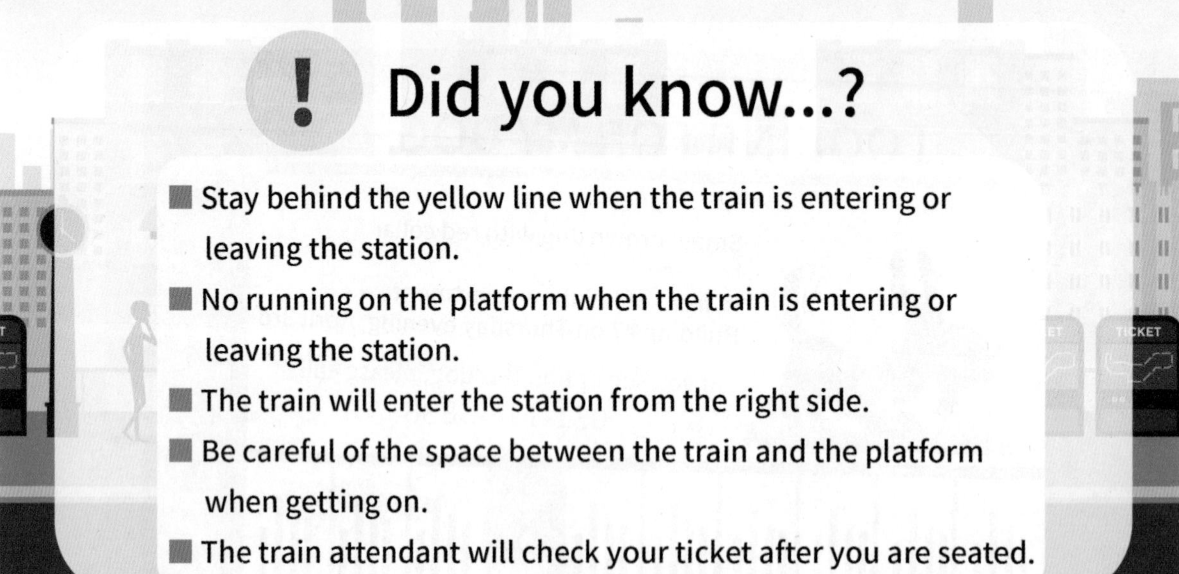

15. What should you NOT do on the station platform?

(A) run to get on the train before it leaves

(B) run with the train as it leaves to say goodbye

(C) watch the train enter the station from the right side

(D) stand behind the yellow line when the train is entering

16. What should you do when getting on the train?

(A) wait behind the yellow line

(B) look right to watch for the train

(C) show your ticket to the train attendant

(D) be careful of the space between the train and the platform

QUESTIONS 17-18. Refer to the following information.

17. What is the sale price on the teddy bear?

(A) 10% off

(B) 30% off

(C) 70% off

(D) not on sale

18. If the regular price of the model airplane is $100, how much is the sale price?

(A) $30

(B) $50

(C) $70

(D) $90

QUESTIONS 19-20. Refer to the following information.

Model	Phone Type	Camera	MP3 Player	Memory	Price
GL50	Folding	✕	✓	1GB	$100
XB870	Sliding	✓	✓	1GB	$150
P10	Regular	✕	✕	64MB	$40
SM60	Folding	✓	✓	2GB	$200

19. What type of phone is the cheapest model?

(A) sliding phone

(B) regular phone

(C) camera phone

(D) folding phone

20. Which model has a camera and MP3 player for less than $200?

(A) P10

(B) GL50

(C) SM60

(D) XB870

PART D General Reading and Retelling

DIRECTIONS: For questions 21 to 30, read the passages and choose the BEST answer for each question about the passages.

지시 사항: 21번부터 30번까지는 글을 읽고, 글과 관련된 질문에 답하는 문제입니다. 질문에 가장 알맞은 답을 고르세요.

QUESTIONS 21-22. Refer to the following passage.

You are eating with a friend when he spills his soda. Suddenly, and without thinking, you jump up so you don't get any soda on your clothes. Your brain has just calculated when, where, and how fast you should move. Then it controls your muscles to do so. This information is sent from your brain to your muscles at more than 322 kilometers per hour! So it takes less than one second for you to act.

21. Which is the best title for this passage?

(A) Don't Drink Soda
(B) Our Amazing Brain
(C) Avoiding Accidents
(D) Eating with a Friend

22. Which of the following statements is NOT true?

(A) Your brain controls your muscles.
(B) Your muscles can move 322 kilometers per hour.
(C) Your brain sends information to your muscles very quickly.
(D) Your brain calculates when, where, and how fast you move.

QUESTIONS 23-24. Refer to the following passage.

When photographers take pictures of food for advertisements, they use many tricks to make the food look delicious. For example, they use white glue instead of milk on cereal. This keeps the cereal looking fresh. Roasted chickens are sometimes stuffed with paper to make them look fat and round. Or a little bit of soap is added to milk so that the milk looks bubbly and refreshing.

23. Why are tricks used when taking pictures of food?

(A) to prepare the food for eating
(B) to prepare the food for cooking
(C) to make the food more delicious
(D) to make the food look more delicious

24. What is added to milk to make it look bubbly and refreshing?

(A) glue
(B) soap
(C) paper
(D) cereal

QUESTIONS 25-26. Refer to the following passage.

The word "umbrella" comes from the Latin word "umbra," and it means "shadow." Ancient people used umbrellas to shade themselves from the bright sun. The Chinese were the first to use the umbrella for rain. They covered their umbrellas with wax so no water could go through. Then, umbrellas became popular in Northern Europe in the 16th century. In 1852, Samuel Fox used steel instead of wood to make the umbrella's frame.

25. Who were the first people to use umbrellas for rain?

(A) Samuel Fox
(B) ancient people
(C) Chinese people
(D) Northern Europeans

26. What happened in the 16th century?

(A) People began to use umbrellas for shade.
(B) Steel was used to make the umbrella's frame.
(C) The umbrella became popular in Northern Europe.
(D) The umbrella was waxed so no water could leak through.

QUESTIONS 27-28. Refer to the following passage.

A turtle is from the family of reptiles, like snakes and lizards. But the turtle is the only reptile with a shell. The shell is made of a hard material. The hard material protects the turtle. A turtle can protect itself by pulling its head, tail, and legs into the shell. While turtles on land can protect themselves from enemies, the shape of the shell makes it easier for sea turtles to swim. Turtle shells are brown, black, or dark green. Some turtles have red, orange, or yellow spots. The spots make the shell beautiful.

27. What family is the turtle from?

(A) the family of shells
(B) the family of snakes
(C) the family of lizards
(D) the family of reptiles

28. What is NOT true about turtle shells?

(A) They are all colorful.
(B) They are used for protection.
(C) They can make swimming easier.
(D) They are made from a hard material.

QUESTIONS 29-30. Refer to the following passage.

The pyramids of Egypt are truly amazing. Not only are they thousands of years old, but they are one of the largest man-made objects in the world. The largest of the pyramids, the Great Pyramid of King Khufu, is 147 meters high! That's as tall as a fifty-story building! Each stone block used to build the pyramid weighs as much as 15,000 kilograms! How these giant stones were moved is still somewhat of a mystery. Without a doubt, these pyramids are one of the man-made wonders of the world.

29. What does NOT make the pyramids truly amazing?

(A) They are located in Egypt.
(B) They are thousands of years old.
(C) People are still not sure how they were built.
(D) They are one of the largest man-made objects in the world.

30. What best describes the stones used to build the Great Pyramid of King Khufu?

(A) It is 147 meters tall.
(B) It is fifty stories high.
(C) It weighs 15,000 kilograms.
(D) It is thousands of years old.

Actual Test 3

Section I

Listening and Speaking

Part **A** Listen and Respond
10 Questions

Part **B** Listen and Retell
15 Questions

Part **C** Listen and Speak
5 Questions

PART A Listen and Respond

DIRECTIONS: For questions 1 to 10, listen to the sentences and choose the BEST response. The sentences and the choices will be spoken **TWICE**. The choices are NOT printed on your test paper.

지시 사항: 1번부터 10번까지는 문장을 듣고, 가장 알맞은 대답을 고르는 문제입니다. 문제와 보기는 **두 번씩** 들려주며 보기는 시험지에 표시되지 않습니다.

1. Mark your answer on your answer sheet.

2. Mark your answer on your answer sheet.

3. Mark your answer on your answer sheet.

4. Mark your answer on your answer sheet.

5. Mark your answer on your answer sheet.

6. Mark your answer on your answer sheet.

7. Mark your answer on your answer sheet.

8. Mark your answer on your answer sheet.

9. Mark your answer on your answer sheet.

10. Mark your answer on your answer sheet.

PART B Listen and Retell

DIRECTIONS: For questions 11 to 25, listen to the short talks or conversations and choose the BEST answer for each question. The talks and conversations will be spoken **TWICE**.

지시 사항: 11번부터 25번까지는 짧은 대화나 이야기를 듣고, 가장 알맞은 답을 고르는 문제입니다. 문제는 **두 번씩** 들려줍니다.

11. What happened to the boy?

(A) He is confused.
(B) He fell down.
(C) He lost something.
(D) He broke something.

12. What are they doing now?

(A) eating lunch
(B) watching TV
(C) playing a game
(D) doing their homework

13. Where does the girl want to go?

(A) to the park
(B) to the beach
(C) to the classroom
(D) to the schoolyard

14. What are they looking at?

(A) a flower
(B) a sunset
(C) a picture
(D) a rainbow

15. Who will go with them?

(A) the girl's brother
(B) the boy's brother
(C) the boy's sister
(D) the boy's friend

16. When did the boy finish his book report?

(A) today
(B) yesterday
(C) last week
(D) two days ago

17. How will the boy go to his lesson?

(A) He will walk.
(B) He will take a bus.
(C) He will ride his bicycle.
(D) He will take the subway.

[18-19]

18. What is the girl talking about?

(A) her favorite band
(B) her favorite music
(C) her favorite hobby
(D) her favorite instrument

19. Why does the girl like the trumpet?

(A) It looks simple.
(B) It's easy to play.
(C) It is very popular.
(D) It sounds beautiful.

[20-21]

20. Where is this announcement made?

(A) in a park
(B) in a restaurant
(C) in a skating rink
(D) in a shopping mall

21. How long will it take to clean the ice?

(A) 2 minutes
(B) 10 minutes
(C) 20 minutes
(D) half an hour

[22-23]

22. What is the speaker talking about?

(A) her aunt's wedding
(B) her husband's party
(C) her sister's graduation
(D) her friend's birthday party

23. What made the day most special?

(A) the nice weather
(B) the delicious food
(C) the happy wedding
(D) the beautiful flowers

[24-25]

24. What is this announcement for?

(A) a hospital
(B) a fun park
(C) a restaurant
(D) a shopping mall

25. What time will the food court close?

(A) at 5:00 PM
(B) at 8:30 PM
(C) at 10:00 PM
(D) in 30 minutes

PART C Listen and Speak

DIRECTIONS: For questions 26 to 30, listen to the conversations and choose the BEST response. The conversations will be spoken **TWICE**.

지시 사항: 26번부터 30번까지는 대화를 듣고, 뒤에 이어질 가장 알맞은 응답을 고르는 문제입니다. 문제는 **두 번씩** 들려줍니다.

26. What's next?

(A) I think that's a good idea.
(B) But I'm busy this afternoon.
(C) Tomorrow afternoon sounds great.
(D) I have an English class this afternoon.

27. What's next?

(A) I'm too full to eat.
(B) I'll wait till lunch.
(C) I can't wait till later.
(D) This is delicious, thanks.

28. What's next?

(A) I don't need any money.
(B) A pencil is not expensive.
(C) If not, I can lend you some.
(D) I didn't bring my notebook.

29. What's next?

(A) It was a terrible nightmare.

(B) You have a very good memory.

(C) That sounds like a terrible dream.

(D) Most people don't remember their dreams.

30. What's next?

(A) I also have a watch.

(B) Thanks, green is my favorite.

(C) I don't like wearing watches.

(D) Thanks, but it's an old watch.

Section II

Reading and Writing

Part **A** Sentence Completion
5 Questions

Part **B** Situational Writing
5 Questions

Part **C** Practical Reading and Retelling
10 Questions

Part **D** General Reading and Retelling
10 Questions

PART A Sentence Completion

DIRECTIONS: For questions 1 to 5, fill in the blanks to finish the sentences. Choose the option that BEST completes each blank.

지시 사항: 1번부터 5번까지는 빈칸을 알맞게 채워 대화를 완성하는 문제입니다. 가장 알맞은 답을 고르세요.

1. A: The computer is ________.

B: I know. I will fix it.

(A) break

(B) broke

(C) broken

(D) breaked

2. A: Do you want to go?

B: I will go ________ I have time.

(A) if

(B) for

(C) but

(D) and

3. A: What do you usually do after dinner?

B: I ________ in the living room.

(A) watch TV

(B) will watch TV

(C) am watching TV

(D) have watched TV

4. A: Is there some bread on the table?

B: ______________________

(A) Yes, it is.

(B) No, it isn't.

(C) Yes, there are.

(D) No, there isn't.

5. A: ____________ in Seoul?

B: It is warm in spring.

(A) How the weather is

(B) How is the weather

(C) What the weather is

(D) What it is the weather

DIRECTIONS: For questions 6 to 10, look at the pictures and complete the sentences. Choose the option that BEST completes each sentence.

지시 사항: 6번부터 10번까지는 그림을 보고 문장을 완성하는 문제입니다. 가장 알맞은 답을 고르세요.

6.

The girl is using a ______________________.

(A) cup to water the plant

(B) can to water the plant

(C) hose to clean the plant

(D) towel to clean the plant

7.

The girl and boy are walking ______________________.

(A) behind the dog

(B) next to the dog

(C) far from the dog

(D) in front of the dog

8.

The boy is pushing the girl ______________________.

(A) on the slide

(B) on the swing

(C) to the seesaw

(D) to the merry-go-round

9.

The girl is ________________________.

(A) studying at a library

(B) reading a book at a library

(C) looking for a book at a bookstore

(D) talking to her friend at a bookstore

10.

The teacher is ________________________.

(A) talking to the class

(B) taking a rest during break

(C) writing on the whiteboard

(D) checking the students' homework

PART C Practical Reading and Retelling

DIRECTIONS: For questions 11 to 20, read the practical materials and choose the BEST answer for each question about the materials.

지시 사항: 11번부터 20번까지는 실용적 읽기 자료를 읽고, 자료와 관련된 질문에 답하는 문제입니다. 각 질문에 가장 알맞은 답을 고르세요.

QUESTIONS 11-12. Refer to the following sign.

11. How much is a man's cut for a member?

(A) $7.00

(B) $8.00

(C) $9.00

(D) $10.00

12. How long is a $10.00 membership?

(A) three months

(B) six months

(C) one year

(D) two years

QUESTIONS 13-14. Refer to the following schedule.

13. Which teams will play on September 13?

(A) Teams A and C
(B) Teams B and D
(C) Teams A and D
(D) Teams C and B

14. When will Dan play against Jake?

(A) Saturday, September 12
(B) Saturday, September 19
(C) Sunday, September 6
(D) Sunday, September 20

QUESTIONS 15-16. Refer to the following sign.

Swimming Pool rules

 Shower before entering

 No food, drink, glass, or animal

 No running, splashing, or diving

 Children under 12 years of age should be with an adult

 No swimming allowed when a lifeguard is not on duty

Pool hours are from 9AM to 6PM

15. What should everyone do before entering the pool?

(A) see a doctor

(B) wait for rain

(C) eat some food

(D) take a shower

16. Who must always be at the pool when people are swimming?

(A) a doctor

(B) an adult

(C) an animal

(D) a lifeguard

QUESTIONS 17-18. Refer to the following information.

17. How many bagels can you get for $12.00?

(A) 6

(B) 12

(C) 13

(D) 14

18. What baked goods DOESN'T Bob's Bakery sell?

(A) buns

(B) cakes

(C) bread

(D) croissants

QUESTIONS 19–20. Refer to the following information.

RADIO CONTROLLED CARS

Model	Scale	Power Type	Speed	Price
Stellar	1/10	Battery	35KPH	$110
Fiero	1/8	Gas	50KPH	$150
Rabbit	1/10	Battery	30KPH	$90
Glide	1/12	Battery	40KPH	$100

19. Which car model runs on gas?

(A) Stellar

(B) Fiero

(C) Rabbit

(D) Glide

20. How much does the slowest car cost?

(A) $90

(B) $100

(C) $110

(D) $150

DIRECTIONS: For questions 21 to 30, read the passages and choose the BEST answer for each question about the passages.

지시 사항: 21번부터 30번까지는 글을 읽고, 글과 관련된 질문에 답하는 문제입니다. 질문에 가장 알맞은 답을 고르세요.

QUESTIONS 21-22. Refer to the following passage.

One of the deadliest animals on earth is the box jellyfish. Box jellyfish are found in warm oceans around the world. They are beautiful to look at because you can see through them. They are shaped like bells with long, flowing arms called tentacles. The tentacles have a very strong poison. Jellyfish use this poison to catch small fish to eat. But humans have sometimes died from the jellyfish's poison.

21. Where can box jellyfish be found?

(A) in cold water
(B) in warm oceans
(C) in rivers and lakes
(D) all around the world

22. What does a box jellyfish use to catch small fish?

(A) its mouth
(B) its strong legs
(C) its long tentacles
(D) its bell-shaped body

QUESTIONS 23-24. Refer to the following passage.

Not too many people have heard about the World Pyro Olympics. It is held every year in Manila, Philippines. The word "pyro" means fire. This event is a competition for the world's biggest fireworks companies. The competition lasts for five days. Every day, two countries show off their greatest fireworks. It is an amazing thing to see! The country with the best fireworks gets to be the World Pyro Olympics Champion.

23. Why do they call it World Pyro Olympics?

(A) because it lasts for five days

(B) because it is in Manila, Philippines

(C) because it is a competition of fireworks

(D) because only the biggest companies compete

24. In total, how many countries show off their greatest fireworks?

(A) 2 countries

(B) 5 countries

(C) 10 countries

(D) 20 countries

QUESTIONS 25-26. Refer to the following passage.

Mozart was born in Salzburg, Austria, in 1756. When he was only six years old, he played music for kings and queens. By the time he was eight, Mozart wrote his first symphony. A symphony is a very long and difficult piece of music. All together, Mozart wrote about 600 pieces of music. Sadly, he died a poor man when he was 35 years old. Today, music lovers remember him as one of the greatest musicians in history.

25. What happened when Mozart was eight years old?

(A) He died very poor.
(B) He wrote a symphony.
(C) He wrote 600 pieces of music.
(D) He played for kings and queens.

26. What is NOT true about Mozart?

(A) He was born in Vienna, Austria.
(B) He died when he was 35 years old.
(C) He is one of the greatest musicians.
(D) He could write long, difficult pieces of music.

QUESTIONS 27–28. Refer to the following passage.

Teenagers grow very quickly. Girls usually grow earlier than boys. Girls start growing quickly when they are about 12 to 13 years old. Boys grow quickly when they are about 14 to 15 years old. However, boys can grow faster. Boys can grow about 9cm a year and girls can grow about 8cm a year. The first parts of the body to grow fast are the hands and feet. That's why growing teenagers need to buy new shoes very often.

27. At what age do girls start to grow quickly?

(A) after they are 13 years old
(B) before they are 12 years old
(C) when they are 12 to 13 years old
(D) when they are 14 to 15 years old

28. What is NOT true about the way teenagers grow?

(A) Boys grow earlier than girls.
(B) The hands and feet grow first.
(C) Boys can grow faster than girls.
(D) Girls can grow about 8cm a year.

QUESTIONS 29–30. Refer to the following passage.

The giant sequoia is one of the biggest living things on the planet. Giant sequoia trees can be found in central California. California is a state in the far west of the United States. The largest giant sequoia, called the General Sherman Tree, is 84 meters tall and has a trunk that is 11.1 meters wide. People guess that it weighs as much as 2,500 tons! Many of these giant sequoia trees are thousands of years old.

29. Where can giant sequoia trees be found?

(A) in central California
(B) in southern California
(C) in central United States
(D) in the west of California

30. How wide is the General Sherman Tree's trunk?

(A) 84 meters
(B) 2,500 tons
(C) 11.1 meters
(D) thousands of years

Actual Test 4

Section I

Listening and Speaking

Part **A** Listen and Respond
10 Questions

Part **B** Listen and Retell
15 Questions

Part **C** Listen and Speak
5 Questions

PART A Listen and Respond

DIRECTIONS: For questions 1 to 10, listen to the sentences and choose the BEST response. The sentences and the choices will be spoken **TWICE**. The choices are NOT printed on your test paper.

지시 사항: 1번부터 10번까지는 문장을 듣고, 가장 알맞은 대답을 고르는 문제입니다. 문제와 보기는 **두 번씩** 들려주며 보기는 시험지에 표시되지 않습니다.

1. Mark your answer on your answer sheet.

2. Mark your answer on your answer sheet.

3. Mark your answer on your answer sheet.

4. Mark your answer on your answer sheet.

5. Mark your answer on your answer sheet.

6. Mark your answer on your answer sheet.

7. Mark your answer on your answer sheet.

8. Mark your answer on your answer sheet.

9. Mark your answer on your answer sheet.

10. Mark your answer on your answer sheet.

PART B Listen and Retell

DIRECTIONS: For questions 11 to 25, listen to the short talks or conversations and choose the BEST answer for each question. The talks and conversations will be spoken **TWICE**.

지시 사항: 11번부터 25번까지는 짧은 대화나 이야기를 듣고, 가장 알맞은 답을 고르는 문제입니다. 문제는 **두 번씩** 들려줍니다.

11. What kind of present do they need to buy?

(A) a bitrthday present

(B) a goodbye present

(C) a Mother's Day present

(D) a housewarming present

12. Who sneezes when near a cat?

(A) They both do.

(B) Only the woman does.

(C) Only the man does.

(D) Neither of them does.

13. Where are they?

(A) at a farm

(B) at a restaurant

(C) at a grocery store

(D) at a department store

14. What are they doing?

(A) They are cleaning their rooms.

(B) They are washing their clothes.

(C) They are shopping for clothing.

(D) They are getting ready to go out.

15. Who is the boy waiting for?

(A) his father

(B) his friend

(C) Bill's friend

(D) a soccer player

16. When is the girl's birthday?

(A) this week

(B) next week

(C) next month

(D) in two months

17. How is the boy's brother?

(A) He is hurt.

(B) He feels fine.

(C) He has a cold.

(D) He feels better.

[18-19]

18. Where is this announcement being made?

(A) on a bus
(B) on a subway
(C) in a car wash
(D) on an airplane

19. What did the announcer tell people to do?

(A) close the door
(B) stand near the doors
(C) get off at the next stop
(D) take their things with them

[20-21]

20. What does the woman NOT have an interest in?

(A) eating
(B) cooking
(C) painting the dish
(D) listening to music

21. What does the woman do with her friends?

(A) go to concerts
(B) eat at restaurants
(C) cook in restaurants
(D) paint pictures of food

[22-23]

22. What was the boy doing when he got hurt?

(A) running
(B) swimming
(C) playing tennis
(D) playing soccer

23. What did the boy's mother do for him?

(A) She put a bandage on him.
(B) She drove him to the hospital.
(C)She gave him flowers and a card.
(D) She picked him up off the ground.

[24-25]

24. What is this announcement for?

(A) a bank
(B) a library
(C) a bookstore
(D) a grocery store

25. What day is it today?

(A) Thursday
(B) Friday
(C) Saturday
(D) Sunday

PART C Listen and Speak

DIRECTIONS: For questions 26 to 30, listen to the conversations and choose the BEST response. The conversations will be spoken **TWICE**.

지시 사항: 26번부터 30번까지는 대화를 듣고, 뒤에 이어질 가장 알맞은 응답을 고르는 문제입니다. 문제는 **두 번씩** 들려줍니다.

26. What's next?

(A) He is free.
(B) He is busy.
(C) He has a car.
(D) He will drive.

27. What's next?

(A) I will stay up late tonight.
(B) I could sleep all day long.
(C) Thanks for finishing it for me.
(D) Okay, I'll see you in the morning.

28. What's next?

(A) All my brushes are there.
(B) I needed them to cut my hair.
(C) I have no idea where they are.
(D) You borrowed them last week.

29. What's next?

(A) I think she's very pretty.

(B) She always tells great stories.

(C) She just reads from the textbook.

(D) She's the best teacher I've ever had.

30. What's next?

(A) I'm ready to go.

(B) In a few minutes.

(C) You smell the onion.

(D) I'm really hungry, too.

Section II

Reading and Writing

Part **A** Sentence Completion
5 Questions

Part **B** Situational Writing
5 Questions

Part **C** Practical Reading and Retelling
10 Questions

Part **D** General Reading and Retelling
10 Questions

PART A Sentence Completion

DIRECTIONS: For questions 1 to 5, fill in the blanks to finish the sentences. Choose the option that BEST completes each blank.

지시 사항: 1번부터 5번까지는 빈칸을 알맞게 채워 대화를 완성하는 문제입니다. 가장 알맞은 답을 고르세요.

1. A: There is _________ excuse for what you did.
B: I know. I'm so sorry.

(A) no
(B) not
(C) none
(D) nothing

2. A: _________ one do you like - the green one or the white one?
B: I like the white one better.

(A) Why
(B) Who
(C) What
(D) Which

3. A: Here is my painting, Mrs. Jackson.
B: Great! I'm very pleased with _________ work.

(A) you
(B) your
(C) yours
(D) you're

4. A: Can you help me clean my room?
B: I'm afraid I have _________ free time these days.

(A) few
(B) lots
(C) a lot
(D) little

5. A: I'm a little worried about the cost of the gloves.
B: Don't worry. ________ cheap.

(A) It is
(B) It has
(C) They are
(D) They have

PART B Situational Writing

DIRECTIONS: For questions 6 to 10, look at the pictures and complete the sentences. Choose the option that BEST completes each sentence.

지시 사항: 6번부터 10번까지는 그림을 보고 문장을 완성하는 문제입니다. 가장 알맞은 답을 고르세요.

6.

A girl is ______________________.

(A) skipping rope

(B) stepping over a line

(C) hopping over a stone

(D) jumping over some ropes

7.

The monkey is ______________________.

(A) in front of a deer

(B) next to an elephant

(C) at the back of a giraffe

(D) between a rabbit and a deer

8.

The sharks are swimming ______________________.

(A) under the boat

(B) around the boat

(C) towards each other

(D) away from the boat

9.

The teacher is ______________________.

(A) doing the girl's housework for her

(B) helping the girl do her housework

(C) helping the girl with her schoolwork

(D) listening to the girl explain something

10.

The woman is ______________________.

(A) putting some cake in the refrigerator

(B) cleaning the inside of the refrigerator

(C) searching for something in the refrigerator

(D) taking out some fruit from the refrigerator

DIRECTIONS: For questions 11 to 20, read the practical materials and choose the BEST answer for each question about the materials.

지시 사항: 11번부터 20번까지는 실용적 읽기 자료를 읽고, 자료와 관련된 질문에 답하는 문제입니다. 각 질문에 가장 알맞은 답을 고르세요.

QUESTIONS 11-12. Refer to the following information.

Average Daily Use

Device	Time
MP3 Player	2 hours per day
Bike or Rollerblades	45 minutes per day
Computer	3 hours per day
Cellphone	15 minutes per day
Television	1 hour per day

11. How much time is spent watching television per day?

(A) 1 hour
(B) 2 hours
(C) 3 hours
(D) 4 hours

12. Which will take one hour?

(A) computer
(B) MP3 player
(C) bike and cell phone
(D) rollerblades and television

QUESTIONS 13–14. Refer to the following sign.

13. What time does the store close on Wednesday?

(A) at 11AM

(B) at 4PM

(C) at 6PM

(D) It does not open that day.

14. What can you NOT buy at the store?

(A) plates

(B) chairs

(C) paintings

(D) computers

QUESTIONS 15–16. Refer to the following information.

15. How much is the additional charge to the meal?

(A) $3.31

(B) $4.73

(C) $8.04

(D) $47.30

16. How much does one plate of Chicken Kiev cost?

(A) $9.50

(B) $16.40

(C) $23.65

(D) $32.80

QUESTIONS 17–18. Refer to the following invitation.

Tim and Rebecca Lee wish to invite you
to the 80th birthday of Tim's mother
on Saturday, May 21st at 3PM.

No presents, please.

17. Whose birthday is it?

(A) Tim's

(B) Rebecca's

(C) Tim's mother's

(D) Rebecca's sister's

18. What day is the party?

(A) Thursday

(B) Friday

(C) Saturday

(D) Sunday

QUESTIONS 19–20. Refer to the following information.

Charity Basketball Game

Tickets $10

The Philadelphia Eagles
vs.
Reading Police

Friday, May 18
Doors open at 6PM
Game starts at 7PM

Tickets are available at:

World Gym
The Pike Cafe
Vegas School
Jo's Sporting Goods

19. What time does the game start?

(A) 5 PM

(B) 6 PM

(C) 7 PM

(D) 8 PM

20. Where can you NOT buy the ticket?

(A) World Gym

(B) The Pike Cafe

(C) Charity School

(D) Jo's Sporting Goods

DIRECTIONS: For questions 21 to 30, read the passages and choose the BEST answer for each question about the passages.

지시 사항: 21번부터 30번까지는 글을 읽고, 글과 관련된 질문에 답하는 문제입니다. 질문에 가장 알맞은 답을 고르세요.

QUESTIONS 21-22. Refer to the following passage.

A delicious avocado fruit is good for you, and is one of the healthiest foods you can eat. Cut an avocado from the top to the bottom and separate the two pieces. Remove the stone with a spoon, then place the pieces cut side down and take off the skin using a knife or your fingers. Sprinkle the fruit with lemon juice and enjoy it. The taste is pleasing and feels as smooth as butter in your mouth.

21. What is the first step in preparing an avocado?

(A) Peel the skin.
(B) Remove the pit.
(C) Cut it from top to bottom.
(D) Sprinkle with lemon juice.

22. Which of the following feels like an avocado?

(A) fruit
(B) butter
(C) coconut
(D) vegetable

QUESTIONS 23-24. Refer to the following passage.

The beach may look like a nice place, but there are dangers. Too much sun is bad for anyone, and babies should not be in the sun at all. Playing in the sand is fun, but look at the sand carefully for broken shells or bottles. Wear water shoes to keep the hot sand or dangers in the water from hurting your feet. Wear a sun hat to protect your eyes from the strong sun. Finally, be sure to keep a close watch on children. They may walk down the beach or go into the water alone.

23. According to the passage, which is NOT mentioned as a danger of the beach?

(A) hot sand
(B) big waves
(C) strong sun
(D) broken shells

24. Which is NOT true about the passage?

(A) You must sunbathe with babies.
(B) You should wear water shoes in the sand.
(C) You should keep a close watch on children.
(D) You must wear a sun hat to protect your eyes.

QUESTIONS 25-26. Refer to the following passage.

The highest waterfall in the world is Angel Falls in South America. It is 1,002 meters high, 19 times higher than Niagara Falls. It was discovered in 1935 by Jimmy Angel. He was flying his airplane above the waterfall. He landed his airplane on top of the mountain and found the waterfall. Soon the whole world learned about the waterfall, and it was named after the man who first saw it. Many visitors go to the waterfall each year.

25. How high is Angel Falls?

(A) 19 meters
(B) 1,002 meters
(C) 1,200 meters
(D) 1,935 meters

26. Where did Jimmy Angel land his airplane?

(A) at the airport
(B) by Niagara Falls
(C) on top of a waterfall
(D) on top of a mountain

QUESTIONS 27–28. Refer to the following passage.

Clouds are made when very small water drops stick to very small pieces of dirt in the air. When the cloud meets cold air, the water falls to the ground as rain or snow. This can happen when warm air pushes cool air up the side of a mountain, and it gets colder as it rises. It can also happen when warm air moves over a colder area, like water. It rains or snows because cool air holds less water than warm air.

27. What do small water drops stick to as clouds are made?

(A) air
(B) dirt
(C) water
(D) clouds

28. What happens when the cloud meets cold air?

(A) It turns warm.
(B) The sun shines.
(C) It rains or snows.
(D) The cloud moves away.

QUESTIONS 29–30. Refer to the following passage.

Flying radio control airplanes is one of the most exciting hobbies. You must be able to follow directions, build a small airplane, and learn how to fly it with a radio remote control. Then all you have to do is find an open field. The great thing is you can have fun outside in the fresh air flying the airplane above you. The key is to just have fun and try not to let your airplane hit the ground and break. However, if you do break your plane, you can always fix it.

29. Where do people fly radio control airplanes?

(A) in a classroom
(B) inside the house
(C) outside in a field
(D) in an open market

30. What do you need to fly radio control airplanes?

(A) a radio
(B) a TV set
(C) a computer
(D) a radio remote control

Actual Test 5

Section I

Listening and Speaking

Part **A** Listen and Respond
10 Questions

Part **B** Listen and Retell
15 Questions

Part **C** Listen and Speak
5 Questions

PART A Listen and Respond

DIRECTIONS: For questions 1 to 10, listen to the sentences and choose the BEST response. The sentences and the choices will be spoken **TWICE**. The choices are NOT printed on your test paper.

지시 사항: 1번부터 10번까지는 문장을 듣고, 가장 알맞은 대답을 고르는 문제입니다. 문제와 보기는 **두 번씩** 들려주며 보기는 시험지에 표시되지 않습니다.

1. Mark your answer on your answer sheet.

2. Mark your answer on your answer sheet.

3. Mark your answer on your answer sheet.

4. Mark your answer on your answer sheet.

5. Mark your answer on your answer sheet.

6. Mark your answer on your answer sheet.

7. Mark your answer on your answer sheet.

8. Mark your answer on your answer sheet.

9. Mark your answer on your answer sheet.

10. Mark your answer on your answer sheet.

PART B Listen and Retell

DIRECTIONS: For questions 11 to 25, listen to the short talks or conversations and choose the BEST answer for each question. The talks and conversations will be spoken **TWICE**.

지시 사항: 11번부터 25번까지는 짧은 대화나 이야기를 듣고, 가장 알맞은 답을 고르는 문제입니다. 문제는 **두 번씩** 들려줍니다.

11. Where did the boy see the theater?

(A) in a photo

(B) in a TV ad

(C) in a painting

(D) in a drawing

12. What are the boy and girl doing?

(A) They are making plans.

(B) They don't like to be outside.

(C) They are eating at a restaurant.

(D) They are thinking about their futures.

13. Why does the girl feel better?

(A) The boy gave her flowers.

(B) The boy likes her painting.

(C) She likes the boy's painting.

(D) The boy will buy her a painting.

14. Where are they going?

(A) to the village
(B) to the video shop
(C) to the parking lot
(D) to the supermarket

15. Who will the girl visit?

(A) her uncle
(B) her friend
(C) her teacher
(D) her grandparents

16. What is the problem?

(A) The boy doesn't swim very well.
(B) The boy is worried about the girl.
(C) The swimming place is dangerous.
(D) The boy doesn't know how to swim.

17. What is true?

(A) They weigh the same.
(B) The boy weighs less than the girl.
(C) The girl weighs less than her sister.
(D) The boy weighs more than the girl.

[18-19]

18. What was the bridge made of?

(A) spaghetti
(B) sticks
(C) paper
(D) glue

19. How much weight made the bridge break?

(A) three kilos
(B) six kilos
(C) ten kilos
(D) twelve kilos

[20-21]

20. When will the gift shop close?

(A) at four-thirty
(B) at five o'clock
(C) at six o'clock
(D) at nine o'clock

21. What is this talk about?

(A) location of the gift shop
(B) directions to the museum
(C) operating hours of the museum
(D) special exhibits in the museum

[22-23]

22. What is the speaker mainly talking about?

(A) watching a fire

(B) driving in traffic

(C) playing in the street

(D) a visit from his grandparents

23. How did his grandparents feel?

(A) glad

(B) tired

(C) afraid

(D) worried

[24-25]

24. What is the speaker mainly talking about?

(A) how to give a speech

(B) how to write a speech

(C) how to take better notes

(D) how to improve pronunciation

25. What should you remember?

(A) to speak quickly

(B) to look at the class

(C) to practice only a little

(D) to look at your paper often

PART C Listen and Speak

DIRECTIONS: For questions 26 to 30, listen to the conversations and choose the BEST response.
The conversations will be spoken **TWICE**.

지시 사항: 26번부터 30번까지는 대화를 듣고, 뒤에 이어질 가장 알맞은 응답을 고르는 문제입니다.
문제는 **두 번씩** 들려줍니다.

26. What's next?

(A) I'll go with you.

(B) That's not right.

(C) That sounds good.

(D) When did you go?

27. What's next?

(A) Okay, let's wait.

(B) I'll help you look.

(C) Let's ask that man.

(D) We won't ask anyone.

28. What's next?

(A) Why? What's wrong with them?

(B) Thanks. That's really nice of you.

(C) Thanks. You can pay me back later.

(D) This time you can borrow my money.

29. What's next?

(A) I didn't think of flowers.

(B) I don't want any flowers.

(C) When are you having a party?

(D) Your mom's flowers are beautiful.

30. What's next?

(A) Is it hot enough?

(B) That's a great idea.

(C) I just love a surprise.

(D) Okay, what's your plan?

Section II

Reading and Writing

Part **A** Sentence Completion
5 Questions

Part **B** Situational Writing
5 Questions

Part **C** Practical Reading and Retelling
10 Questions

Part **D** General Reading and Retelling
10 Questions

PART A Sentence Completion

DIRECTIONS: For questions 1 to 5, fill in the blanks to finish the sentences. Choose the option that BEST completes each blank.

지시 사항: 1번부터 5번까지는 빈칸을 알맞게 채워 대화를 완성하는 문제입니다. 가장 알맞은 답을 고르세요.

1. A: Where is __________________?

B: Sorry, we ate all of it after dinner.

(A) I baked the cake

(B) the cake I baked

(C) the cake baked

(D) baked the cake

2. A: ________ I go to the dentist today?

B: Of course. It's time for a checkup.

(A) Am

(B) Have

(C) Must

(D) Would

3. A: Did you see ________ found the bag?

B: Yes, and I thanked him.

(A) when

(B) who

(C) what

(D) whom

4. A: ________ very dark outside.

B: Don't worry. My dad will drive you to your house.

(A) It get

(B) It was

(C) It going

(D) It's getting

5. A: What will you do tonight?

B: I will go out for dinner ________ I finish early.

(A) if

(B) for

(C) but

(D) and

PART B Situational Writing

DIRECTIONS: For questions 6 to 10, look at the pictures and complete the sentences. Choose the option that BEST completes each sentence.

지시 사항: 6번부터 10번까지는 그림을 보고 문장을 완성하는 문제입니다. 가장 알맞은 답을 고르세요.

6.

They are ______________________.

(A) fishing

(B) watering

(C) feeding fish

(D) taking a walk

7. 

The cat has ____________________.

(A) taken the cup

(B) drunk the milk

(C) broken the cup

(D) spilled the milk

8. 

My shirt is too ____________________.

(A) tight

(B) loose

(C) thick

(D) wide

9. 

She is looking into the ____________________.

(A) screen

(B) window

(C) closet

(D) mirror

10. 

The boy is ____________________ the girl.

(A) behind

(B) next to

(C) in front of

(D) far away from

PART C Practical Reading and Retelling

DIRECTIONS: For questions 11 to 20, read the practical materials and choose the BEST answer for each question about the materials.

지시 사항: 11번부터 20번까지는 실용적 읽기 자료를 읽고, 자료와 관련된 질문에 답하는 문제입니다. 각 질문에 가장 알맞은 답을 고르세요.

QUESTIONS 11–12. Refer to the following schedule.

OCEAN BEACH
CHILDREN'S ANIMATION FILM FESTIVAL
August 5-7

Feature Films (Sun Theater)		Classic Films (Star Theater)	
UP!	3:00 p.m	CINDERELLA	3:00 p.m
BOLT	4:30 p.m	101 DALMATIANS	5:00 p.m
MADAGASCAR	6:00 p.m	LION KING	6:30 p.m
TALE of DESPEREAUX	7:30 p.m	FINDING NEMO	8:00 p.m
WALL-E Late feature	9:00 p.m		

TICKET PRICES: Feature Films: $6.00 Classic Films: $4.00

11. Where are the feature films being shown?

(A) at Sun Theater

(B) at Star Theater

(C) at Beach Theater

(D) at Classic Theater

12. How much does it cost when you see UP and LION KING?

(A) 6 dollars

(B) 8 dollars

(C) 10 dollars

(D) 12 dollars

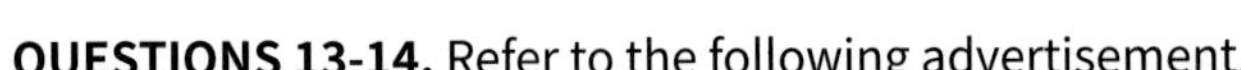

QUESTIONS 13-14. Refer to the following advertisement.

The Pancake Mill Restaurant

Now celebrating Our 27th Year!
BREAKFAST - LUNCH - PIE SHOP
OPEN FROM 6 A.M. TO 3 P.M.

2 For 1 SPECIALS

Ham & Cheese Omelet	**$6.00**
Pancakes (comes with your choice of sausage or ham)	**$5.00**
Strawberry Pancakes	**$4.00**

2 for 1 Specials Available on Sundays only
Monday Lunch Special $5.99
Wednesday BBQ Lunch-All You Can Eat $5.99

13. How long has the restaurant been open?

(A) three years
(B) four years
(C) twenty years
(D) twenty-seven years

14. When can you have the two-for-one special?

(A) on Sunday
(B) on Monday
(C) on Wednesday
(D) on Friday

QUESTIONS 15–16. Refer to the following notice.

15. What will only mothers receive on May 10?

    (A) a rose

    (B) a daisy

    (C) a violin

    (D) a cookie

16. Where will visitors have tea?

    (A) in the kitchen

    (B) in the restaurant

    (C) in the greenhouse

    (D) in the rose garden

QUESTIONS 17–18. Refer to the following information.

VOLLEYBALL	BASKETBALL	SOCCER
Girls Aug. 17-21 $120	Girls July 13-17 $125	Girls / Boys Aug. 24-27 $100
Girls / Boys Aug. 24-27 $120	Boys Aug. 10-14 $125	

Times: All school camps run from **9 AM** to **noon.**

17. How much does it cost for the girls' basketball camp?

(A) one hundred dollars

(B) two hundred dollars

(C) one hundred and twenty dollars

(D) one hundred and twenty-five dollars

18. When do boys have basketball camp?

(A) July 13-17

(B) August 10-14

(C) August 17-21

(D) August 24-27

QUESTIONS 19–20. Refer to the following notice.

GRADE 12 FINAL EXAM SCHEDULE

All morning exams begin at 9:00 a.m. and end at 11:30 a.m.
All afternoon exams begin at 1:00 p.m. and end at 3:30 p.m.

History students may have an extra half hour to complete their essays.

Monday	Tuesday	Thursday
AM Biology	AM Mathematics	AM Physics
PM History	PM Geography	PM Chemistry

PLEASE OBSERVE THE FOLLOWING RULES

Do not start until you are told to begin.
No cell phones, dictionaries or calculators
(calculators allowed for Mathematics and Chemistry exams)
Do not look at another person's work.
Do not talk.
When the time is up, you must stop.

19. Which of the following exams permits a calculator?

(A) Biology

(B) Physics

(C) Chemistry

(D) Geography

20. Which exam has a four o'clock finish time?

(A) History

(B) Physics

(C) Chemistry

(D) Geography

PART D General Reading and Retelling

DIRECTIONS: For questions 21 to 30, read the passages and choose the BEST answer for each question about the passages.

지시 사항: 21번부터 30번까지는 글을 읽고, 글과 관련된 질문에 답하는 문제입니다. 질문에 가장 알맞은 답을 고르세요.

QUESTIONS 21–22. Refer to the following passage.

At one time crocodile farms were popular in Australia. Visitors came to see saltwater crocodiles being caught because these crocodiles are so dangerous. They can grow up to 6.2 meters and weigh 1.5 tons. The shows were exciting for the visitors. In one show, a man put his head inside the open mouth of a crocodile. Today, most of the farms have closed. People began to think that dangerous crocodile shows were not such a good idea after all.

21. What is the best title for the passage?

(A) Tips on Feeding Crocodiles
(B) Last of the Crocodile Farms
(C) The Dangers of Saltwater Crocodiles
(D) Australia's Most Interesting Crocodiles

22. What happened to the crocodile farms?

(A) They became safer.
(B) They became less popular.
(C) They became more popular.
(D) They became more dangerous.

QUESTIONS 23-24. Refer to the following passage.

Taste is one of the five senses, and there are four tastes that people have. The first taste is sweet. Try putting sugar or honey on your tongue. The second taste is salty. Try licking a little salt. The third taste is sour, the taste of a lemon, and the fourth taste is bitter. Bite into an olive or taste coffee. Taste is not the same as flavor. Flavor is the smell of a food with its taste.

23. Which of these has a sour taste?

(A) salt
(B) olives
(C) coffee
(D) lemons

24. What is flavor?

(A) the taste of a food
(B) the look of a food
(C) the taste and smell of a food
(D) the look and smell of a food

QUESTIONS 25–26. Refer to the following passage.

One of the most well-known and popular games in the world is chess. Chess began over 1,600 years ago in India. It is a game that requires a lot of thinking about how the other player will move his or her game pieces. For many years scientists even tried to create a chess-playing computer. In 1997, Deep Blue became the first computer to win a chess game. It beat the world champion chess player, Garry Kasparov.

25. When did people start playing chess?

(A) in 1997
(B) 600 years ago
(C) 1,000 years ago
(D) 1,600 years ago

26. What is the name of the computer that won a chess game?

(A) India
(B) Deep Blue
(C) Blue Chess
(D) Garry Kasparov

QUESTIONS 27–28. Refer to the following passage.

The most beautiful villages in Mexico are called the "Magical Villages." One of these villages is Tapalpa. The country around this village has high mountains, beautiful waterfalls and a green jungle. The houses and buildings in the village are some of the oldest in Mexico. The food is wonderful, and every week there are colorful festivals to enjoy. A trip to the magical village of Tapalpa is a surprise for many travelers to Mexico.

27. What is Tapalpa?

(A) a high mountain in Mexico
(B) the oldest village in Mexico
(C) a beautiful waterfall in Mexico
(D) one of Mexico's magical villages

28. How do many visitors feel when they first see Tapalpa?

(A) bored
(B) afraid
(C) magical
(D) surprised

QUESTIONS 29–30. Refer to the following passage.

Cleaning one's teeth is something people have done for a very long time. Long ago, people chewed on small sticks to clean their teeth. As the years passed, the sticks became bigger until they were the size of a pencil. One end was chewed until it became soft and like a brush. The first true toothbrush was made by the Chinese, who used animal hairs for the brush. This toothbrush was introduced to the rest of the world by travelers to China.

29. How did people clean their teeth before toothbrushes?

(A) They used pencils.
(B) They chewed on leaves.
(C) They chewed on small sticks.
(D) They chewed on animal hair.

30. Who introduced the toothbrush to the rest of the world?

(A) traveling doctors
(B) travelers to China
(C) Chinese dentists
(D) Chinese travelers

Appendix

A

a few	어느 정도, 조금
about	adv.거의
above all	무엇보다도, 특히
advertisement	n. 광고
advice	n. 조언, 충고
after	prep. 후에
after all	adj. 결국에는
afternoon	n. 오후
again	adv. 한 번 더, 다시
against	prep. ~에 맞서
agree	v. 동의하다, 의견이 일치하다
all-you-can-eat	양껏 먹을 수 있는, 뷔페식의
almost	adv. 거의
along	prep. ~을 따라
already	adv. 이미, 벌써
always	adv. 항상
amazing	adj. 놀라운
ambulance	n. 구급차
ancient	adj. 고대의, 아주 오래된
animation	n. 만화
announce	v. 발표하다, 알리다
another	adj. 다른, 또 하나
answer	v. 대답하다, 대응하다
antique	n. 골동품
anyone	pron. 누구, 아무
anyway	adv. 어쨌든
apologize	v. 사과하다
appetizer	n. 전채 요리
around	prep. 주위에
arrive	v. 도착하다
at the back of	prep. ~의 뒤에
at this time	이맘때에
athletics	n. 육상
attendant	n. 종업원, 안내원
attention	n. 주의, 주목
aunt	n. 이모
available	adj. 구할 수 있는
average	n. 평균
avocado	n. 아보카도
avoid	v. 방지하다, 막다, 피하다
away	adv. 떨어져
awesome	adj. 어마어마한, 엄청난, 굉장한

B

bake	v. 굽다, 구워지다
bakery	n. 빵집, 제과점
bandage	n. 붕대
bathroom	n. 욕실
be sure to do something	꼭[반드시] ~을 하다
beach	n. 해변
beach volleyball	n. 비치 발리볼
beak	n. 부리

beat	v. 이기다
beautiful	adj. 아름다운
behind	prep. 뒤에
bell	n. 종
beside	prep. 옆에
better	adj. 더 좋은, 더 나은
between	prep. 사이에
bill	n. 영수증
bite	v. 물다
book	v. 예약하다
bookstore	n. 서점
borrow	v. 빌리다
both	pron. 둘 다의
bottle	n. 병
bought	v. (buy의 과거형) 샀다
bread	n. 빵
break	v. 깨다, 부수다, (기록을) 깨다 (break-broke-broken)
break up	(관계 등을) 끝내다
breakfast	n. 아침식사
bring	v. 가져오다
bronze	n. 동
broom	n. 빗자루
bubbly	adj. 거품이 나는
bun	n. 번빵, 둥글 납작한 빵
busy	adj. 바쁜
button	n. (옷의) 단추

C

calculate	v. 계산하다, 산출하다
calculator	n. 계산기
can	n. (깡통)분무기
catch	v. 버스/기차를 타다
catch a cold	감기에 걸리다
celebrate	v. 축하하다
central	adj. 중앙의
champion	n. 챔피온
charity	n. 자선 단체, 자선
cheap	adj. 싼, 저렴한
cheaper	adj. 더 싼(cheap-cheaper-cheapest)
check	v. 확인하다, 검사하다
check out	대출하다
checkup	n. 검진
chef	n. 요리사
chew	v. 씹다
chubby	adj. 통통한, 토실토실한
class	n. 반, 학급
classic film	n. 고전 영화
classmate	n. 반 친구, 급우
clean	v. 닦다, 청소하다
cliff	n. 절벽
clock	n. 시계
closet	n. 벽장
clothing	n. 옷

coat	n. 코트, 외투
cockroach	n. 바퀴벌레
collar	n. 칼라, 깃, (개 등의 목에 거는) 목걸이
color	v. 색을 칠하다
coloring	n. 염색
combination	n. 조합
come by	잠깐 들르다
comic book	n. 만화책
compete	v. 경쟁하다
competition	n. 경쟁
completely	adv. 완전히, 전적으로
cookie	n. 쿠키
cooking	n. 요리
cool off	식히다
cooperation	n. 협력, 협조
cost	n. 비용
couch	n. 긴 의자, 침상, 소파
country	n. 지역, 고장
cousin	n. 사촌
cover for	대신하다, 보호하다
crazy about	...에 (푹) 빠져 있는
create	v. 창조하다
crocodile	n. 악어
croissant	n. 크루아상
crumple	v. 구기다, 구겨지다
cry out	비명을 지르다
curl	n. 곱슬, 컬
customer	n. 고객

D

daily	adj. 나날의
danger	n. 위험
dangerous	adj. 위험한
deadly	adj. 치명적인
delay	n. 지연, 지체; v. 미루다, 연기하다
delicious	adj. 맛있는
dental	adj. 이[치아/치과]의
dentist	n. 치과, 치과의사
denture	n. 틀니, 의치
department store	n. 백화점
device	n. 장치
different	adj. 다른
direction	n. 방향, 위치, 지시
dirt	n. 먼지
discount	n. 할인
discover	v. 발견하다
dish	n. 요리, 음식
diving	n. 다이빙
dozen	n. 12개 묶음
drink	n. 음료
drive	v. 운전하다, 태워다 주다
drop by	잠깐 들르다

dye	v. 염색하다
E	
early	adj. 초기의, 이른, 빠른
enemy	n. 적
enjoy	v. 즐기다
enough	adv. 충분히
enter	v. 들어가다
essay	n. 에세이, 과제물, 글
even though	비록 ~일지라도
event	n. 행사
excuse	n. 변명
expect	v. 기대하다
expensive	adj. 비싼
explain	v. 설명하다
F	
fall	v. 넘어지다 (fall-fell-fallen)
far from	멀리
farm	n. 농장
fat	adj. 뚱뚱한
favorite	adj. 매우 좋아하는, 마음에 드는
feature film	n. 장편 영화
fee	n. 비용, 요금
feed	v. 먹이를 주다
feel	v. 느끼다, ~감정이 들다
fever	n. 열
fiber	n. 섬유질
field	n. 들판
finally	adv. 마침내
fine	adj. 좋은, 건강한
finest	adj. 최상의
finish	v. 끝내다
fire truck	n. 소방차
fireworks	n. 폭죽
fix	v. 수리하다, 고치다
flight	n. 비행
flowing	adj. 물결 같은
fog	n. 안개
fold	v. 접다
following	adj. 다음의, 다음에 나오는
food court	n. 푸드코트
fountain	n. 분수, 식수대
frame	n. 틀, 뼈대
free	adj. 무료의, 여유로운
free time	n. 여가 시간
fresh	adj. 신선한
friendship	n. 우정, 교우 관계
fries	n. 감자튀김
front	n. 앞쪽
front desk	n. 프런트(안내 데스크)
full	adj. 가득 찬, 배부른
furniture	n. 가구

G

gallery	n. 미술관
game	n. 경기
gardener	n. 정원사
gardening	n. 정원 가꾸기
garlic	n. 마늘
gate	n. 탑승구
germ	n. 세균
get better	좋아지다, 호전되다
get off	내리다, 하차하다
get ready	준비를 하다
giant	adj. 거대한
gift shop	n. 기념품샵
glad	adj. 기쁜, 고마운
glass	n. 유리
gloves	n. 장갑
glue	n. 접착제
go away	(떠나)가다
goodbye	n. 작별
grade	n. 학년
graduation	n. 졸업, 졸업식
grandparent	n. 조부[모]
great	adj. 엄청난, 대단한
green	n. 초록색
greenhouse	n. 온실
grocery store	n. 식료품점

H

hair	n. 털
hair salon	n. 미용실
half an hour	30분
hard	adv. 심하게, 많이
harden	v. 굳다, 경화되다
hardly	adv. 거의 ~아니다[없다]
harmless	adj. 해가 없는, 무해한
hear	v. 듣다(hear-heard-heard)
here	adv. 여기에[에서/로]
hit	v. 때리다, ~와 부딪치다
hoop	n. (농구의)링
hope	v. 바라다, 희망하다
hose	n. 호스
housewarming	n. 집들이
housework	n. 집안일
hurry	v. 서두르다; n. 서두름
hurt	adj. 다친
husband	n. 남편

I

I'm afraid	유감이지만
idea	n. 발상, 생각
if	conj. 만약, ~면
improve	v. 나아지다, 향상되다
in front of	~의 앞에
ingredient	n. 재료

inside	prep. 내부에
instead	adv. 대신에
instrument	n. 악기
insurance	n. 보험
interesting	adj. 흥미로운, 재미있는
introduce	v. 소개하다
invite	v. 초대하다
iron	n. 다리미; v .다리미질을 하다
item	n. 물품
J	
jewelry	n. 보석
journalist	n. 기자
jungle	n. 정글
K	
kayak	n. 카약
keep a close watch on	잘 지켜보다
knee	n. 무릎
knock	v. 두드리다, 치다
kph	시간 당 킬로미터
L	
land	v. 착륙하다
last	v. 계속하다, 지속하다, 오래가다
late	adj. 늦은
lay	v. 알을 낳다
learn	v. 배우다, 학습하다
lend	v. 빌려주다
less	adj. 더 적은, 덜한
library	n. 도서관
lifeguard	n. 안전 요원
little	adv. 조금, 약간
living room	n. 거실
look	v. 찾다, 찾아보다
look for	찾다
look forward to	~을 기대하다
look up	쳐다보다
loose	adj. 헐렁한, 느슨한
lost	adj. 길을 잃은
loud	adj. 큰, 시끄러운
lower	v. 낮추다, 내리다
lunch	n. 점심식사
M	
mall	n. 쇼핑 몰
man-made	사람이 만든, 인공의
material	n. 재료
medal	n. 메달
member	n. 회원
membership	n. 회원자격
memory	n. 기억, 기억력
merry-go-round	n. 회전목마
mess up	엉망으로 만들다
mill	n. 방앗간
mine	pron. 나의 것

mixture	n. 혼합물
model	n. 모형, 모델
mop	n. 대걸레
mountain biking	n. 산악 자전거 타기
movie	n. 영화
muscle	n. 근육
museum	n. 박물관
N	
name	v. 명명하다
nap	n. 낮잠
National Archive	n. 국가 기록 보관소, 국가 문서 보관소
natural	adj. 자연의, 천연의
near	adv. 가까이
nearly	adv. 거의
necessary	adj. 필요한
need	v. 필요로 하다
neither	pron. (둘 중)어느 것도 …아니다
next to	~의 옆에
nice	adj. 친절한, 좋은, 멋진
nightmare	n. 악몽
no longer	더 이상 ~ 않다
no wonder	~는 놀랍지도 않다, 그도 그럴 것이
notebook	n. 공책
nothing	pron. 아무것도, 단 하나도
O	
object	n. 물건, 물체
observe	v. 준수하다
office	n. 사무소, 사무실
Olympic	adj. 올림픽(대회)의
on duty	근무 중
on time	시간을 어기지 않고, 정각에
one on one	일대일로
onion	n. 양파
only	adj. 유일한
order	v. 주문하다
original	adj. 원래의; n. 원본
owner	n. 주인, 소유주
P	
painting	n. 그림 그리기, (물감으로 그린) 그림
parking lot	n. 주차장
partial	adj. 부분적인
pass	v. 지나가다, 흐르다
passenger	n. 승객, 탑승객
patience	n. 인내심
pay	v. 지불하다
pay off	성공하다, 성과를 올리다
pay somebody back	~에게 갚다
peel	v. 껍질을 벗기다
per	prep. 각, ~당[마다]
perform	v. 행하다, 공연하다
pet dog	n. 애완견
photographer	n. 사진작가, 사진사

pick	v. 따다, 고르다
piece	n. 조각
piece of music	음악 작품
pit	n. 씨
place	v. 두다
planet	n. 지구, 행성
plant	n. 식물
platform	n. 플랫폼
please	v. 기쁘게 하다, 기분을 맞추다
pleased	adj. 기쁜, 만족해하는
pleasing	adj. 만족스러운
plug	n. 플러그
poison	n. 독
poor	adj. 가난한
popular	adj. 인기 있는
porcelain	n. 자기
pot	n. 화분
pottery	n. 도자기
practice	n. 연습; v. 연습하다
prefer	v. 선호하다
present	n. 선물
president	n. 대통령
price	n. 값, 가격
protect	v. 보호하다, 지키다
pull	v. 끌다, 당기다
push	v. 밀다
put	v. 놓다, 넣다, 두다
Q	
quarantine	n. (전염병 확산을 막기 위한 동물, 사람의) 격리
quickly	adv. 빠르게
quiet	v. 조용해지다, 조용히 시키다
R	
rabies	n. 광견병
radio control	무선 조종의
radio-controlled	무선으로 조종되는
rake	n. 갈퀴
reach	v. ~에 이르다, 닿다
ready	adj. 준비가 된, 완성된
refrigerator	n. 냉장고
regular	adj. 규칙적인, 정기적인
reline	v. 선을 새로 긋다, 안감을 갈다
remote control	n. 원격 조종, 리모콘
remove	v. 제거하다
repair	v. 수리[보수/수선]하다
reptile	n. 파충류
require	v. 요구하다
rest	n. 나머지, 다른 사람들; v. 쉬다
restroom	n. 화장실
rise	v. 오르다
roasted	adj. 구운
rollerblade	n. 롤러블레이드
rule	n. 규칙

run away	도망치다
S	
safe	adj. 안전한
saltwater	adj. 바다의
same	adj. 같은
schedule	n. 일정, 스케줄
schoolwork	n. 학교 공부
scissors	n. 가위
scooter	n. 스쿠터, 소형 오토바이
seagull	n. 갈매기
search	v. 찾다
section	n. 부분, 부문
seesaw	n. 시소
separate	v. 분리하다
serve	v. 제공하다
shade	v, 가리다; n. 그늘
shake hands	악수하다
shark	n. 상어
shell	n. 껍질, 껍데기
shopper	n. 쇼핑객
shovel	n. 삽
show up	눈에 띄다 [나타나다]
shrimp	n. 새우
shy	adj. 수줍음을 많이 타는, 수줍어하는
side	n. 쪽, 측
sign	n. 표지판, 서명

silverware	n. 은 식기류
simple	adj. 간단한, 단순한
since	conj. 때문에; 한 이후로
skater	n. 스케이트 타는 사람
skeleton	n. 뼈대, 골격
skin	n. 피부, 껍질
skip rope	v. 줄넘기하다
sky blue	하늘색
sleep	v. 자다
sleepy	adj. 졸음이 오는
sleeve	n. 소매
slide	v. 미끄러지다; n. 미끄럼틀
slope	n. 경사지, 경사면
smell	n. 냄새; v. 냄새가 나다
smooth	adj. 부드러운
sneeze	n. 재채기; v. 재채기하다
social studies	사회학
some	adj. 약간의
somewhat	adv. 어느 정도, 약간, 다소
sound	v. ~처럼 들리다, ~인 것 같다; n. 소리
space	n. 공간, 장소
special	n. 특별 상품
speech	n. 연설
spider	n. 거미
spill	v. 흐르다, 흘리다, 쏟다
splash	v. (물을) 튀기다, 끼얹다

splitting	adj. 깨질듯한
spring	n. 봄
sprinkle	v. 뿌리다
stand back	물러서다
stand somebody up	~를 바람맞히다
state	n. 국가, 주
station	n. 역, 정거장
stay	v. 머무르다
stay healthy	건강을 유지하다
stick	v. 달라붙다; n. 막대기, 나뭇가지
stone	n. 씨, 돌
street	n. 거리, 가
strong	adj. 강한
stuck	adj. 움직일 수 없는
stuff	v. 채워 넣다, 쑤셔 넣다
subtotal	n. 소계
subway	n. 지하철, 지하도
suddenly	adv. 갑자기, 불현듯
supermarket	n. 슈퍼마켓
supplement	n. 보충(물)
surprise	n. 뜻밖의 일, 놀라움
sweater	n. 스웨터
sweep	v. 쓸다, 털다
swim	v. 헤엄치다
swimmer	n. 수영을 할 줄 아는 사람, 수영을 하고 있는 사람
swimming pool	n. 수영장
swing	n. 그네
symphony	n. 교향곡, 심포니

T

table tennis	n. 탁구
tablet	n. 정제
take	v. 가지고 가다, (얼마의 시간이)걸리다
take a rest	쉬다
take off	벗기다
take out	꺼내다, 가지고 나가다
taste	v. 맛이 나다
tax	n. 세금
teacher	n. 선생님
tear	v. 찢다, 뜯다
tentacle	n. 촉수
terrible	adj. 끔직한
textbook	n. 교과서
thank	v. 감사하다, 고마워하다
theater	n. 극장
these days	요즘에는
thick	adj. 굵은, 두꺼운
thinking	n. 생각
thirsty	adj. 목이 마른, 갈증이 나는
tight	adj. (옷이) 꽉 조이는
tip	n. 팁, 봉사료
tired	adj. 피곤한
tissue	n. 휴지

together	adv. 함께, 같이
tongue	n. 혀
too	adv. 너무, ~도
toothbrush	n. 칫솔
tournament	n. 대회, 경기
toward	prep. ~을 향하여
towards	prep. 쪽으로, 향하여
towel	n. 수건
traffic	n. 교통
transfer	v. 환승하다
traveler	n. 여행자
trick	n. 속임수, 장난
trip	v. 발을 헛디디다
truly	adv. 정말로, 진심으로
trumpet	n. 트럼펫
trunk	n. 나무의 몸통

U

ugly	adj. 못생긴
uncle	n. 삼촌
under	prep. 아래에
university	n. 대학교
unscrew	v. 열다
use	n. 사용
usually	adv. 주로, 보통

V

vacuum cleaner	n. 진공청소기
vet	n. 수의사
veteran	n. 베테랑, 전문가
video shop	n. 비디오 가게
village	n. 마을
visit	v. 방문하다; n. 방문
visitor	n. 방문객
volleyball	n. 배구

W

wait	v. 기다리다; n. 기다림
wait for	~를 기다리다
walk along	따라 걷다
want	v. 원하다
warm	adj. 따뜻한
watch	n. 손목시계
water	v. 물을 주다
water drop	n. 물방울
waterfall	n. 폭포
watering can	n. 물뿌리개
weather	n. 날씨
wedding	n. 결혼식
weekend	n. 주말
weigh	v. 무게가 ~이다
well-known	adj. 잘 알려진
west	n. 서쪽
while	conj. ~하는 동안
white	n. 흰색

whiteboard	n. (흰색) 칠판
whole	adj. 전체의
wide	adj. 폭이 ...인
wipe	v. 닦다; n. 행주
without	prep. ~없이
wonder	n. 경이, 불가사의
wonderful	adj. 훌륭한
wooden sticks	n. 나무 막대기
work	n. 작품
would like to	~하고 싶다
wrestling	n. 레슬링
Y	
yearbook	n. 연감, 연보, 졸업 앨범
yet	adv. 아직
Z	
zoo	n. 동물원

국제영어능력인증시험 (TOSEL)

* 연습을 위한 OMR 카드 샘플입니다.

JUNIOR	한글이름		감독확인	

수 험 번 호

				-				-						
(1)				-				-						
(2)	0	0	0	-	0	0	0	-	0	0	0	0	0	0
	1	1	1		1	1	1		1	1	1	1	1	1
	2	2	2		2	2	2		2	2	2	2	2	2
	3	3	3		3	3	3		3	3	3	3	3	3
	4	4	4		4	4	4		4	4	4	4	4	4
	5	5	5		5	5	5		5	5	5	5	5	5
	6	6	6		6	6	6		6	6	6	6	6	6
	7	7	7		7	7	7		7	7	7	7	7	7
	8	8	8		8	8	8		8	8	8	8	8	8
	9	9	9		9	9	9		9	9	9	9	9	9

주의사항

1. 수험번호 및 답안은 검은색 사인펜을 사용해서 <보기>와 같이 표기합니다.
   <보기> 바른표기 : ● 틀린표기 : ⓥ ⓧ ⊙ ◑ ◎
2. 수험번호(1)에는 아라비아 숫자로 쓰고, (2)에는 해당란에 ● 표기합니다.
3. 답안 수정은 수정 테이프로 흔적을 깨끗이 지웁니다.
4. 수험번호 및 답안 작성란 이외의 여백에 낙서를 하지 마시기 바랍니다. 이로 인한 불이익은 수험자 본인 책임입니다.
5. 마킹오류로 채점 불가능한 답안은 0점 처리되오니, 이점 유의하시기 바랍니다.

* 정기시험 OMR로 사용이 불가합니다.

SECTION Ⅰ

문항	A	B	C	D	문항	A	B	C	D
1	A	B	C	D	16	A	B	C	D
2	A	B	C	D	17	A	B	C	D
3	A	B	C	D	18	A	B	C	D
4	A	B	C	D	19	A	B	C	D
5	A	B	C	D	20	A	B	C	D
6	A	B	C	D	21	A	B	C	D
7	A	B	C	D	22	A	B	C	D
8	A	B	C	D	23	A	B	C	D
9	A	B	C	D	24	A	B	C	D
10	A	B	C	D	25	A	B	C	D
11	A	B	C	D	26	A	B	C	D
12	A	B	C	D	27	A	B	C	D
13	A	B	C	D	28	A	B	C	D
14	A	B	C	D	29	A	B	C	D
15	A	B	C	D	30	A	B	C	D

SECTION Ⅱ

문항	A	B	C	D	문항	A	B	C	D
1	A	B	C	D	16	A	B	C	D
2	A	B	C	D	17	A	B	C	D
3	A	B	C	D	18	A	B	C	D
4	A	B	C	D	19	A	B	C	D
5	A	B	C	D	20	A	B	C	D
6	A	B	C	D	21	A	B	C	D
7	A	B	C	D	22	A	B	C	D
8	A	B	C	D	23	A	B	C	D
9	A	B	C	D	24	A	B	C	D
10	A	B	C	D	25	A	B	C	D
11	A	B	C	D	26	A	B	C	D
12	A	B	C	D	27	A	B	C	D
13	A	B	C	D	28	A	B	C	D
14	A	B	C	D	29	A	B	C	D
15	A	B	C	D	30	A	B	C	D

국제토셀위원회

국제영어능력인증시험 (TOSEL)

* 연습을 위한 OMR 카드 샘플입니다.

JUNIOR

한글이름		감독확인	

수 험 번 호

				–				–						
(1)				–				–						
(2)	0	0	0	–	0	0	0	–	0	0	0	0	0	0
	1	1	1		1	1	1		1	1	1	1	1	1
	2	2	2		2	2	2		2	2	2	2	2	2
	3	3	3		3	3	3		3	3	3	3	3	3
	4	4	4		4	4	4		4	4	4	4	4	4
	5	5	5		5	5	5		5	5	5	5	5	5
	6	6	6		6	6	6		6	6	6	6	6	6
	7	7	7		7	7	7		7	7	7	7	7	7
	8	8	8		8	8	8		8	8	8	8	8	8
	9	9	9		9	9	9		9	9	9	9	9	9

주의사항

1. 수험번호 및 답안은 검은색 사인펜을 사용해서 〈보기〉와 같이 표기합니다.
   〈보기〉 바른표기 : ● 틀린표기 : ✓ ⊗ ⊙ ◑ ◎
2. 수험번호(1)에는 아라비아 숫자로 쓰고, (2)에는 해당란에 ● 표기합니다.
3. 답안 수정은 수정 테이프로 흔적을 깨끗이 지웁니다.
4. 수험번호 및 답안 작성란 이외의 여백에 낙서를 하지 마시기 바랍니다. 이로 인한 불이익은 수험자 본인 책임입니다.
5. 마킹오류로 채점 불가능한 답안은 0점 처리되오니, 이점 유의하시기 바랍니다.

* 정기시험 OMR로 사용이 불가합니다.

SECTION Ⅰ

문항	A	B	C	D	문항	A	B	C	D
1	Ⓐ	Ⓑ	Ⓒ	Ⓓ	16	Ⓐ	Ⓑ	Ⓒ	Ⓓ
2	Ⓐ	Ⓑ	Ⓒ	Ⓓ	17	Ⓐ	Ⓑ	Ⓒ	Ⓓ
3	Ⓐ	Ⓑ	Ⓒ	Ⓓ	18	Ⓐ	Ⓑ	Ⓒ	Ⓓ
4	Ⓐ	Ⓑ	Ⓒ	Ⓓ	19	Ⓐ	Ⓑ	Ⓒ	Ⓓ
5	Ⓐ	Ⓑ	Ⓒ	Ⓓ	20	Ⓐ	Ⓑ	Ⓒ	Ⓓ
6	Ⓐ	Ⓑ	Ⓒ	Ⓓ	21	Ⓐ	Ⓑ	Ⓒ	Ⓓ
7	Ⓐ	Ⓑ	Ⓒ	Ⓓ	22	Ⓐ	Ⓑ	Ⓒ	Ⓓ
8	Ⓐ	Ⓑ	Ⓒ	Ⓓ	23	Ⓐ	Ⓑ	Ⓒ	Ⓓ
9	Ⓐ	Ⓑ	Ⓒ	Ⓓ	24	Ⓐ	Ⓑ	Ⓒ	Ⓓ
10	Ⓐ	Ⓑ	Ⓒ	Ⓓ	25	Ⓐ	Ⓑ	Ⓒ	Ⓓ
11	Ⓐ	Ⓑ	Ⓒ	Ⓓ	26	Ⓐ	Ⓑ	Ⓒ	Ⓓ
12	Ⓐ	Ⓑ	Ⓒ	Ⓓ	27	Ⓐ	Ⓑ	Ⓒ	Ⓓ
13	Ⓐ	Ⓑ	Ⓒ	Ⓓ	28	Ⓐ	Ⓑ	Ⓒ	Ⓓ
14	Ⓐ	Ⓑ	Ⓒ	Ⓓ	29	Ⓐ	Ⓑ	Ⓒ	Ⓓ
15	Ⓐ	Ⓑ	Ⓒ	Ⓓ	30	Ⓐ	Ⓑ	Ⓒ	Ⓓ

SECTION Ⅱ

문항	A	B	C	D	문항	A	B	C	D
1	Ⓐ	Ⓑ	Ⓒ	Ⓓ	16	Ⓐ	Ⓑ	Ⓒ	Ⓓ
2	Ⓐ	Ⓑ	Ⓒ	Ⓓ	17	Ⓐ	Ⓑ	Ⓒ	Ⓓ
3	Ⓐ	Ⓑ	Ⓒ	Ⓓ	18	Ⓐ	Ⓑ	Ⓒ	Ⓓ
4	Ⓐ	Ⓑ	Ⓒ	Ⓓ	19	Ⓐ	Ⓑ	Ⓒ	Ⓓ
5	Ⓐ	Ⓑ	Ⓒ	Ⓓ	20	Ⓐ	Ⓑ	Ⓒ	Ⓓ
6	Ⓐ	Ⓑ	Ⓒ	Ⓓ	21	Ⓐ	Ⓑ	Ⓒ	Ⓓ
7	Ⓐ	Ⓑ	Ⓒ	Ⓓ	22	Ⓐ	Ⓑ	Ⓒ	Ⓓ
8	Ⓐ	Ⓑ	Ⓒ	Ⓓ	23	Ⓐ	Ⓑ	Ⓒ	Ⓓ
9	Ⓐ	Ⓑ	Ⓒ	Ⓓ	24	Ⓐ	Ⓑ	Ⓒ	Ⓓ
10	Ⓐ	Ⓑ	Ⓒ	Ⓓ	25	Ⓐ	Ⓑ	Ⓒ	Ⓓ
11	Ⓐ	Ⓑ	Ⓒ	Ⓓ	26	Ⓐ	Ⓑ	Ⓒ	Ⓓ
12	Ⓐ	Ⓑ	Ⓒ	Ⓓ	27	Ⓐ	Ⓑ	Ⓒ	Ⓓ
13	Ⓐ	Ⓑ	Ⓒ	Ⓓ	28	Ⓐ	Ⓑ	Ⓒ	Ⓓ
14	Ⓐ	Ⓑ	Ⓒ	Ⓓ	29	Ⓐ	Ⓑ	Ⓒ	Ⓓ
15	Ⓐ	Ⓑ	Ⓒ	Ⓓ	30	Ⓐ	Ⓑ	Ⓒ	Ⓓ

국제토셀위원회

국제영어능력인증시험 (TOSEL)

* 연습을 위한 OMR 카드 샘플입니다.

JUNIOR

한글이름		감독확인	

수 험 번 호

(1)				–				–							
(2)	0	0	0	–	0	0	0	–	0	0	0	0	0	0	0
	1	1	1		1	1	1		1	1	1	1	1	1	1
	2	2	2		2	2	2		2	2	2	2	2	2	2
	3	3	3		3	3	3		3	3	3	3	3	3	3
	4	4	4		4	4	4		4	4	4	4	4	4	4
	5	5	5		5	5	5		5	5	5	5	5	5	5
	6	6	6		6	6	6		6	6	6	6	6	6	6
	7	7	7		7	7	7		7	7	7	7	7	7	7
	8	8	8		8	8	8		8	8	8	8	8	8	8
	9	9	9		9	9	9		9	9	9	9	9	9	9

주의사항

1. 수험번호 및 답안은 검은색 사인펜을 사용해서 <보기>와 같이 표기합니다.
   <보기> 바른표기 : ● 틀린표기 : ✓ ⊗ ⊙ ◑ ◎
2. 수험번호(1)에는 아라비아 숫자로 쓰고, (2)에는 해당란에 ● 표기합니다.
3. 답안 수정은 수정 테이프로 흔적을 깨끗이 지웁니다.
4. 수험번호 및 답안 작성란 이외의 여백에 낙서를 하지 마시기 바랍니다. 이로 인한 불이익은 수험자 본인 책임입니다.
5. 마킹오류로 채점 불가능한 답안은 0점 처리되오니, 이점 유의하시기 바랍니다.

* 정기시험 OMR로 사용이 불가합니다.

SECTION Ⅰ

문항	A	B	C	D	문항	A	B	C	D
1	A	B	C	D	16	A	B	C	D
2	A	B	C	D	17	A	B	C	D
3	A	B	C	D	18	A	B	C	D
4	A	B	C	D	19	A	B	C	D
5	A	B	C	D	20	A	B	C	D
6	A	B	C	D	21	A	B	C	D
7	A	B	C	D	22	A	B	C	D
8	A	B	C	D	23	A	B	C	D
9	A	B	C	D	24	A	B	C	D
10	A	B	C	D	25	A	B	C	D
11	A	B	C	D	26	A	B	C	D
12	A	B	C	D	27	A	B	C	D
13	A	B	C	D	28	A	B	C	D
14	A	B	C	D	29	A	B	C	D
15	A	B	C	D	30	A	B	C	D

SECTION Ⅱ

문항	A	B	C	D	문항	A	B	C	D
1	A	B	C	D	16	A	B	C	D
2	A	B	C	D	17	A	B	C	D
3	A	B	C	D	18	A	B	C	D
4	A	B	C	D	19	A	B	C	D
5	A	B	C	D	20	A	B	C	D
6	A	B	C	D	21	A	B	C	D
7	A	B	C	D	22	A	B	C	D
8	A	B	C	D	23	A	B	C	D
9	A	B	C	D	24	A	B	C	D
10	A	B	C	D	25	A	B	C	D
11	A	B	C	D	26	A	B	C	D
12	A	B	C	D	27	A	B	C	D
13	A	B	C	D	28	A	B	C	D
14	A	B	C	D	29	A	B	C	D
15	A	B	C	D	30	A	B	C	D

국제토셀위원회

국제영어능력인증시험 (TOSEL)

* 연습을 위한 OMR 카드 샘플입니다.

JUNIOR	한글이름		감독확인	

수 험 번 호

				–				–						
(1)				–				–						
(2)	0	0	0	–	0	0	0	–	0	0	0	0	0	0
	1	1	1		1	1	1		1	1	1	1	1	1
	2	2	2		2	2	2		2	2	2	2	2	2
	3	3	3		3	3	3		3	3	3	3	3	3
	4	4	4		4	4	4		4	4	4	4	4	4
	5	5	5		5	5	5		5	5	5	5	5	5
	6	6	6		6	6	6		6	6	6	6	6	6
	7	7	7		7	7	7		7	7	7	7	7	7
	8	8	8		8	8	8		8	8	8	8	8	8
	9	9	9		9	9	9		9	9	9	9	9	9

주의사항

1. 수험번호 및 답안은 검은색 사인펜을 사용해서 〈보기〉와 같이 표기합니다.
   〈보기〉 바른표기 : ●　　틀린표기 : ✓ ⊗ ⊙ ◑ ◉
2. 수험번호(1)에는 아라비아 숫자로 쓰고, (2)에는 허당란에 ● 표기합니다.
3. 답안 수정은 수정 테이프로 흔적을 깨끗이 지웁니다.
4. 수험번호 및 답안 작성란 이외의 여백에 낙서를 하지 마시기 바랍니다. 이로 인한 불이익은 수험자 본인 책임입니다.
5. 마킹오류로 채점 불가능한 답안은 0점 처리되오니, 이점 유의하시기 바랍니다.

* 정기시험 OMR로 사용이 불가합니다.

SECTION Ⅰ

문항	A	B	C	D	문항	A	B	C	D
1	A	B	C	D	16	A	B	C	D
2	A	B	C	D	17	A	B	C	D
3	A	B	C	D	18	A	B	C	D
4	A	B	C	D	19	A	B	C	D
5	A	B	C	D	20	A	B	C	D
6	A	B	C	D	21	A	B	C	D
7	A	B	C	D	22	A	B	C	D
8	A	B	C	D	23	A	B	C	D
9	A	B	C	D	24	A	B	C	D
10	A	B	C	D	25	A	B	C	D
11	A	B	C	D	26	A	B	C	D
12	A	B	C	D	27	A	B	C	D
13	A	B	C	D	28	A	B	C	D
14	A	B	C	D	29	A	B	C	D
15	A	B	C	D	30	A	B	C	D

SECTION Ⅱ

문항	A	B	C	D	문항	A	B	C	D
1	A	B	C	D	16	A	B	C	D
2	A	B	C	D	17	A	B	C	D
3	A	B	C	D	18	A	B	C	D
4	A	B	C	D	19	A	B	C	D
5	A	B	C	D	20	A	B	C	D
6	A	B	C	D	21	A	B	C	D
7	A	B	C	D	22	A	B	C	D
8	A	B	C	D	23	A	B	C	D
9	A	B	C	D	24	A	B	C	D
10	A	B	C	D	25	A	B	C	D
11	A	B	C	D	26	A	B	C	D
12	A	B	C	D	27	A	B	C	D
13	A	B	C	D	28	A	B	C	D
14	A	B	C	D	29	A	B	C	D
15	A	B	C	D	30	A	B	C	D

국제토셀위원회

국제영어능력인증시험 (TOSEL)

* 연습을 위한 OMR 카드 샘플입니다.

JUNIOR

한글이름		감독확인	

수 험 번 호

(1)				—				—					
(2)	0	0	0		0	0	0		0	0	0	0	0	0
	1	1	1		1	1	1		1	1	1	1	1	1
	2	2	2		2	2	2		2	2	2	2	2	2
	3	3	3		3	3	3		3	3	3	3	3	3
	4	4	4	—	4	4	4	—	4	4	4	4	4	4
	5	5	5		5	5	5		5	5	5	5	5	5
	6	6	6		6	6	6		6	6	6	6	6	6
	7	7	7		7	7	7		7	7	7	7	7	7
	8	8	8		8	8	8		8	8	8	8	8	8
	9	9	9		9	9	9		9	9	9	9	9	9

주의사항

1. 수험번호 및 답안은 검은색 사인펜을 사용해서 <보기>와 같이 표기합니다.
   <보기> 바른표기 : ● 틀린표기 : ✓ ⊗ ⊙ ◑ ◉
2. 수험번호(1)에는 아라비아 숫자로 쓰고, (2)에는 해당란에 ● 표기합니다.
3. 답안 수정은 수정 테이프로 흔적을 깨끗이 지웁니다.
4. 수험번호 및 답안 작성란 이외의 여백에 낙서를 하지 마시기 바랍니다. 이로 인한 불이익은 수험자 본인 책임입니다.
5. 마킹오류로 채점 불가능한 답안은 0점 처리되오니, 이점 유의하시기 바랍니다.

* 정기시험 OMR로 사용이 불가합니다.

SECTION Ⅰ

문항	A	B	C	D	문항	A	B	C	D
1	A	B	C	D	16	A	B	C	D
2	A	B	C	D	17	A	B	C	D
3	A	B	C	D	18	A	B	C	D
4	A	B	C	D	19	A	B	C	D
5	A	B	C	D	20	A	B	C	D
6	A	B	C	D	21	A	B	C	D
7	A	B	C	D	22	A	B	C	D
8	A	B	C	D	23	A	B	C	D
9	A	B	C	D	24	A	B	C	D
10	A	B	C	D	25	A	B	C	D
11	A	B	C	D	26	A	B	C	D
12	A	B	C	D	27	A	B	C	D
13	A	B	C	D	28	A	B	C	D
14	A	B	C	D	29	A	B	C	D
15	A	B	C	D	30	A	B	C	D

SECTION Ⅱ

문항	A	B	C	D	문항	A	B	C	D
1	A	B	C	D	16	A	B	C	D
2	A	B	C	D	17	A	B	C	D
3	A	B	C	D	18	A	B	C	D
4	A	B	C	D	19	A	B	C	D
5	A	B	C	D	20	A	B	C	D
6	A	B	C	D	21	A	B	C	D
7	A	B	C	D	22	A	B	C	D
8	A	B	C	D	23	A	B	C	D
9	A	B	C	D	24	A	B	C	D
10	A	B	C	D	25	A	B	C	D
11	A	B	C	D	26	A	B	C	D
12	A	B	C	D	27	A	B	C	D
13	A	B	C	D	28	A	B	C	D
14	A	B	C	D	29	A	B	C	D
15	A	B	C	D	30	A	B	C	D

국제토셀위원회

memo

memo

엄선된 **100만 명**의 응시자 성적 데이터를 활용한 **AI기반** 데이터 공유 및 가치 고도화 **플랫폼**

TOSEL® Lab

공동기획
- 고려대학교 문과대학 언어정보연구소
- 국제토셀위원회

TOSEL Lab 이란?

국내외 15,000여 개 학교·학원 단체응시인원 중 엄선한 100만 명 이상의 실제 TOSEL 성적 데이터와, 정부(과학기술정보통신부)의 AI 바우처 지원 사업 수행기관 선정으로 개발된 맞춤식 AI 빅데이터 기반 영어성장 플랫폼입니다.

TOSEL Lab

지정교육기관 혜택

혜택 1
지역독점권

혜택 2
시험 고사장 자격 부여

혜택 3
고려대학교 field trip

혜택 4
토셀 영어학습 패키지

혜택 5
단체 성적분석자료
특강반, 신설반 교재추천

혜택 6
진단평가 기반
무료 영어학습 컨텐츠
Placement Test / Self Study / Monthly Test

학원장의 실질적인 비용부담 없이
TOSEL® Lab
브랜드를 사용할 수 있는 기회

TOSEL Lab 에는 어떤 콘텐츠가 있나요?

진단 맞춤형 레벨테스트로 정확한 평가 제공

응시자 빅데이터 분석에 기반한 테스트로 신규 상담 학생의 영어능력을 정확하게 진단하고 효과적인 영어 교육을 실시하기 위한 객관적인 가이드라인을 제공합니다.

교재 세분화된 레벨로 실력에 맞는 학습 제공

TOSEL의 세분화된 교재 레벨은 각 연령에 맞는 어휘와 읽기 지능 및 교과 과정과의 연계가 가능하도록 설계된 교재들로 효과적인 학습 커리큘럼을 제공합니다.

학습 다양한 교재연계 콘텐츠로 효과적인 자기주도학습

TOSEL 시험을 대비한 다양한 콘텐츠를 제공해 영어 학습에 시너지 효과를 기대할 수 있으며, 학생들의 자기주도 학습 습관을 더 탄탄하게 키울 수 있습니다.

Reading Series

내신과 토셀 고득점을 한꺼번에

Pre-Starter | Starter | Basic | Junior | High-Junior

- 각 단원 학습 도입부에 주제와 관련된 이미지를 통한 말하기 연습
- 각 Unit 별 4-6개의 목표 단어 제시, 그림 또는 영문으로 단어 뜻을 제공하여 독해 학습 전 단어 숙지
- 독해&실용문 연습을 위한 지문과 Comprehension 문항을 10개씩 수록하여 이해도 확인 및 진단
- 숙지한 독해 지문을 원어민 음성으로 들으며 듣기 학습 , 듣기 전, 듣기 중, 듣기 후 학습 커리큘럼 마련

Listening Series

한국 학생들에게 최적화된 듣기 실력 완성!

Pre-Starter | Starter | Basic | Junior | High-Junior

- 초등 / 중등 교과과정 연계 말하기&듣기 학습과 세분화된 레벨
- TOSEL 기출 문장과 실생활에 자주 활용되는 문장 패턴을 통해 듣기 및 말하기 학습
- 실제 TOSEL 지문의 예문을 활용한 실용적 학습 제공
- 실전 감각 향상과 점검을 위한 기출 문제 수록

Speaking Series
출간예정

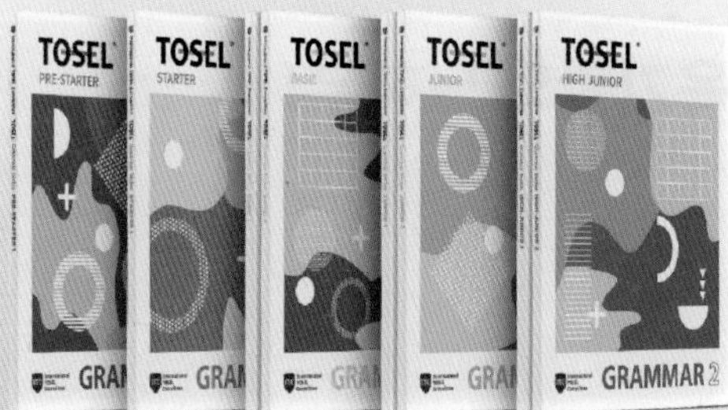

Grammar Series

체계적인 단계별 **문법 지침서**

Pre-Starter | Starter | Basic | Junior | High-Junior

- 초등 / 중등 교과과정 연계 문법 학습과 세분화된 레벨
- TOSEL 기출 문제 연습과 최신 수능 출제 문법을 포함하여 수능 / 내신 대비 가능
- 이해하기 쉬운 그림, 깔끔하게 정리된 표와 설명, 다양한 문제를 통해 문법 학습
- 실전 감각 향상과 점검을 위한 기출 문제 수록

Voca Series

학년별 꼭 알아야하는 **단어 수록!**

Pre-Starter | Starter | Basic | Junior | High-Junior

- 각 단어 학습 도입부에 주제와 관련된 이미지를 통한 말하기 연습
- TOSEL 시험을 기준으로 빈출 지표를 활용한 예문과 문제 구성
- 실제 TOSEL 지문의 예문을 활용한 실용적 학습 제공
- 실전 감각 향상과 점검을 위한 실전 문제 수록

Story Series

읽는 재미에 실력까지 **동시에!**

Pre-Starter | Starter | Basic | Junior

- 초등 / 중등 교과과정 연계 영어 학습과 세분화된 레벨
- 이야기 지문과 단어를 함께 연결지어 학생들의 독해 능력을 평가
- 이해하기 쉬운 그림, 깔끔하게 정리된 표와 설명, 다양한 문제, 재미있는 스토리를 통한 독해 학습
- 다양한 단계의 문항을 풀어보고 학생들의 읽기, 듣기, 쓰기, 말하기 실력을 집중적으로 향상

교재를 100% 활용하는 TOSEL Lab 지정교육기관의 노하우!

Teaching Materials

TOSEL에서 제공하는 수업 자료로
교재 학습을 더욱 효과적으로 진행!

Study Content

철저한 자기주도학습 콘텐츠로
교재 수업 후 효과적인 복습!

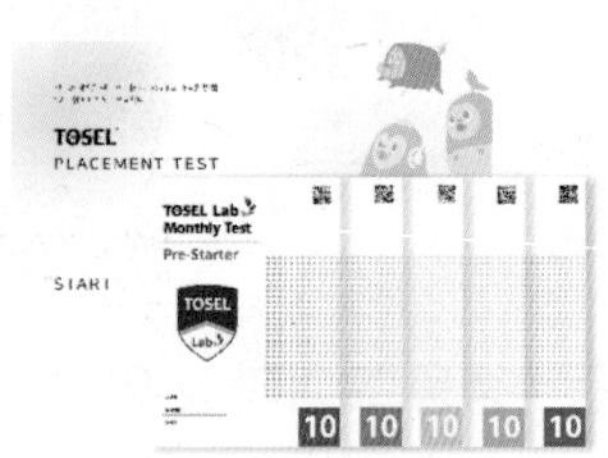

Test Content

교재 학습과 더불어 학생 맞춤형
시험으로 실력 점검 및 향상

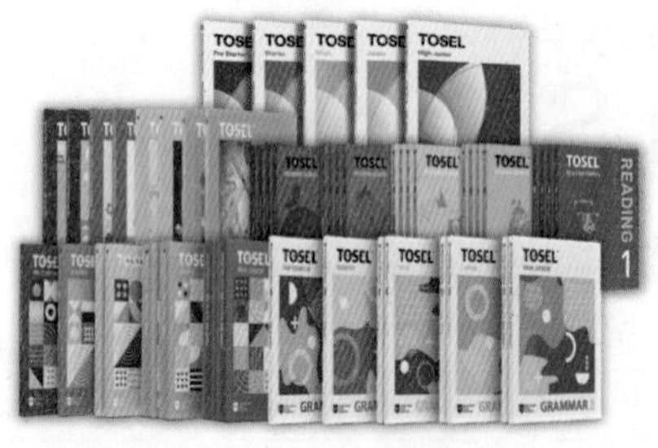

100만 명으로 엄선된 **TOSEL**
성적 데이터로 탄생!

TOSEL Lab 지정교육기관을 위한 콘텐츠로 더욱 효과적인 수업을 경험하세요.

국제토셀위원회는 TOSEL Lab 지정교육기관에서 교재로 수업하는 학원을 위해 교재를 잘 활용할 수 있는 다양한 콘텐츠를 제공 및 지원합니다.

TOSEL Lab 지정교육기관은

국제토셀위원회 직속 TOSEL연구소에서 20년 동안 보유해온 전국 15,000여 개 교육기관 토셀 응시자들의 영어성적 분석데이터를 공유받아, 통계를 기반으로 한 전문적이고 과학적인 커리큘럼을 설계하고, 영어학습 방향을 제시하여,경쟁력있는 기관, 잘 가르치는 기관으로 해당 지역에서 입지를 다지게 됩니다.

TOSEL Lab 지정교육기관으로 선정되기 위해서는 소정의 심사 절차가 수반됩니다.

TOSEL Lab
심사신청

TOSEL Lab
더 알아보기

TOSEL® Lab

국제토셀위원회

TOSEL 실전문제집 2

JUNIOR
정답 및 해설

ITC 국제토셀위원회

TOSEL® 실전문제집 2

Junior

정답 및 해설

TOSEL Junior

실전 1회

Section I Listening and Speaking

1 (B)	2 (C)	3 (C)	4 (D)	5 (A)
6 (D)	7 (C)	8 (D)	9 (C)	10 (B)
11 (B)	12 (D)	13 (C)	14 (B)	15 (A)
16 (C)	17 (B)	18 (B)	19 (A)	20 (B)
21 (A)	22 (D)	23 (B)	24 (C)	25 (D)
26 (C)	27 (D)	28 (B)	29 (C)	30 (D)

Section II Reading and Writing

1 (D)	2 (D)	3 (C)	4 (A)	5 (D)
6 (B)	7 (C)	8 (A)	9 (D)	10 (D)
11 (C)	12 (B)	13 (A)	14 (C)	15 (A)
16 (B)	17 (D)	18 (C)	19 (A)	20 (C)
21 (A)	22 (C)	23 (C)	24 (D)	25 (D)
26 (A)	27 (D)	28 (A)	29 (C)	30 (A)

SECTION I LISTENING AND SPEAKING

Part A. Listen and Respond (p.14)

1. Girl: I'm sorry, we no longer sell that juice.
Boy: ________________
(A) Can I have a hamburger?
(B) Well, can I have soda then?
(C) I'd like two tickets please.
(D) I'll buy it anyway.

해석 소녀: 죄송하지만, 저희는 더 이상 그 주스를 팔지 않아요.
소년: ________________
(A) 제가 햄버거를 먹을 수 있을까요?
(B) 음, 그럼 제가 탄산음료는 먹을 수 있나요?
(C) 티켓 두 장 부탁드립니다.
(D) 어쨌든 전 그걸 살 거예요.

풀이 그 주스를 더 이상 판매하지 않는다고 했으므로 다른 음료를 주문하겠다고 대답한 (B)가 정답이다.

Words and Phrases no longer 더 이상 ~ 않다 | anyway 어쨌든

2. Boy: Have you heard about the concert tonight?
Girl: ________________
(A) I heard the TV.
(B) I didn't go yesterday.
(C) Yes. Are you going to go?
(D) They are singers.

해석 소년: 너 오늘 밤에 있을 콘서트에 대해 들었어?
소녀: ________________
(A) 난 TV를 들었어.
(B) 난 어제 안 갔어.
(C) 응. 넌 갈 예정이야?
(D) 그들은 가수이다.

풀이 오늘 밤 있을 콘서트에 대해 들었는지 묻는 질문에 그렇다며 참석 여부를 묻는 (C)가 정답이다.

3. Girl: You'll remember to call me tonight?
Boy: ________________
(A) Around 8am?
(B) I will eat dinner then.
(C) Around 7pm?
(D) It could rain tonight.

해석 소녀: 너 오늘 밤에 나한테 전화하기로 한 거 기억하지?
소년: ________________
(A) 오전 8시쯤?
(B) 그럼 난 저녁 먹을래.
(C) 오후 7시쯤?
(D) 오늘밤 비가 올 수도 있어.

풀이 오늘 밤에 전화하기로 한 것을 기억하냐는 질문에 저녁 7시쯤인지 시간을 확인하는 (C)가 정답이다.

4. Boy: Which do you prefer – the library or the gym?
Girl: ________________
(A) Ok, let's go!
(B) The library is over there.
(C) Will you go to the gym after lunch?
(D) I like reading better.

해석 소년: 넌 도서관이랑 체육관 중에 어느 쪽을 더 선호해?
소녀: ________________
(A) 좋아, 어서 가자!
(B) 도서관은 저기 있어.
(C) 너 점심 먹고 체육관 갈 거야?
(D) 난 책 읽는 걸 더 좋아해.

풀이 도서관과 체육관 중 어느 쪽을 더 좋아하냐는 질문에 (도서관에서) 책을 읽는 걸 더 좋아한다고 말한 (D)가 정답이다.

Words and Phrases prefer 선호하다

5. Girl: Do you think I should buy these shoes?
Boy: ________________
(A) If you have enough money.
(B) They are special.
(C) They are bigger than these ones.
(D) I'm sorry to hear that.

해석 소녀: 너는 내가 이 신발을 사야 한다고 생각해?
소년: ________________
(A) 만약 네가 충분한 돈을 가지고 있다면.
(B) 그들은 특별해.
(C) 그들은 이것들보다 더 커.
(D) 그것 참 안 됐다.

풀이 신발을 사는 것에 대한 의견을 구하는 말에 돈이 충분하다면 사라고 대답하는 (A)가 정답이다.

6. Boy: Could I ask you to buy the tickets for me?
Girl: ________________
(A) Let's go tomorrow.
(B) I will buy apples.
(C) The tickets are cheap.
(D) I'm sorry but I'm really busy.

해석 소년: 너에게 날 위해 표들을 좀 사다달라고 부탁해도 될까?
소녀: ________________
(A) 내일 가자.
(B) 난 사과들을 살 거야.
(C) 그 표들은 저렴하다.
(D) 미안하지만 나 너무 바빠.

풀이 표들을 사다 줄 수 있냐는 질문에 바쁘다고 거절을 표현하는 (D)가 정답이다.

7. Girl: If I were you, I'd study for the test.
Boy: ________________
(A) Really? I didn't know that.
(B) The teacher is here.
(C) Ok, I will go to the library.
(D) I am reading.

해석 소녀: 만약 내가 너라면, 난 시험을 위해 공부할 거야.
소년: ________________
(A) 정말? 난 그건 몰랐어.
(B) 선생님은 여기 계셔.
(C) 알았어, 도서관에 갈게.
(D) 난 읽는 중이야.

풀이 시험 공부할 것을 우회적으로 제안하는 말에 수긍하는 대답을 하는 (C)가 정답이다.

8. Boy: May I help you?
Girl: ________________
(A) My mother is here.
(B) Please go away.
(C) I like shirts.
(D) Thanks but I'm just looking.

해석 소년: 제가 도와드릴까요?
소녀: ________________
(A) 제 어머니가 여기 계세요.
(B) 제발 가 주세요.
(C) 전 셔츠가 좋아요.
(D) 고맙지만 그냥 둘러보는 중이에요.

풀이 도움이 필요한지 묻는 말에 둘러보는 중이라며 거절하는 (D)가 정답이다.
Words and Phrases go away (떠나)가다

9. Girl: Do you know the ambulance was here?
Boy: ________________
(A) I saw the star.
(B) I don't like loud noise.
(C) Did something happen?
(D) Nobody was here.

해석 소녀: 너 여기 구급차 있던 거 알아?
소년: ________________
(A) 나는 별을 봤어.
(B) 난 시끄러운 소음이 싫어.
(C) 무슨 일 있었어?
(D) 여긴 아무도 없었어.

풀이 구급차가 왔었다는 말에 무슨 일이 있었는지 묻는 (C)가 정답이다.
Words and Phrases ambulance 구급차

10. Boy: May I have another cookie?
Girl: ________________
(A) There are only two people left.
(B) Of course.
(C) Please don't do it.
(D) There is no one here.

해석 소년: 내가 쿠키 하나 더 먹어도 될까?
소녀: ________________
(A) 단 두 명밖에 안 남았어.
(B) 당연하지.
(C) 제발 그거 하지 마.
(D) 여기 아무도 없어.

풀이 쿠키를 하나 더 먹어도 될지 허락을 구하는 말에 그렇다고 답하는 (B)가 정답이다.

Part B. Listen and Retell (p.15)

11. Girl: I'm scared of cockroaches.
Boy: Yeah, me too, but spiders are worse.
Girl: I'm OK with spiders.
Question: Are they both scared of spiders?
(A) Only the girl is.
(B) Only the boy is.
(C) They like cockroaches.
(D) They don't like any bugs.

해석 소녀: 난 바퀴벌레를 무서워해.
소년: 맞아, 나도 그래, 근데 거미는 더 싫어.
소녀: 난 거미는 괜찮아.
질문: 그들은 둘 다 거미를 무서워하는가?
(A) 소녀만 그렇다.
(B) 소년만 그렇다.
(C) 그들은 바퀴벌레를 좋아한다.
(D) 그들은 어떤 벌레도 좋아하지 않는다.

풀이 소년은 거미를 싫어하고 소녀는 괜찮다고 했으므로 (B)가 정답이다.
Words and Phrases cockroach 바퀴벌레 | spider 거미

12. Boy: I think I will have the beef.
Girl: Really? I prefer the pork.
Boy: The beef looks better to me.
Question: Where are they?
(A) at a bakery
(B) at an airport
(C) at a stadium
(D) at a restaurant

해석 소년: 난 소고기를 먹을 생각이야.
소녀: 그래? 난 돼지고기가 더 좋아.
소년: 나한텐 소고기가 더 좋아 보여.
질문: 그들은 어디에 있는가?
(A) 빵집에
(B) 공항에
(C) 경기장에
(D) 식당에

풀이 어느 고기를 먹을지에 대한 이야기를 하고 있으므로 (D)가 정답이다.

13. Boy: Can you check the calendar?
Girl: Yes, we're free on the 16th.
Boy: Ok, if it is fine, let's go.
Question: What are they doing?
(A) They are reading.
(B) They are at home.
(C) They are making plans.
(D) They are eating breakfast.

해석 소년: 달력 좀 확인해 줄래?
소녀: 응, 우리는 16일에 시간이 돼.
소년: 좋아, 괜찮다면, 가자.
질문: 그들은 무엇을 하고 있는가?
(A) 그들은 읽고 있다.
(B) 그들은 집에 있다.
(C) 그들은 계획을 짜고 있다.
(D) 그들은 아침을 먹고 있다.

풀이 달력을 보고 시간이 되는 날짜를 확인하고 있으므로 (C)가 정답이다.

14. Boy: When is your friend arriving?
Girl: Tomorrow at three.
Boy: I'll go and pick her up then.
Question: What will the boy do?
(A) He will catch a bus at 3 p.m.
(B) He will meet the friend at 3 p.m.
(C) He will look for the friend at 3 p.m.
(D) He will buy dinner for the friend at 3 p.m.

해석 소년: 네 친구는 언제 와?
소녀: 내일 3시에.
소년: 그럼 내가 가서 그녀를 데려올게.
질문: 소년은 무엇을 할 것인가?
(A) 그는 오후 3시에 버스를 탈 것이다.
(B) 그는 오후 3시에 그 친구를 만날 것이다.
(C) 그는 오후 3시에 그 친구를 찾을 것이다.
(D) 그는 오후 3시에 그 친구에게 저녁을 살 것이다.

풀이 소년이 3시에 소녀의 친구를 데리러 가겠다고 했으므로 (B)가 정답이다.

Words and Phrases arrive 도착하다

15. Girl: How is your mother's health now?
Boy: She is doing better, thanks.
Girl: I'm glad she has improved.
Question: How was the boy's mother?
(A) She was sick.
(B) She was healthy.
(C) She was doing great.
(D) She was at the party.

해석 소녀: 요즘 너네 어머니 건강은 어떠셔?
소년: 점점 더 나아지고 있어, 고마워.
소녀: 그녀가 나아지고 계시다니 나는 기뻐.
질문: 소년의 어머니는 어떤 상태였는가?
(A) 그녀는 아프셨다.
(B) 그녀는 건강하셨다.
(C) 그녀는 잘 지내고 계셨다.
(D) 그녀는 파티에 계셨다.

풀이 건강이 점점 나아지는 중이라고 했으므로 과거에는 건강이 좋지 못했음을 알 수 있다. 그러므로 (A)가 정답이다.

Words and Phrases improve 나아지다, 향상되다

16. Girl: Why did you knock the water over?
Boy: Sorry. Is your book ok?
Girl: It's a mess!
Question: How is the book?
(A) It is old.
(B) It is lost.
(C) It is wet.
(D) It is clean.

해석 소녀: 너 물은 왜 쏟은 거야?
소년: 미안. 네 책은 괜찮아?
소녀: 엉망이야!
질문: 책 상태는 어떤가?
(A) 오래됐다.
(B) 잃어버렸다.
(C) 젖었다.
(D) 깨끗하다.

풀이 물을 엎질러서 책이 엉망이라고 했으므로 (C)가 정답이다.

Words and Phrases knock 두드리다, 치다

17. Boy: I'd like to be a journalist.
Girl: Do you like talking with people?
Boy: Yes, so it would be a good job for me.
Question: What does the boy like to do?
(A) He likes to be on TV.
(B) He likes to interview people.
(C) He likes to ask the girl questions.
(D) He likes to write letters to friends.

해석 소년: 나는 기자가 되고 싶어.
소녀: 너 사람들이랑 말하는 거 좋아해?
소년: 응, 그래서 그게 나한테 좋은 직업이 될 것 같아.
질문: 소년은 무엇을 하는 것을 좋아하는가?
(A) 그는 TV에 나오는 것을 좋아한다.
(B) 그는 사람들을 인터뷰하는 것을 좋아한다.
(C) 그는 소녀에게 질문하는 걸 좋아한다.
(D) 그는 친구들에게 편지 쓰는 걸 좋아한다.

풀이 소년이 사람들과 이야기하는 걸 좋아한다고 했으므로 (B)가 정답이다.

Words and Phrases journalist 기자

[18-19]

Boy: The Summer Olympic Games was held in Beijing, China from August 8 to August 24. People from around the world competed for the gold, silver or bronze medals. Athletics and wrestling are the oldest sports in the Olympic Games. The original games were held in Greece over 2500 years ago. Kayaking, mountain biking, baseball and beach volleyball are some new Olympic sports.

18. When were the first games held?
(A) less than 600 years ago
(B) more than 2,000 years ago
(C) more than 3,000 years ago
(D) from August 8th until the 24th

19. What is NOT a new Olympic sport?
(A) wrestling
(B) baseball
(C) mountain biking
(D) beach volleyball

해석 소년: 하계올림픽이 중국 베이징에서 8월 8일부터 24일까지 열렸습니다. 전세계의 사람들이 금, 은, 동메달을 위해 경쟁했습니다. 육상과 레슬링은 올림픽 경기 중에 가장 오래된 종목입니다. 최초의 경기들은 2500년 전 그리스에서 열렸습니다. 카약, 산악자전거, 야구와 비치 발리볼은 새 올림픽 종목들입니다.

18. 첫 경기는 언제 열렸는가?
(A) 600년 전이 안됐을 때
(B) 2000년 전보다 더 오래 전에
(C) 3000년 전보다 더 오래 전에
(D) 8월 8일부터 24일까지

19. 새 올림픽 종목이 아닌 것은 무엇인가?
(A) 레슬링
(B) 야구
(C) 산악자전거
(D) 비치 발리볼

풀이 지문에서 올림픽 첫경기가 그리스에서 2500년 전에 열렸다고 이야기하고 있으므로 18번의 정답은 (B)이다.

카약, 산악자전거, 야구와 비치 발리볼이 새 올림픽 종목이므로 19번의 정답은 (A)이다. 레슬링은 가장 오래된 올림픽 종목이다.

Words and Phrases Olympic 올림픽 (대회)의 | compete 경쟁하다 | bronze 동 | medal 메달 | athletics 육상 | wrestling 레슬링 | kayak 카약 | mountain biking 산악 자전거 타기 | beach volleyball 비치 발리볼

[20-21]

Girl: Hello. Passengers of flight 18 Paris, with a stop in Hong Kong, your gate has been changed to 28A. Please go to 28A. There will also be a delay for flights to Sydney due to fog. We apologize for the changes. Thank you for your patience.

20. Where is this?
(A) at a hospital
(B) at an airport
(C) at a train station
(D) at a bus station

21. Why do the flights to Sydney have to be delayed?
(A) because of the weather
(B) because of the gate change
(C) because of a stop in Hong Kong
(D) because of too many passengers

해석 소녀: 안녕하세요. 홍콩을 경유해 파리로 가는 항공편 18 탑승객 여러분, 탑승구가 28A로 변경되었습니다. 28A 탑승구로 가주시길 바랍니다. 시드니로 가는 비행편은 안개로 인한 지연이 있을 예정입니다. 변경사항에 대해 죄송하다는 말씀드립니다. 양해 부탁드립니다.

20. 이곳은 어디인가?
(A) 병원에
(B) 공항에
(C) 기차역에
(D) 버스정류장에

21. 시드니로 가는 비행편은 어떤 이유로 인해 지연되는가?
(A) 날씨 때문에
(B) 탑승구 변동 때문에
(C) 홍콩에서의 경유 때문에
(D) 탑승객이 너무 많기 때문에

풀이 지문은 공항 내 탑승구 변경 및 항공편 지연과 관련해 이야기하고 있으므로 20번의 정답은 (D)이다.

시드니로 가는 비행편은 안개로 인해 지연이 있을 것이라고 하였으므로 21번의 정답은 (A)이다.

Words and Phrases passenger 승객, 탑승객 | flight 비행 | gate 탑승구 | delay 지연, 지체; 미루다, 연기하다 | fog 안개 | apologize 사과하다 | patience 인내심

[22-23]

Boy: Many people catch a cold at this time of year. Here is some advice for staying healthy. Wash your hands before eating, after eating and after going to the bathroom. Eating garlic is also very useful to fight germs and keep away colds. Some people think that eating yoghurt is another good way to fight colds. Maybe someone should make garlic yoghurt!

22. What is the advice for?
(A) to help people eat better
(B) to help people eat yoghurt
(C) to help supermarkets sell garlic
(D) to help people from getting colds

23. What is NOT the advice for staying healthy in winter?
(A) eating garlic
(B) taking a bath
(C) washing hands
(D) eating yoghurt

해석 소년: 매년 이맘때마다 많은 사람들이 감기에 걸린다. 다음은 건강을 유지하기 위한 조언들이다. 먹기 전, 먹고 난 후, 화장실에 갔다 와서 손을 씻어라. 마늘을 먹는 것은 세균과 싸우고 감기에 걸리지 않는 데에 매우 유용하다. 어떤 사람들은 요거트를 먹는 것이 감기에 걸리지 않게하는 또다른 좋은 방법이라고 생각한다. 아마 누군가가 마늘 요거트를 만들어야할지도 모른다!

22. 이 조언들은 무엇을 위한 것인가?
(A) 사람들이 더 잘 먹게 하기 위해서
(B) 사람들이 요거트를 먹게 하기 위해서
(C) 슈퍼마켓들이 마늘을 파는 데에 도움이 되기 위해서
(D) 사람들이 감기에 걸리지 않게 하기 위해서

23. 겨울에 건강을 지키기 위한 조언이 아닌 것은 무엇인가?
(A) 마늘 먹기
(B) 목욕하기
(C) 손씻기
(D) 요거트 먹기

풀이 지문에서 겨울에 감기에 걸리지 않고 건강을 유지하는 방법에 관해 이야기하고 있으므로 22번의 정답은 (D)이다.

겨울에 건강을 지키기 위해 손을 씻고, 마늘과 요거트를 먹으라고 하였으므로 23번의 정답은 (B)이다.

Words and Phrases catch a cold 감기에 걸리다 | advice 조언, 충고 | stay healthy 건강을 유지하다 | garlic 마늘 | germ 세균

[24-25]

Girl: There is a beach near my house that I walk along every morning. I see lots of things, shells washed up on the sand, seagulls flying high talking loudly to each other, and always one duck. Ducks don't usually live on beaches, but this one is there every day and it likes to follow me on my walks.

24. Where does she live?
(A) on the path
(B) near the lake
(C) near the beach
(D) next to the store

25. Where does the duck walk?
(A) in the park
(B) in the water
(C) near her farm
(D) after the woman

해석 소녀: 우리 집 근처에는 내가 매일 아침 걸어다니는 해변이 있다. 나는 많은 것들을 본다, 모래에 닦여진 조개껍질들, 서로에게 시끄럽게 이야기하며 높이 날아다니는 갈매기들, 그리고 오리 한 마리. 오리들은 주로 해변에 살지 않지만, 이 오리는 매일 거기에 있고 나를 따라 거닐기를 좋아한다.

24. 그녀는 어디에 사는가?
(A) 길에
(B) 호수 주변에
(C) 해변 주변에
(D) 상점 옆에

25. 오리는 어디를 걷는가?
(A) 공원 안
(B) 물 속
(C) 그녀의 농장 주변
(D) 여자를 따라

풀이 지문에서 소녀가 자신의 집 근처에는 해변이 있다고 하였으므로 24번의 정답은 (C)이다.

해변에 있는 유일한 오리는 소녀를 따라 거닐기를 좋아한다고 하였으므로 25번의 정답은 (D)이다.

Words and Phrases walk along 따라 걷다 | shell 껍데기 | seagull 갈매기

PART C. Listen and Speak (p.19)

26. Girl: Did you ask your father if you could go?
Boy: Yes. He said no.
Girl: Really? Why is that?
Boy: ________________
(A) He said that I had to play.
(B) He said that he was writing.
(C) He said that I was too young.
(D) He said that he was watching TV.

해석 소녀: 네 아버지께 네가 갈 수 있는지 여쭤봤니?
소년: 응. 그는 안된다고 하셨어.
소녀: 진짜? 어째서?
소년: ________________
(A) 그는 내가 놀았었어야 한다고 하셨어.
(B) 그는 쓰는 중이라고 하셨어.
(C) 그는 내가 너무 어리다고 하셨어.
(D) 그는 TV를 보고 있었다고 하셨어.

풀이 대화에서 소년의 아버지가 소년을 가지 못하게 하는 이유에 대해 물어봤으므로 (C)가 정답이다.

27. Girl: Did you finish your social studies homework?
Boy: Nearly.
Girl: Could you help me with it?
Boy: ________________
(A) Sure, but I can't talk well.
(B) Sure, but I can't add well.
(C) Sure, but I haven't been there.
(D) Sure, but I don't know much about it.

해석 소녀: 너 사회 숙제 다 했니?
소년: 거의.
소녀: 나 좀 도와줄 수 있니?
소년: ________________
(A) 그럼, 그런데 나 말을 잘 못해.
(B) 그럼, 그런데 나 더하기를 잘 못해.
(C) 그럼, 그런데 나 거기 가본 적이 없어.
(D) 그럼, 그런데 나 그것에 대해 잘 몰라.

풀이 대화에서 소녀가 소년에게 사회 숙제를 도와줄 수 있는지 물어봤으므로 (D)가 정답이다.

Words and Phrases social studies 사회학 | nearly 거의

28. Boy: Ah! I lost my button.
Girl: Oops! Where did you see it last?
Boy: I'm not sure.
Girl: ________________
(A) I think I know.
(B) O.K. Let's look for it.
(C) O.K. Let's buy lunch.
(D) O.K. What do you need it for?

해석 소년: 아! 나 단추를 잃어버렸어.
소녀: 앗! 마지막으로 어디서 봤니?
소년: 나도 잘 모르겠어.
소녀: ________________
(A) 나 알 것 같아.
(B) 알았어. 같이 찾아보자.
(C) 알았어. 같이 점심 사 먹자.
(D) 알았어. 뭐에 필요 한데?

풀이 대화에서 소년이 단추를 어디서 잃어버렸는지 모른다고 했으므로 (B)가 정답이다.

Words and Phrases button (옷의) 단추 | last 마지막에 | look for 찾다

29. Boy: There is something on your bag.
Girl: Ah! It's dirty with ketchup.
Boy: I'll get a tissue.
Girl: ________________
(A) Thanks. It must be yours.
(B) Thanks. It must be stuck.
(C) Thanks. It must be from lunch.
(D) Thanks. It must be the teachers.

해석 소년: 네 가방 위에 뭐가 있어.
소녀: 아! 케첩으로 더럽혀졌어.
소년: 휴지 가져올게.
여: ________________
(A) 고마워. 아마 네 것 일 거야.
(B) 고마워. 아마 끼어있나 봐.
(C) 고마워. 아마 점심 때 그랬나 봐.
(D) 고마워. 아마 선생님들이 그랬나 봐.

풀이 대화에서 소녀의 가방에 케첩이 묻어있으므로 (C)가 정답이다.

Words and Phrases tissue 휴지 | stuck 움직일 수 없는 | lunch 점심

30. Girl: There is the president!
Boy: Let's take a photo.
Girl: Do you think I can shake his hand?
Boy: ________________
(A) No, it's not clean.
(B) Everyone knows that.
(C) Don't think about him.
(D) That would be wonderful.

해석 소녀: 저기 대통령이 있어!
소년: 우리 가서 사진 찍자.
소녀: 네가 생각했을 때 내가 그랑 악수할 수 있을 것 같아?
남: ________________
(A) 아니, 그것은 깨끗하지 않아.
(B) 모두 그것을 알아.
(C) 그에 대해 생각하지 마.
(D) 그거 정말 좋겠다.

풀이 대화에서 소녀가 대통령과 악수할 수 있는지 물어봤으므로 (D)가 정답이다.

Words and Phrases president 대통령 | shake hands 악수하다

SECTION II READING AND WRITING

Part A. Sentence Completion (p.21)

1. A: Did you get the CD?
B: I got a CD. ___________, it is the wrong one.
(A) Since
(B) So that
(C) Instead
(D) However

해석 A: 너는 CD 받았어?
B: 나는 CD 받았어. 그런데, 그것은 잘못된 거야.
(A) 왜냐하면
(B) 그래서
(C) 대신에
(D) 그런데
풀이 CD는 받았지만 잘못된 CD였다는 내용이 이어지므로 (D)가 정답이다.
Words and Phrases since 때문에; 한 이후로 | instead 대신에

2. A: You were here last night, ___________?
B: Yeah.
(A) can't you
(B) didn't you
(C) wasn't you
(D) weren't you
해석 A: 당신은 어젯밤에 여기 계셨죠, 아닌가요?
B: 네.
(A) 할 수 없나요?
(B) 하지 않았나요?
(C) 아닌가요?
(D) 아닌가요?
풀이 be동사 문장의 부가의문문이므로 (D)가 정답이다. (C)는 2인칭 주어 'you'와 맞지 않는 be동사이므로 오답이다.
Words and Phrases here 여기에[에서/로]

3. A: Pencils are made ___________ wood.
B: That's right.
(A) in
(B) at
(C) of
(D) to
해석 A: 연필들은 나무로 만들어졌어.
B: 맞아.
(A) 안에서
(B) 에서
(C) 로
(D) 에게
풀이 연필이 나무로 만들어졌다는 의미의 문장이므로 (C)가 정답이다.

4. A: ___________ you have any questions, drop by my office.
B: Okay, I will.
(A) If
(B) As
(C) Since
(D) Because
해석 A: 궁금한 게 있으면 제 사무실로 오세요.
B: 알겠습니다. 그렇게 하겠습니다.
(A) (만약) ...면
(B) 때문에, -아서[-어서/-므로]
(C) ...때문에, ...므로[여서]
(D) ... 때문에, -해서[여서/니까]
풀이 조건을 나타내는 접속사 (A)가 정답이다.
Words and Phrases drop by 잠깐 들르다

5. A: Taking the bus is ___________ than the subway.
B: Then, I'll take a bus.
(A) great
(B) good
(C) best
(D) better
해석 A: 버스를 타는 게 지하철보다 더 나아.
B: 그럼, 나는 버스를 탈게.
(A) 대단해
(B) 좋아
(C) 가장 좋아
(D) 더 나아
풀이 버스와 지하철을 비교하는 문장이므로 비교급 표현이 쓰인 (D)가 정답이다.
Words and Phrases great 엄청난, 대단한

Part B. Situational Writing (p.23)

6. The boy at the front is about to ___________.
(A) cry out
(B) fall down
(C) run away
(D) clap his hands
해석 앞에 있는 소년은 막 넘어지려고 한다.
(A) 비명을 지르려고
(B) 넘어지려고
(C) 도망가려고
(D) 박수를 치려고
풀이 그림에서 소년이 넘어지기 직전이므로 (B)가 정답이다.
Words and Phrases front 앞쪽 | cry out 비명을 지르다 | run away 도망치다

7. The man is holding ___________.
(A) a couch
(B) a popcorn
(C) a remote control
(D) an air conditioner

해석 그 남자는 리모컨을 들고 있다.

(A) 침상

(B) 팝콘

(C) 리모컨

(D) 에어컨

풀이 그림에서 남자가 리모컨을 들고 있으므로 (C)가 정답이다.

Words and Phrases remote control 원격 조종, 리모콘 | couch 긴 의자, 침상, 소파

8. The box is ___________.

(A) wet

(B) torn

(C) opened

(D) crumpled

해석 그 박스는 젖어 있다.

(A) 젖어 있다.

(B) 찢어져 있다.

(C) 열려 있다.

(D) 구겨져 있다.

풀이 그림에서 박스가 젖어 있으므로 (A)가 정답이다.

Words and Phrases tear 찢다, 뜯다 | crumple 구기다, 구겨지다

9. My father is using ___________.

(A) a mop

(B) a wipe

(C) a watering can

(D) a vacuum cleaner

해석 우리 아빠는 진공청소기를 사용 중이시다.

(A) 대걸레

(B) 행주

(C) 물뿌리개

(D) 진공청소기

풀이 그림에서 아빠는 청소기를 사용하여 집안 청소를 하고 있으므로 (D)가 정답이다.

Words and Phrases wipe 닦다; 행주 | mop 대걸레 | vacuum cleaner 진공청소기 | watering can 물뿌리개

10. Let's play ___________.

(A) baseball

(B) volleyball

(C) badminton

(D) table tennis

해석 우리 탁구 하자.

(A) 야구

(B) 배구

(C) 배드민턴

(D) 탁구

풀이 그림에서 탁구를 묘사하고 있으므로 (D)가 정답이다.

Words and Phrases table tennis 탁구 | volleyball 배구

Part C. Practical Reading and Retelling (p.26)

[11-12]

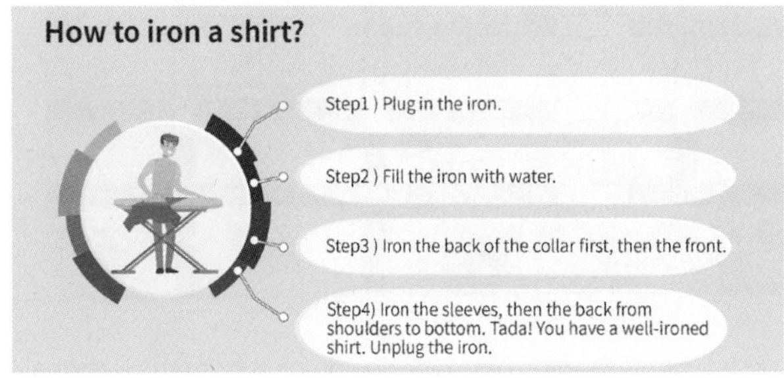

11. What happens before filling the iron with water?

(A) Iron the collar.

(B) Unplug the iron.

(C) Plug in the iron.

(D) Iron the shoulders.

12. Which happens last?

(A) Iron the collar.

(B) Unplug the iron.

(C) Iron the sleeves.

(D) Fill the iron with water.

해석

셔츠를 다림질하는 방법

1단계: 다리미의 플러그를 꽂습니다.

2단계: 다리미에 물을 채웁니다.

3단계: 옷깃의 뒷부분을 먼저 다리고, 그 뒤에 앞부분을 다립니다.

4단계: 소매를 다린 후에, 등 부분을 어깨에서부터 아래로 다립니다. 짜잔! 당신은 이제 잘 다려진 셔츠를 갖게 됩니다. 다리미의 플러그를 뽑으세요.

11. 다리미에 물을 채우기 전에 무슨 일이 일어나는가?

(A) 옷깃을 다린다.

(B) 다리미의 플러그를 뽑는다.

(C) 다리미의 플러그를 꽂는다.

(D) 어깨를 다린다.

12. 마지막으로 무슨 일이 일어나는가?

(A) 옷깃을 다린다.

(B) 다리미의 플러그를 뽑는다.

(C) 소매를 다린다.

(D) 다리미에 물을 채운다.

풀이 다리미에 물을 채우기 전, 먼저 다리미의 플러그를 꽂아야 하므로 11번의 정답은 (C)이다.

마지막으로 다리미의 플러그를 뽑아야 하므로 12번의 정답은 (B)이다.

Words and Phrases iron 다리미; 다리미질을 하다 | plug 플러그 | collar 칼라, 깃 | sleeve 소매

[13-14]

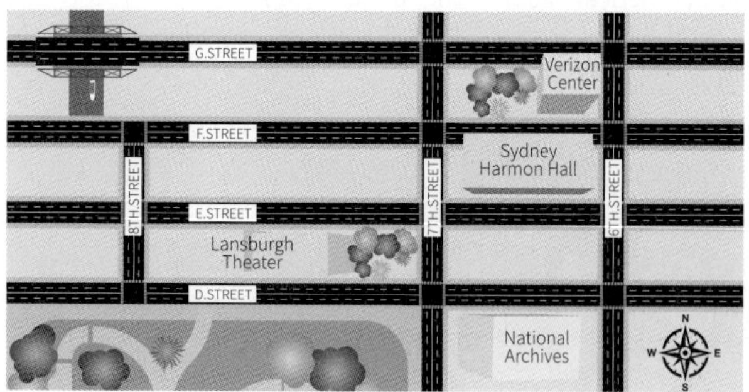

13. At least how many crossroads do you pass from the National Archives to Sydney Harman Hall?

(A) 2
(B) 4
(C) 6
(D) 8

14. In what direction does F.STREET take?

(A) D.STREET
(B) to the right
(C) East - West
(D) North - South

해석

13. 국가 기록 보관소에서 Sydney Harman 홀까지 최소한 몇 개의 교차로를 지나야 하는가?

(A) 2
(B) 4
(C) 6
(D) 8

14. F.가는 어느 방향에 위치하는가?

(A) D.가
(B) 오른쪽으로
(C) 동쪽 – 서쪽
(D) 북쪽 – 남쪽

풀이 국가 기록 보관소에서 Sydney Harman 홀은 최소한 두 개의 교차로를 지나야 하므로 13번의 정답은 (A)이다.

F.가는 지도와 평행하게 동-서 방향으로 위치하므로 14번의 정답은 (C)이다.

Words and Phrases street 거리, 가 | National Archive 국가 기록 보관소, 국가 문서 보관소

[15-16]

Show your smile!
DENTAL CLINIC
Welcoming Veterans of All Ages!
New Complete and Partial Dentures
Same Day Relines and Repairs
Mouth Guards and Tooth Whitening
All Insurance Plans Accepted
- Announcement -
We are thrilled and honored to welcome MR. WILSON TAM, DD to Show Your Smile. Mr. Tam brings years of experience and is highly respected by customers. Welcome, Wilson!
8763 Bayview Ave. #7
Richmond hill
905-764-7222
WILSON TAM, DD / MONA GALLIERA, DD

15. Who is the new dentist?

(A) Wilson Tam
(B) Veteran Ages
(C) Richmond Hill
(D) Mona Galliera

16. What information does this brochure NOT have?

(A) address
(B) office hours
(C) dentists' name
(D) dental services

해석

'당신의 미소를 보여주세요' 치과
모든 연령대의 전문가들을 환영합니다!
8763 Bayview가, #7
Richmond hill
905-764-7222
새로운 전체 및 부분 틀니
당일 (틀니)조정과 수리
구강 보호와 치아 미백
모든 보험 가능
치의사 Wilson Tam, 치의사 Mona Galliera
공지사항: 우리는 '당신의 미소를 보여주세요' 치과에 치의사 Wilson Tam씨를 맞이하게 되어 기쁘고 영광입니다. Tam씨는 다년간의 경험을 가지고 있으며 고객들에게 큰 존경을 받고 있습니다. 환영합니다, Wilson!

15. 새로 온 치과의사는 누구인가?

(A) Wilson Tam
(B) Veteran Ages
(C) Richmond Hill
(D) Mona Galleria

16. 이 책자에 없는 정보는 무엇인가?

(A) 주소
(B) 근무 시간
(C) 치과의사의 이름
(D) 치과 서비스

풀이 치의사 Wilson Tam을 맞이하게 되어 기쁘다고 언급하였으므로 15번의 정답은 (A)이다.

근무 시간에 대한 언급은 없으므로 16번의 정답은 (B)이다.

Words and Phrases dental 이[치아/치과]의 | partial 부분적인 | denture 틀니, 의치 | repair 수리[보수/수선]하다 reline 선을 새로 긋다, 안감을 갈다 | insurance 보험 | veteran 베테랑, 전문가

[17–18]

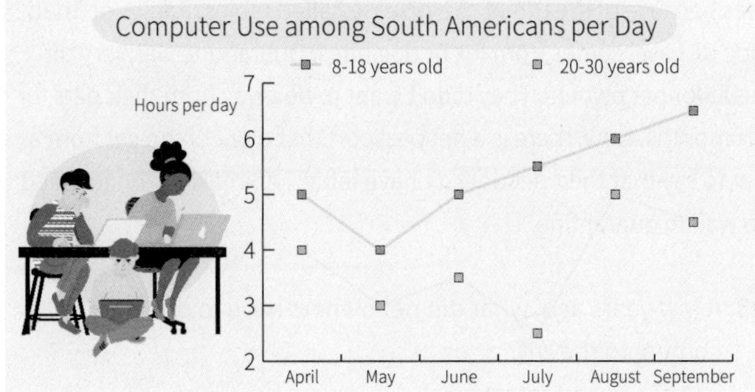

17. Which month did 20–30 year olds use the computer the least?

(A) April
(B) May
(C) June
(D) July

18. About how many hours did the younger group use the computer in August?

(A) 2
(B) 5
(C) 6
(D) 8

해석

남미인들 사이의 일일 컴퓨터 사용량

17. 20–30세가 컴퓨터를 가장 적게 사용한 달은 언제인가?

(A) 4월
(B) 5월
(C) 6월
(D) 7월

18. 나이가 더 적은 집단은 8월에 컴퓨터를 몇 시간 사용했는가?

(A) 2
(B) 5
(C) 6
(D) 8

풀이 20–30세 집단이 컴퓨터를 가장 적게 사용한 것은 7월이므로 17번의 정답은 (D)이다.

나이가 더 적은 8–18세 집단이 8월에 컴퓨터를 사용한 시간은 6시간이므로 18번의 정답은 (C)이다.

Words and Phrases per 각, ~당[마다]

[19–20]

Supplement Facts
Serving size: 5 tablets (800 mg)

Amount Per Serving	%Daily Value
Vitamin A 1.36 I.U	0%
Vitamin C .05 mg	0%
Vitamin D .05 mg	0%

-Daily value not established

Milk & Cookies is a delicious combination of milk and cookies.
Pop the top off for yummy chocolate cookies, then unscrew the cap to drink milk.

19. Where are the cookies?

(A) in the cap
(B) in the milk
(C) under the milk
(D) next to the milk

20. What is NOT true about this product?

(A) It has two tastes.
(B) It has less fat in milk.
(C) It serves plenty of protein.
(D) It is a mixture of milk and cookies.

해석

병 포함: 2% 저지방 우유 (20 온스)
뚜껑 포함: 미니 초콜릿 샌드위치 쿠키
영양성분표
1회 제공량: 5조각 (800mg)

제공량 당	일일 기준량 대비%
비타민 A 1.36 I.U	0%
비타민 C 0.05mg	0%
비타민 D 0.05mg	0%

일일 기준량이 정해져 있지 않음

'Milk & Cookies'는 우유와 쿠키의 맛있는 조합입니다. 윗부분을 뜯어 맛있는 초콜릿 쿠키를, 그리고 뚜껑을 열어 우유를 드세요.

19. 쿠키들은 어디에 있는가?

(A) 뚜껑 안에
(B) 우유 안에
(C) 우유 아래에
(D) 우유 옆에

20. 해당 제품에 관해 사실이 아닌 것은 무엇인가?

(A) 두 가지 맛을 가진다.
(B) 우유에 지방이 적다.
(C) 단백질이 풍부하다.
(D) 우유와 쿠키의 조합이다.

풀이 뚜껑에 쿠키가 포함되어 있고, 쿠키를 먹기 위해서는 윗부분을 뜯어야 한다고 했으므로 19번의 정답은 (A)이다.

영양성분표에 단백질에 관한 언급이 없으므로 20번의 정답은 (C)이다.

Words and Phrases supplement 보충(물) | tablet 정제 | combination 조합 | unscrew 열다 | mixture 혼합물

Part D. General Reading and Retelling (p.31)

[21-22]
I got chosen for the basketball team! It's one of the happiest days of my life. Every morning I wake up and practice basketball before school. I play one on one with another friend. We run around the track for 30 minutes and do other exercises to make us stronger. Then we shoot hoops for 30 minutes. The one with fewer goals has to buy the other one a drink. I usually lost. I didn't think I would make the basketball team but I did. All that practice paid off.

21. If he gets fewer goals than his friend, what does he have to do?
(A) He has to buy a drink.
(B) He has to shoot hoops.
(C) He has to do exercises.
(D) He has to run around the track.

22. When does he practice?
(A) at night
(B) in the evening
(C) in the morning
(D) in the afternoon

해석 나는 농구팀에 선발되었다! 내 인생에서 가장 행복한 날들 중 하나이다. 나는 매일 아침 일어나서 학교에 가기 전에 농구 연습을 한다. 나는 다른 친구와 일대일로 경기한다. 우리는 30분 동안 운동장을 돌고 우리를 강하게 만들기 위해 다른 운동들을 한다. 그리고 우리는 30분 동안 골대에 골을 넣는다. 더 적은 골을 넣은 사람이 다른 사람에게 음료수를 사야 한다. 나는 종종 진다. 나는 내가 농구팀에 들어갈 것이라 생각하지 않았지만 나는 해냈다. 그 모든 연습이 성과를 냈다.

21. 만약 그가 그의 친구보다 골을 적게 넣는다면, 그는 무엇을 해야 하는가?
(A) 그는 음료수를 사야 한다.
(B) 그는 골대에 골을 넣어야 한다.
(C) 그는 운동을 해야 한다.
(D) 그는 운동장을 달려야 한다.

22. 그는 언제 연습을 하는가?
(A) 밤에
(B) 저녁에
(C) 아침에
(D) 오후에

풀이 골을 더 적게 넣은 사람이 다른 사람에게 음료수를 사야 한다고 했으므로 21번의 정답은 (A)이다.

화자는 매일 아침 학교에 가기 전 농구 연습을 한다고 했으므로 22번의 정답은 (C)이다.

Words and Phrases one on one 일대일로 | hoop (농구의) 링 | pay off 성공하다, 성과를 올리다

[23-24]
Until a few years ago, all animals entering the UK had to spend six months in quarantine—away from people and other animals. This was because of the threat of a disease called rabies. Rabies or 'mad dog disease' comes from fox or dog bites. Quarantine was very difficult for pet owners. They didn't want to be away from their pets for six months. Now, there is a pet passport that owners can get from a vet to say that their pet doesn't have rabies. Animals no longer need to wait in quarantine.

23. A few years ago, what did pet owners have to do when coming to the UK?
(A) They had to get a vet.
(B) They had to use a passport.
(C) They had to keep their pet away from people.
(D) They had to buy special medicine so they didn't bite.

24. Why is it easier to bring your pet to the UK now?
(A) You don't need a vet.
(B) You can have a holiday.
(C) Your pet doesn't have rabies.
(D) You can get a pet passport from a vet.

해석 몇 년 전까지만 해도, 영국에 들어오는 모든 동물들은 사람이나 다른 동물들로부터 떨어져 격리되어 6개월을 보내야 했다. 이것은 광견병이라고 불리는 질병의 위협 때문이었다. 광견병 또는 '미친 개 질환'은 여우나 개가 물었을 때 발생한다. 반려동물의 주인들에게 격리는 매우 어려웠다. 그들은 그들의 반려동물과 6개월간 떨어져 있기를 바라지 않았다. 이제, 주인들이 수의사로부터 그들의 반려동물이 광견병을 가지고 있지 않다고 말할 수 있는 반려동물 여권을 받을 수 있다. 동물들은 더 이상 격리될 필요가 없다.

23. 몇 년 전에, 반려동물의 주인들은 영국에 오면 무엇을 해야 했는가?
(A) 그들은 수의사를 불러야 했다.
(B) 그들은 여권을 사용해야만 했다.
(C) 그들은 그들의 반려동물을 사람들로부터 멀리해야 했다.
(D) 그들은 그들이 물지 않도록 특별한 약을 사야만 했다.

24. 왜 이제는 당신의 반려동물을 영국으로 데려오는 것이 더 쉬워졌는가?
(A) 당신은 수의사가 필요 없기 때문이다.
(B) 당신은 휴일을 보낼 수 있기 때문이다.
(C) 당신의 반려동물은 광견병을 갖고 있지 않기 때문이다.
(D) 당신은 수의사로부터 반려동물 여권을 받을 수 있기 때문이다.

풀이 몇 년 전까지만 해도 영국에 들어오는 모든 동물들은 6개월의 격리 기간이 있었다고 했으므로 23번의 정답은 (C)이다.

현재는 반려동물 여권이 생겨 격리가 필요 없어졌다고 했으므로 24번은 (D)가 정답이다.

Words and Phrases quarantine (전염병 확산을 막기 위한 동물, 사람의) 격리 | rabies 광견병 | vet 수의사

[25–26]

The Beatles was a British pop and rock group from Liverpool. They are the most famous band in the world. There were four male members to the Beatles. Many girls around the world were crazy about them. The group broke many sales records and charted more than 50 top 40 hit singles, including 20 #1's in USA alone. The band has sold over a billion records worldwide. The band broke up in 1970.

25. How do you know the Beatles was popular?

(A) They were British.
(B) They were handsome.
(C) They are a rock group.
(D) They sold many records.

26. Which sentence means the same as 'the band broke up in 1970'?

(A) The band separated in 1970.
(B) The band went to Liverpool in 1970.
(C) The band broke record sales in 1970.
(D) The band was famous in USA alone in 1970.

해석 비틀즈는 리버풀 출신의 영국 팝과 록 그룹이었다. 그들은 세계에서 가장 유명한 밴드이다. 비틀즈에는 4명의 남성 멤버가 있었다. 전 세계의 많은 소녀들이 그들에게 열광했다. 그 그룹은 많은 판매 기록을 깼고 미국에서만 20번의 1위를 포함하여, 히트 싱글 차트 40위권 이상을 50번 이상 기록했다. 그 밴드는 전 세계적으로 10억 장 이상의 음반을 팔았다. 그 밴드는 1970년에 해체했다.

25. 비틀즈가 인기 있었다는 것을 어떻게 알 수 있는가?

(A) 그들은 영국인이었다.
(B) 그들은 잘생겼다.
(C) 그들은 록 그룹이다.
(D) 그들은 많은 음반을 팔았다.

26. 다음 중 '그 밴드는 1970년에 해체했다'와 같은 의미의 문장은 무엇인가?

(A) 그 밴드는 1970년에 해체되었다.
(B) 그 밴드는 1970년에 리버풀에 갔다.
(C) 그 밴드는 1970년에 음반 판매 기록을 깼다.
(D) 그 밴드는 1970년에 미국에서만 유명했다.

풀이 그들의 판매 기록과 음원 차트 기록을 통해 인기를 확인할 수 있으므로 25번의 정답은 (D)이다.

'해체했다(broke up)'와 동일한 의미는 '해체되었다(separated)'이므로 26번의 정답은 (A)이다.

Words and Phrases crazy about ...에 (푹) 빠져 있는 | break (기록을) 깨다 | break up (관계 등을) 끝내다

[27–28]

Birds are warm-blooded animals that have wings, feathers, a beak, no teeth, a skeleton in which many bones are joined together. Most birds can fly. Birds have a very strong heart and a good way of breathing—these are necessary for birds to fly. Birds use a lot of energy while flying and need to eat a lot of food so they can fly. Birds do not have any teeth. Birds have a tongue, but a bird's tongue is hard. Birds build nests in trees, on cliffs, or on the ground. Birds bear their young in hard-shelled eggs which hatch after some time. Some birds, like chickens, lay eggs each day, others only once every few years.

27. Why do birds need to eat often?

(A) because they are hungry
(B) because they lay big eggs
(C) because they have a good heart
(D) because they need strength to fly

28. Where can birds lay their eggs?

(A) on cliffs
(B) in the ocean
(C) in hard shells
(D) under the ground

해석 새는 날개, 깃털, 부리를 가지고, 이빨이 없으며, 여러 개의 뼈가 합쳐진 뼈대를 가진 온혈동물이다. 대부분의 새들은 날 수 있다. 새는 매우 강한 심장과 좋은 호흡법을 가지고 있는데, 이것들은 새가 나는 데에 필수적이다. 새는 날 때 많은 에너지를 사용하고 날기 위해 많은 양의 음식을 필요로 한다. 새들은 이빨을 가지고 있지 않다. 새는 혀를 가지고 있지만, 새의 혀는 단단하다. 새는 나무와 절벽, 또는 땅에 둥지를 짓는다. 새는 시간이 지나면 부화하는 단단한 껍질의 알 속에 있는 새끼를 낳는다. 닭과 같은 일부 새들은, 매일 알을 낳고, 다른 새들은 몇 년에 한 번씩만 알을 낳기도 한다.

27. 왜 새들은 자주 먹어야 하는가?

(A) 그들이 배가 고프기 때문에
(B) 그들이 큰 알을 낳기 때문에
(C) 그들이 좋은 심장을 가졌기 때문에
(D) 그들이 날기 위해 힘을 필요로 하기 때문에

28. 새들은 어디에 그들의 알을 낳을 수 있는가?

(A) 절벽에
(B) 바다에
(C) 딱딱한 껍질에
(D) 지하에

풀이 새는 날 때 많은 에너지를 사용하고, 날기 위해 많은 양의 음식을 필요로 한다고 했으므로 27번의 정답은 (D)이다.

새들은 나무와 절벽, 또는 땅에 둥지를 짓고 알을 낳는다고 했으므로 28번의 정답은 (A)이다.

Words and Phrases beak 부리 | skeleton 뼈대, 골격 | necessary 필요한 | tongue 혀 | cliff 절벽 | lay 알을 낳다

[29-30]
A man was walking along the street when he found a penguin. He picked it up and took it to the police station. He said to the policeman, "I found this penguin on the street. What should I do with it?" The policeman looked at the man and said, "Take the penguin to the zoo." The man said, "Of course, I'll take it to the zoo." He left the police station with the penguin under his arm. The next day the policeman saw the man walking along the street with the penguin next to him. The policeman stopped the man and said, "I thought I told you to take the penguin to the zoo." The man replied, "Yes, I took it to the zoo yesterday. Today I'm taking it to see a movie."

29. Why was the policeman surprised?
(A) He didn't know what to do.
(B) He saw a penguin in the city.
(C) The man didn't leave the penguin at the zoo.
(D) The man was going to take the penguin to the zoo.

30. Where should the penguin be now?
(A) at the zoo
(B) on the street
(C) at the movies
(D) at the police station

해석 한 남자가 길을 걷다가 펭귄을 발견했다. 그는 그것을 집어들어 경찰서로 가져갔다. 그는 경찰관에게, "제가 이 펭귄을 길에서 발견했습니다. 그것을 어떻게 하면 좋을까요?"라고 말했다. 그 경찰관은 그 남자를 보고는 "펭귄을 동물원으로 데려가세요."라고 말했다.
그 남자는 "물론이죠, 제가 그것을 동물원에 데려가겠습니다."라고 말했다. 그는 펭귄을 팔에 끼고 경찰서를 떠났다. 다음날 경찰관은 그 남자가 옆의 펭귄과 함께 길을 걷고 있는 것을 보았다. 경찰관은 남자를 멈춰 세우고 "제가 당신에게 펭귄을 동물원에 데려가라고 말했던 것 같은데요."라고 말했다. 그 남자는 "네, 어제 동물원에 데려갔습니다. 오늘은 영화를 보러 갈 거예요."라고 대답했다.

29. 그 경찰관은 왜 놀랐는가?
(A) 그가 무엇을 해야 할지 몰랐기 때문이다.
(B) 그가 도시에서 펭귄을 보았기 때문이다.
(C) 그 남자가 동물원에 펭귄을 두고 오지 않았기 때문이다.
(D) 그 남자가 펭귄을 동물원에 데려가려고 했기 때문이다.

30. 펭귄은 현재 어디에 있어야 하는가?
(A) 동물원에
(B) 거리에
(C) 영화관에
(D) 경찰서에

풀이 경찰관이 남자에게 동물원에 펭귄을 데려가라고 말했으나 남자가 펭귄을 그곳에 두고 오지 않았다는 걸 알았으므로 29번의 정답은 (C)이다.
예정대로라면 펭귄은 동물원에 있어야만 했으므로 30번의 정답은 (A)이다.

Words and Phrases along ~을 따라 | zoo 동물원

TOSEL Junior

실전 2회

Section I Listening and Speaking

1 (A)	2 (B)	3 (B)	4 (A)	5 (B)
6 (D)	7 (D)	8 (B)	9 (B)	10 (D)
11 (A)	12 (A)	13 (B)	14 (C)	15 (C)
16 (D)	17 (A)	18 (B)	19 (A)	20 (B)
21 (C)	22 (C)	23 (D)	24 (D)	25 (B)
26 (C)	27 (C)	28 (D)	29 (C)	30 (C)

Section II Reading and Writing

1 (A)	2 (A)	3 (A)	4 (A)	5 (C)
6 (C)	7 (C)	8 (B)	9 (A)	10 (C)
11 (C)	12 (C)	13 (A)	14 (D)	15 (B)
16 (D)	17 (A)	18 (A)	19 (B)	20 (D)
21 (B)	22 (B)	23 (D)	24 (B)	25 (C)
26 (C)	27 (D)	28 (A)	29 (A)	30 (C)

SECTION I LISTENING AND SPEAKING

Part A. Listen and Respond (p.38)

1. Girl: Is this shirt too big on me?
Boy: ________________
(A) Yes, try a smaller one.
(B) Yes, try a bigger one.
(C) Yes, it's perfect.
(D) Yes, it's too small.

해석 소녀: 이 셔츠가 나에게 너무 커?
소년: ________________
(A) 응, 더 작은 것을 입어봐.
(B) 응, 더 큰 것을 입어봐.
(C) 응, 그것은 완벽해.
(D) 응, 그것은 너무 작아.

풀이 셔츠가 너무 크냐고 묻는 소녀의 질문에 긍정하는 대답이므로 (A)가 정답이다.

Words and Phrases too 너무, ~도

2. Boy: How does it sound?
Girl: ________________
(A) I can't see it.
(B) It's too loud.
(C) It's very soft.
(D) It's not sweet enough.

해석 소년: 듣기에 어떤 것 같아?

소녀: ________________

(A) 나는 그것을 볼 수 없어.

(B) 너무 시끄러워.

(C) 매우 부드러워.

(D) 충분히 달지 않아.

풀이 듣기에 어떻냐는 질문에 대해 시끄럽다고 대답한 (B)가 정답이다.

Words and Phrases sound ~처럼 들리다, ~인 것 같다, 소리 | enough 충분히

3. Girl: Do you know where we are?

Boy: ________________

(A) No, this is the place.

(B) No, I think we're lost.

(C) Yes, I've never been here.

(D) Yes, let's ask for directions.

해석 소녀: 너는 우리가 어디에 있는지 알아?

소년: ________________

(A) 아니, 여기가 그곳이야.

(B) 아니, 내가 생각하기엔 우리가 길을 잃은 것 같아.

(C) 응, 나는 여기에 와 본 적 없어.

(D) 응, 방향을 물어보자.

풀이 우리가 어디에 있는지 묻는 소녀의 질문에 부정하며 길을 잃었다고 대답하는 (B)가 정답이다.

Words and Phrases direction 방향, 위치

4. Boy: Who is the girl?

Girl: ________________

(A) She is my classmate.

(B) She feels fine.

(C) She's not very nice.

(D) She went to the toilet.

해석 소년: 그 소녀는 누구야?

소녀: ________________

(A) 그녀는 나의 반 친구야.

(B) 그녀는 기분이 좋아.

(C) 그녀는 그다지 친절하지 않아.

(D) 그녀는 화장실에 갔어.

풀이 그 소녀가 누구인지 묻는 질문에 대한 대답이므로 자신과의 관계를 설명하는 (A)가 정답이다.

Words and Phrases classmate 반 친구, 급우 | nice 친절한, 좋은, 멋진

5. Girl: Why do you like this zoo?

Boy: ________________

(A) I can go to the zoo.

(B) I can see a lot of interesting animals.

(C) I can read many good books.

(D) I can play sports with my friends.

해석 소녀: 너는 이 동물원을 왜 좋아해?

소년: ________________

(A) 나는 그 동물원에 갈 수 있어.

(B) 나는 많은 흥미로운 동물들을 볼 수 있어.

(C) 나는 많은 좋은 책들을 읽을 수 있어.

(D) 나는 내 친구들과 운동할 수 있어.

풀이 그 동물원을 좋아하는 이유를 설명해야 하므로 (B)가 정답이다.

Words and Phrases interesting 흥미로운, 재미있는

6. Boy: What kind of ice cream do you want?

Girl: ________________

(A) You're very kind.

(B) That's a good idea.

(C) I'll have another one.

(D) My favorite kind is chocolate.

해석 소년: 너는 어떤 종류의 아이스크림을 원해?

소녀: ________________

(A) 너는 정말 친절하다.

(B) 그거 좋은 생각이다.

(C) 나는 다른 걸로 할래.

(D) 내가 가장 좋아하는 종류는 초콜릿이야.

풀이 어떤 아이스크림이 좋은지 묻는 질문이므로 초콜릿이라고 답하는 (D)가 정답이다.

Words and Phrases another 다른, 또 하나 | favorite 매우 좋아하는, 마음에 드는

7. Girl: When are you coming back?

Boy: ________________

(A) It's time to go.

(B) Come back here.

(C) I just came back.

(D) I'll come back soon.

해석 소녀: 너는 언제 돌아와?

소년: ________________

(A) 가야 할 시간이야.

(B) 여기로 돌아와.

(C) 나는 막 돌아왔어.

(D) 나는 곧 돌아올 거야.

풀이 언제 돌아올 것인지 묻는 질문이므로 곧 돌아오겠다고 답하는 (D)가 정답이다.

8. Boy: I'm sorry to make you wait.

Girl: ________________

(A) Take some more.

(B) Take your time.

(C) Wait for me.

(D) Wait a minute.

해석 소년: 너를 기다리게 만들어서 미안해.

소녀: ________________

(A) 좀 더 먹어.

(B) 천천히 해.

(C) 나를 기다려 줘.

(D) 잠깐 기다려봐.

풀이 기다리게 해서 미안하다는 말에 대한 대답이므로 천천히 하라고 답하는 (B)가 정답이다.
Words and Phrases wait 기다리다, 기다림

9. Girl: I bought a new bicycle.
Boy: ________________
(A) Try it again.
(B) Good for you.
(C) You can do it.
(D) The bicycle is new.
해석 소녀: 나는 새 자전거를 샀어.
소년: ________________
(A) 다시 도전해봐.
(B) 잘됐네.
(C) 너는 할 수 있어.
(D) 그 자전거는 새 것이다.
풀이 새 자전거를 샀다는 말에 대한 대답이므로 축하의 표현인 (B)가 정답이다.
Words and Phrases again 한 번 더, 다시

10. Boy: I have to go to class now.
Girl: ________________
(A) I don't need it.
(B) Okay, I can go.
(C) I'll be right back.
(D) Okay, see you later.
해석 소년: 나는 지금 수업에 가야 해.
소녀: ________________
(A) 나는 그것이 필요하지 않아.
(B) 알았어, 나는 갈 수 있어.
(C) 바로 돌아올게.
(D) 알았어, 나중에 봐.
풀이 수업에 가야 한다는 말에 대한 대답이므로 나중에 보자고 말하는 (D)가 정답이다.
Words and Phrases class 수업

Part B. Listen and Retell (p.39)

11. Girl: Are you tired yet?
Boy: A little. But I want to go up once more.
Girl: Okay, let's wait for the ski lift.
Question: Where are the girl and the boy?
(A) at a ski slope
(B) in a shopping mall
(C) at a swimming pool
(D) in an amusement park
해석 소녀: 아직 안 피곤해?
소년: 조금. 하지만 나는 한 번 더 올라가고 싶어.
소녀: 알았어, 스키 리프트를 기다리자.
질문: 그 소녀와 소년은 어디에 있는가?
(A) 스키 경사면에
(B) 쇼핑몰에
(C) 수영장에
(D) 놀이공원에
풀이 소녀가 스키 리프트를 기다리자고 제안했으므로 (A)가 답이다.
Words and Phrases slope 경사지, 경사면

12. Boy: What do you want for your birthday?
Girl: You don't have to buy me a gift.
Boy: I want to because you're my friend.
Question: What kind of gift will the boy buy?
(A) a birthday gift
(B) a Christmas gift
(C) a friendship gift
(D) a graduation gift
해석 소년: 너는 네 생일 선물로 무엇을 원해?
소녀: 너는 내게 선물을 사 주지 않아도 돼.
소년: 너는 내 친구니까 그렇게 하고 싶어.
질문: 그 소년은 어떤 종류의 선물을 살 예정인가?
(A) 생일 선물
(B) 크리스마스 선물
(C) 우정 선물
(D) 졸업 선물
풀이 소년이 소녀에게 생일 선물로 무엇을 원하는지 물었으므로 (A)가 답이다.
Words and Phrases friendship 우정, 교우 관계 | graduation 졸업, 졸업식

13. Boy: Do you think the cookies are ready?
Girl: Yes, I think so.
Boy: Okay, I'll take them out of the oven.
Question: What are they doing now?
(A) They're eating cookies.
(B) They're baking cookies.
(C) They're cleaning the oven.
(D) They're getting ready to go out.
해석 소년: 네가 생각하기에 그 쿠키들이 다 된 것 같아?
소녀: 응, 나는 그렇게 생각해.
소년: 좋아, 내가 그것들을 오븐 밖으로 꺼낼게.
질문: 그들은 지금 무엇을 하고 있는가?
(A) 그들은 쿠키를 먹는 중이다.
(B) 그들은 쿠키를 굽는 중이다.
(C) 그들은 오븐을 청소하는 중이다.
(D) 그들은 나갈 준비를 하는 중이다.
풀이 소년이 쿠키를 오븐 밖으로 꺼내겠다고 대답했으므로 (B)가 답이다.
Words and Phrases ready 준비가 된, 완성된

14. Boy: The library is about to close.
Girl: Yes, we should go back home.
Boy: Okay, let's take a bus.
Question: Why are they going back home?

(A) Because it is early.
(B) Because it is getting dark.
(C) Because the library is closing.
(D) Because they want to take a bus.

해석 소년: 도서관이 거의 닫을 때야.
소녀: 응, 우리는 집에 돌아가야 해.
소년: 알았어, 버스를 타자.
질문: 그들은 왜 집으로 돌아가는가?
(A) 시간이 이르기 때문이다.
(B) 어두워지는 중이기 때문이다.
(C) 도서관이 닫고 있기 때문이다.
(D) 그들이 버스를 타고 싶기 때문이다.

풀이 소년이 도서관이 닫을 때가 되었다고 했으므로 (C)가 답이다.

Words and Phrases early 초기의, 이른, 빠른

15. Girl: Do you want to play basketball tomorrow?
Boy: I have to visit my grandparents. Sorry.
Girl: That's okay, I'll ask someone else.
Question: Who will the boy visit?
(A) his parents
(B) another friend
(C) his grandparents
(D) a basketball player

해석 소녀: 너는 내일 농구를 하길 원해?
소년: 나는 나의 조부모님 댁에 가야 해. 미안해.
소녀: 괜찮아, 내가 다른 사람한테 물어 볼게.
질문: 소년은 누구를 방문하는가?
(A) 그의 부모님
(B) 다른 친구
(C) 그의 조부모님
(D) 농구 선수

풀이 소년이 조부모님 댁에 가야 한다고 했으므로 (C)가 답이다.

Words and Phrases grandparent 조부[모]

16. Girl: When did you come back?
Boy: About 15 minutes ago.
Girl: Really? I looked for you for an hour!
Question: When did the boy come back?
(A) an hour ago
(B) half an hour ago
(C) fifty minutes ago
(D) fifteen minutes ago

해석 소녀: 너는 언제 돌아왔어?
소년: 약 15분 전에.
소녀: 정말? 나는 너를 한 시간 동안 찾았어!
질문: 소년은 언제 돌아왔는가?
(A) 1시간 전에
(B) 30분 전에
(C) 50분 전에
(D) 15분 전에

풀이 소년이 약 15분 전에 돌아왔다고 했으므로 (D)가 답이다.

Words and Phrases half an hour 반 시간, 30분

17. Boy: It's too late to walk there.
Girl: Should we take the subway?
Boy: Let's take a bus. It's faster.
Question: How does the boy want to get there?
(A) He wants to take a bus.
(B) He wants to take a taxi.
(C) He wants to walk faster.
(D) He wants to take the subway.

해석 소년: 그곳까지 걸어가기에는 너무 늦었어.
소녀: 우리가 지하철을 타야 할까?
소년: 버스를 타자. 그게 더 빨라.
질문: 소년은 그곳에 어떻게 가고 싶어 하는가?
(A) 그는 버스를 타고 싶어한다.
(B) 그는 택시를 타고 싶어한다.
(C) 그는 더 빠르게 걷고 싶어한다.
(D) 그는 지하철을 타고 싶어한다.

풀이 소년이 버스를 타자고 했으므로 (A)가 답이다.

Words and Phrases late 늦은 | subway 지하철, 지하도

[18–19]
Girl: Hi, everyone! Today, I want to tell you about my pet snake. Many people are afraid of snakes because they think snakes are dangerous. But my snake is completely harmless. It does not bite humans. It likes to eat worms. And it is very shy and lazy.

18. What is the girl talking about?
(A) shy people
(B) her pet snake
(C) her pet worm
(D) dangerous snakes

19. What is true about the girl's snake?
(A) It is lazy.
(B) It's not shy.
(C) It bites humans.
(D) It is dangerous.

해석 소녀: 안녕하세요, 여러분! 오늘, 저는 여러분에게 저의 애완 뱀에 대해 말하고 싶어요. 많은 사람들은 뱀이 위험하다고 생각하기 때문에 뱀을 두려워합니다. 그러나 저의 뱀은 완전히 무해해요. 그것은 사람을 물지 않습니다. 그것은 애벌레를 먹는 걸 좋아하죠. 그리고 그것은 매우 수줍음이 많고 게을러요.

18. 소녀는 무엇에 대해 말하는 중인가?
(A) 수줍음이 많은 사람들
(B) 그녀의 애완 뱀
(C) 그녀의 애완 애벌레
(D) 위험한 뱀들

19. 소녀의 뱀에 관해 사실인 것은 무엇인가?
(A) 그것은 게으르다.
(B) 그것은 수줍음이 많지 않다.
(C) 그것은 사람을 문다.
(D) 그것은 위험하다.

풀이 소녀가 자신의 애완 뱀에 대해 말하고 싶다고 했으므로 18번의 정답은 (B)이다.

소녀의 뱀은 매우 수줍음이 많고 게으르다고 했으므로 19번의 정답은 (A)이다.

Words and Phrases completely 완전히, 전적으로 | harmless 해가 없는, 무해한 | bite 물다 | shy 수줍음을 많이 타는, 수줍어하는

[20-21]
Boy: Hi, Jin! This is Billy. I've been trying to reach you all day. Why don't you answer your phone? Anyway, I'm calling because I want to go to the park this afternoon. Maybe we can go together. Call me back when you get this message. Bye!

20. What kind of message is this?
(A) a radio message
(B) a phone message
(C) a computer message
(D) a television message

21. What does Billy want?
(A) He wants to go home.
(B) He wants to call Jin again.
(C) He wants to go to the park.
(D) He wants to answer a question.

해석 소년: 안녕, Jin! 나 Billy야. 나는 하루종일 너랑 연락하려고 했어. 너는 왜 네 휴대폰 연락을 안 받아? 어쨌든, 나는 오늘 오후에 공원에 가고 싶어서 연락하는 중이야. 아마도 우리가 같이 갈 수 있을 것 같다. 이 메시지 받으면 다시 연락해. 안녕!

20. 이것은 어떤 종류의 메시지인가?
(A) 라디오 메시지
(B) 휴대폰 메시지
(C) 컴퓨터 메시지
(D) 텔레비전 메시지

21. Billy는 무엇을 원하는가?
(A) 그는 집에 가기를 원한다.
(B) 그는 Jin에게 다시 연락하길 원한다.
(C) 그는 공원에 가기를 원한다.
(D) 그는 질문에 대답하기를 원한다.

풀이 Billy가 Jin에게 왜 휴대폰 연락을 받지 않느냐고 물었으므로 20번의 정답은 (B)이다.

Billy가 오후에 공원에 가고 싶어서 연락하는 중이라고 했으므로 21번의 정답은 (C)이다.

Words and Phrases reach ~에 이르다, 닿다 | together 함께, 같이

[22-23]
Girl: Dear shoppers. We are pleased to announce that our store is having a fruit sale. You can now get 5 oranges for $2. You can also get 3 apples for $1. Please come to the fruit section of our store. Hurry! This sale will not last long!

22. Where is this announcement made?
(A) in a school
(B) on television
(C) in a supermarket
(D) in a clothing store

23. Which statement is true?
(A) You can get 3 apples for $2.
(B) You can get 5 apples for $1.
(C) You can get 3 oranges for $1.
(D) You can get 5 oranges for $2.

해석 소녀: 쇼핑객 분들께. 우리는 우리 매장이 과일 세일을 진행 중이라는 사실을 알릴 수 있어 기쁩니다. 여러분은 지금 오렌지 5개를 2달러에 살 수 있습니다. 여러분은 또한 사과 3개를 1달러에 살 수 있습니다. 우리 매장의 과일 코너로 와 주시길 바랍니다. 서둘러 주세요! 이 세일은 오래 지속되지 않을 것입니다!

22. 이 안내는 어디에서 만들어졌는가?
(A) 학교에서
(B) 텔레비전에서
(C) 슈퍼마켓에서
(D) 옷 가게에서

23. 어느 문장이 사실인가?
(A) 당신은 사과 3개를 2달러에 살 수 있다.
(B) 당신은 사과 5개를 1달러에 살 수 있다.
(C) 당신은 오렌지 3개를 1달러에 살 수 있다.
(D) 당신은 오렌지 5개를 2달러에 살 수 있다.

풀이 과일 세일을 진행하는 매장이라고 했으므로 22번의 정답은 (C)이다.

오렌지 5개를 2달러에, 사과 3개를 1달러에 살 수 있다고 했으므로 23번의 정답은 (D)가 답이다.

Words and Phrases shopper 쇼핑객 | please 기쁘게 하다, 기분을 맞추다 | announce 발표하다, 알리다 | section 부분, 부문 | last 계속하다, 지속하다, 오래가다

[24-25]
M: Your attention, please. Good morning to all teachers and students. This is your principal speaking. We will take pictures for the school yearbook tomorrow in the gym. All 3rd and 4th grade classes should come to the gym by 9:00 AM. 5th and 6th grade classes should come by 2:00 PM.

24. Who is speaking?
(A) a school teacher
(B) the gym teacher
(C) the photographer
(D) the school principal

25. What should the 6th grade students do tomorrow?
(A) They should go to the gym at 2:00 AM.
(B) They should go to the gym at 2:00 PM.
(C) They should go to the gym at 9:00 AM.
(D) They should go to the gym at 9:00 PM.

해석 남자: 주목 부탁 드립니다. 모든 선생님들 그리고 학생들, 좋은 아침입니다. 여러분의 교장 선생님이 말하는 중입니다. 우리는 내일 체육관에서 학교 연감을 위한 사진을 찍을 예정입니다. 모든 3, 4학년 학급은 오전 9시까지 체육관으로 와 주세요. 5, 6학년 학급은 오후 2시까지 오셔야 합니다.

24. 누가 말하고 있는가?
(A) 학교 선생님
(B) 체육 선생님
(C) 사진 작가
(D) 학교 교장 선생님

25. 6학년 학생들은 내일 무엇을 해야 하는가?
(A) 그들은 오전 2시까지 체육관으로 가야 한다.
(B) 그들은 오후 2시까지 체육관으로 가야 한다.
(C) 그들은 오전 9시까지 체육관으로 가야 한다.
(D) 그들은 오후 9시까지 체육관으로 가야 한다.

풀이 여러분의 교장 선생님이 말하는 중이라고 했으므로 24번의 정답은 (D)이다.

5, 6학년 학급은 오후 2시까지 체육관으로 가야 한다고 했으므로 25번의 정답은 (B)이다.

Words and Phrases yearbook 연감, 연보, 졸업 앨범

PART C. Listen and Speak (p.43)

26. Boy: Why are you talking so loud?
Girl: I'm sorry. I'm just really excited.
Boy: Can you please quiet down? I'm trying to study.
Girl: ________________
(A) Okay, I'll finish soon.
(B) Sure, I'll take it with me.
(C) Okay, I'll lower my voice.
(D) Okay, I'll speak a little louder.

해석 소년: 너는 왜 그렇게 크게 말해?
소녀: 미안해. 내가 그냥 너무 신났나봐.
소년: 조용히 해 줄 수 있어? 나는 공부하려고 하고 있거든.
여: ________________
(A) 응, 내가 곧 끝낼게.
(B) 당연하지, 내가 가지고 갈게.
(C) 응, 내가 목소리를 낮출게.
(D) 응, 내가 조금 더 크게 말할게.

풀이 소년이 공부하기 위해 조용히 해 달라고 부탁했으므로 (C)가 정답이다.

Words and Phrases loud 큰, 시끄러운 | quiet 조용해지다, 조용히 시키다 | lower 낮추다, 내리다

27. Girl: How many apples did you pick?
Boy: I have 12. What about you?
Girl: I've picked about 20 so far.
Boy: ________________
(A) Wow! I have more than you.
(B) Wow! You have less than me.
(C) Wow! You have more than me.
(D) Wow! We have the same number.

해석 소녀: 너는 사과를 몇 개나 땄어?
소년: 나는 12개를 가지고 있어. 너는 어때?
소녀: 나는 지금까지 약 20개를 땄어.
소년: ________________
(A) 와! 내가 너보다 많이 가지고 있어.
(B) 와! 네가 나보다 적게 가지고 있어.
(C) 와! 네가 나보다 많이 가지고 있어.
(D) 와! 우리는 같은 개수를 가지고 있어.

풀이 소년이 12개를 가지고 있고, 소녀가 20개를 가지고 있다고 했으므로 소녀가 사과를 더 많이 가지고 있다. 그러므로 (C)가 정답이다.

Words and Phrases pick 따다, 고르다

28. Boy: It's so sunny today.
Girl: Yeah, I'm glad I brought my hat.
Boy: I should've brought mine, too.
Girl: ________________
(A) You can wear it now.
(B) Your hat looks good.
(C) Don't take it with you.
(D) Don't forget it next time.

해석 소년: 오늘 날씨가 정말 화창하네.
소녀: 응, 내가 내 모자를 챙겨와서 기뻐.
소년: 나도 내 것을 챙겨왔어야 했는데.
소녀: ________________
(A) 너는 그것을 지금 착용할 수 있어.
(B) 네 모자는 좋아 보인다.
(C) 그것을 가져가지 마.
(D) 다음에는 잊지 마.

풀이 모자를 챙겨오지 않은 것을 후회하는 소년에게 하는 말이므로 (D)가 정답이다.

Words and Phrases glad 기쁜, 고마운 | forget 잊다, 잊어버리다

29. Boy: Which one do you like better?
Girl: I think that one is nicer.
Boy: Me, too.
Girl: ________________
(A) I don't think so.
(B) How about you?
(C) I'm glad we agree.
(D) You don't agree with me?

해석 소년: 너는 어느 쪽이 더 좋아?
소녀: 내가 생각하기엔 저게 더 멋진 것 같아.
소년: 나도 그래.
소녀: ________________
(A) 나는 그렇게 생각하지 않아.
(B) 너는 어때?
(C) 우리가 의견이 일치해서 기뻐.
(D) 너는 나한테 동의하지 않아?

풀이 자신의 말에 동의하는 소년에게 하는 말이므로 (C)가 정답이다.

Words and Phrases better 더 좋은, 더 나은 | agree 동의하다, 의견이 일치하다

30. Girl: Is there a fountain in this park?
Boy: Why? Are you thirsty?
Girl: No, I just want to wash my hands.
Boy: ________________
(A) Let's look for a park.
(B) I washed mine already.
(C) Okay, let's look for one.
(D) Okay, you can have some water.

해석 소녀: 이 공원에 식수대가 있어?
소년: 왜? 너 목말라?
소녀: 아니, 나는 그냥 내 손을 씻고 싶어.
소년: ________________
(A) 공원을 찾아보자.
(B) 나는 이미 내 것을 씻었어.
(C) 알았어, 한 번 찾아보자.
(D) 알았어, 너는 물을 마셔도 돼.

풀이 소녀가 손을 씻을 수 있는 식수대가 있는지 물었으므로 식수대를 찾아보자고 말하는 (C)가 정답이다. (A)는 식수대가 아닌 공원을 찾아보자는 내용이므로 오답이다.

Words and Phrases fountain 분수, 식수대 | thirsty 목이 마른, 갈증이 나는

SECTION II READING AND WRITING

Part A. Sentence Completion (p.46)

1. A: ____________ can I fix it?
B: You have to use some glue.
(A) How
(B) Who
(C) What
(D) When

해석 A: 어떻게 내가 그것을 고칠 수 있을까?
B: 너는 약간의 접착제를 사용해야 해.
(A) 어떻게
(B) 누가
(C) 무엇을
(D) 언제

풀이 질문에 대한 대답으로 고치는 방법을 제시하고 있으므로 방법을 묻는 (A)가 정답이다.

Words and Phrases fix 수리하다, 고치다 | glue 접착제

2. A: Your phone is ringing.
B: Thanks, I should ____________ it.
(A) answer
(B) answered
(C) answering
(D) have answer

해석 A: 네 휴대폰이 울리는 중이야.
B: 고마워, 나는 그것을 받아야(대답해야) 해.
(A) 받아야 (대답해야)
(B) 받았어야
(C) 받는 중이어야
(D) 틀린 표현

풀이 조동사 should 뒤에는 동사원형이 와야 하므로 (A)가 정답이다.

Words and Phrases answer 대답하다, 대응하다

3. A: It's raining very ____________.
B: We'd better take an umbrella.
(A) hard
(B) hardly
(C) harden
(D) was hard

해석 A: 비가 아주 심하게 오고 있어.
B: 우리는 우산을 챙기는 편이 좋겠어.
(A) 심하게
(B) 거의 안
(C) 굳다
(D) 심했다

풀이 비가 심하게 온다는 의미로, 동사 'is raining'을 수식하는 부사 자리이므로 (A)가 정답이다. (C)와 (D)는 동사이므로 오답이다.

Words and Phrases hard 심하게, 많이 | hardly 거의 ~아니다[없다] | harden 굳다, 경화되다

4. A: What does a chef ___________?
B: He cooks food.
(A) do
(B) did
(C) does
(D) doing

해석 A: 요리사는 무슨 일을 해?
B: 그는 음식을 요리해.
(A) 해
(B) 했어
(C) 해
(D) 하는 중이야

풀이 조동사 'does' 뒤에는 동사원형이 와야 하므로 (A)가 정답이다.

Words and Phrases chef 요리사

5. A: Do you want to buy it?
B: Yes, I do. ___________ I don't have any money.
(A) If
(B) Or
(C) But
(D) And

해석 A: 너는 그것을 사고 싶니?
B: 응, 사고 싶어. 하지만 나는 돈이 아예 없어.
(A) 만약
(B) 혹은
(C) 하지만
(D) 그리고

풀이 물건을 사고 싶지만 돈이 없다는 상반된 내용을 이어주는 접속사이므로 (C)가 정답이다.

Part B. Situational Writing (p.47)

6. The boy is using a ___________.
(A) mop to melt the snow
(B) rake to move the snow
(C) shovel to clear the snow
(D) broom to sweep the snow

해석 그 소년은 눈을 치우기 위해 삽을 사용하고 있다.
(A) 눈을 녹이기 위해 대걸레를
(B) 눈을 옮기기 위해 갈퀴를
(C) 눈을 치우기 위해 삽을
(D) 눈을 쓸기 위해 빗자루를

풀이 그림에서 삽을 이용해 눈을 치우고 있으므로 (C)가 정답이다.

Words and Phrases mop 대걸레 | rake 갈퀴 | shovel 삽 | broom 빗자루 | sweep 쓸다, 털다

7. The girl and boy are swimming ___________.
(A) side by side
(B) next to each other
(C) towards each other
(D) away from each other

해석 그 소녀와 소년은 서로를 향해 수영하고 있다.
(A) 나란히
(B) 서로의 옆에서
(C) 서로를 향해
(D) 서로에게서 멀어지며

풀이 그림에서 소녀와 소년이 서로를 향해 수영하고 있으므로 (C)가 정답이다.

Words and Phrases towards 쪽으로, 향하여 | away 떨어져

8. The boy is pulling the girl ___________.
(A) on her bicycle
(B) with his bicycle
(C) on his rollerblades
(D) with his rollerblades

해석 그 소년은 그의 자전거에 탄 채로 소녀를 끌고 있다.
(A) 그녀의 자전거를 탄
(B) 그의 자전거에 탄 채로
(C) 그의 롤러를 탄
(D) 그의 롤러를 탄 채로

풀이 그림에서 소년이 자전거를 탄 채로 소녀를 끌고 있으므로 (B)가 정답이다.

Words and Phrases pull 끌다, 당기다 | rollerblade 롤러블레이드

9. The boy is ___________.
(A) waiting in line
(B) watching a movie
(C) walking to the office
(D) waiting to buy popcorn

해석 그 소년은 줄을 서고 있다.
(A) 줄을 서고 있다.
(B) 영화를 보고 있다.
(C) 사무실로 걸어가고 있다.
(D) 팝콘을 사기 위해 기다리고 있다.

풀이 그림에서 소년은 티켓을 사기 위해 줄을 서고 있으므로 (A)가 정답이다.

Words and Phrases office 사무소, 사무실

10. The piano teacher is ___________.
(A) playing the piano
(B) learning to play the piano
(C) helping the girl play the piano
(D) helping the girl move the piano

해석 그 피아노 선생님은 소녀가 피아노를 연주하는 것을 돕고 있다.
(A) 피아노를 연주하고 있다.
(B) 피아노를 연주하는 것을 배우고 있다.
(C) 소녀가 피아노를 연주하는 것을 돕고 있다.
(D) 소녀가 피아노를 이동시키는 것을 돕고 있다.

풀이 그림에서 선생님은 소녀가 연주하는 것을 돕고 있으므로 (C)가 정답이다.

Words and Phrases learn 배우다, 학습하다

Part C. Practical Reading and Retelling (p.50)

[11–12]

11. Which day is not on the schedule?

(A) Monday
(B) Tuesday
(C) Wednesday
(D) Thursday

12. What day must Peter clean the classroom?

(A) Monday
(B) Tuesday
(C) Thursday
(D) Friday

해석

그룹 A	그룹 B	그룹 C	그룹 D
Mark	John	Linda	Sally
Tony	Wendy	Peter	Tom
Mandy	Susie	Bob	Bill

교실 청소 일정표
월요일: 그룹 A
화요일: 그룹 B
목요일: 그룹 C
금요일: 그룹 D

11. 일정에 없는 것은 어느 요일인가?

(A) 월요일
(B) 화요일
(C) 수요일
(D) 목요일

12. Peter가 교실을 청소해야 하는 날은 무슨 요일인가?

(A) 월요일
(B) 화요일
(C) 목요일
(D) 금요일

풀이 그림의 일정표에는 수요일이 적혀 있지 않으므로 11번의 정답은 (C)이다.

그림의 일정표에서 Peter는 그룹 C에 속하므로 12번의 정답은 (C)이다.

Words and Phrases schedule 일정, 스케줄 | clean 닦다, 청소하다

[13–14]

13. Who do you think made this sign?

(A) the owner of the lost dog
(B) a person who wants to sell a dog
(C) a person who wants to buy a dog
(D) the person who found the lost dog

14. Where was the dog last seen?

(A) a small, brown dog
(B) wearing a red collar
(C) on Thursday, April 3rd
(D) in front of Rainbow Apartment

해석

제 강아지를 찾습니다!
묘사: 빨간색 목줄을 한 작은, 갈색의 강아지
마지막 목격: 4월 3일 목요일 저녁, Rainbow 아파트 #7 건물 앞
만약 이 강아지를 보시거나 찾으신다면, 031-710-3838로 연락 주세요.

13. 이 공고문은 누가 만든 것인가?

(A) 잃어버린 강아지의 주인
(B) 강아지를 팔고사 하는 사람
(C) 강아지를 사고자 하는 사람
(D) 잃어버린 강아지를 찾은 사람

14. 강아지는 어디에서 마지막으로 목격되었는가?

(A) 작은, 갈색의 강아지
(B) 빨간색 목줄을 착용하고 있음
(C) 4월 3일, 목요일
(D) Rainbow 아파트 앞

풀이 자신의 강아지를 찾는다는 제목의 공고문이므로 13번의 정답은 (A)이다.

마지막 목격 장소를 묻는 질문이므로 14번의 정답은 (D)이다.

Words and Phrases sign 표지판, 서명 | owner 주인, 소유주 | collar 목걸이

[15-16]

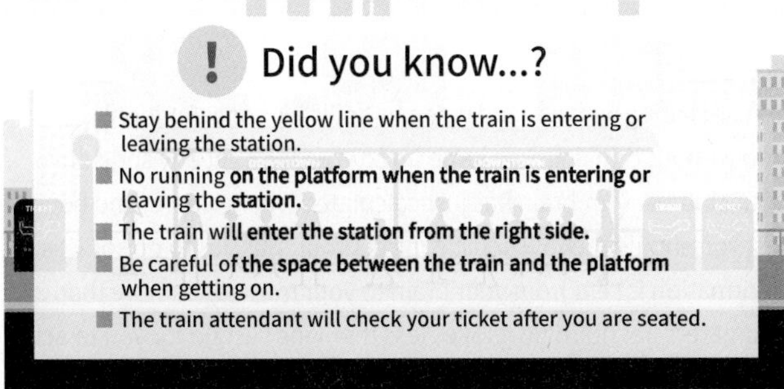

15. What should you NOT do on the station platform?

(A) run to get on the train before it leaves

(B) run with the train as it leaves to say goodbye

(C) watch the train enter the station from the right side

(D) stand behind the yellow line when the train is entering

16. What should you do when getting on the train?

(A) wait behind the yellow line

(B) look right to watch for the train

(C) show your ticket to the train attendant

(D) be careful of the space between the train and the platform

해석

당신은 알고 계셨습니까…?
* 열차가 역에 들어오거나 역을 떠나는 중일 때는 노란 선 뒤에 서세요.
* 열차가 역에 들어오거나 역을 떠나는 중일 때는 승강장에서 달리지 마세요.
* 열차는 오른쪽에서 역으로 들어올 것입니다.
* 열차에 탈 때, 열차와 승강장 사이의 공간을 조심하세요.
* 당신이 착석하신 후에 열차의 승무원이 당신의 탑승권을 확인할 것입니다.

15. 당신은 승강장에서 무엇을 해서는 안 되는가?

(A) 열차가 떠나기 전에 그것을 타기 위해 달리는 것

(B) 열차가 떠날 때 작별 인사를 하기 위해 열차와 함께 달리는 것

(C) 열차가 역의 오른쪽에서 들어오는 것을 지켜보는 것

(D) 열차가 들어올 때 노란 선 뒤에 서는 것

16. 당신은 열차를 탈 때 무엇을 해야 하는가?

(A) 노란 선 뒤에서 기다린다.

(B) 열차를 보기 위해 오른쪽을 바라본다.

(C) 열차 승무원에게 탑승권을 보여준다.

(D) 열차와 승강장 사이의 공간을 조심한다.

풀이 열차가 역에 들어오거나 역을 떠나는 중일 때는 달리지 말라고 했으므로 15번의 정답은 (B)이다.

열차에 탈 때 열차와 승강장 사이의 공간을 조심하라고 했으므로 16번의 정답은 (D)이다.

Words and Phrases station 역, 정거장 | platform 플랫폼 | enter 들어가다 | attendant 종업원, 안내원 | space 공간, 장소

[17-18]

17. What is the sale price on the teddy bear?

(A) 10% off

(B) 30% off

(C) 70% off

(D) not on sale

18. If the regular price of the model airplane is $100, how much is the sale price?

(A) $30

(B) $50

(C) $70

(D) $90

해석

빅 세일!
표시 없는 모든 장난감 10% 할인
파란색 표시가 붙은 모든 장난감 30% 할인
빨간색 표시가 붙은 모든 장난감 70% 할인

17. 곰인형의 할인 가격은 얼마인가?

(A) 10% 할인

(B) 30% 할인

(C) 70% 할인

(D) 할인 대상이 아님

18. 만약 장난감 비행기의 정가가 100달러라면, 할인 가격은 얼마인가?

(A) 30달러

(B) 50달러

(C) 70달러

(D) 90달러

풀이 표시가 없는 장난감은 10% 할인이므로 17번의 정답은 (A)이다.

빨간색 표시가 붙은 장난감은 70% 할인이므로 18번의 정답은 (A)이다.

Words and Phrases price 값, 가격 | regular 규칙적인, 정기적인 | model 모형, 모델

[19-20]

Model	Phone Type	Camera	MP3 Player	Memory	Price
GL50	Folding	✕	✓	1GB	$100
XB870	Sliding	✓	✓	1GB	$150
P10	Regular	✕	✕	64MB	$40
SM60	Folding	✓	✓	2GB	$200

19. What type of phone is the cheapest model?

(A) sliding phone
(B) regular phone
(C) camera phone
(D) folding phone

20. Which model has a camera and MP3 player for less than $200?

(A) P10
(B) GL50
(C) SM60
(D) XB870

해석

모델명	휴대폰 종류	카메라	MP3 플레이어	저장용량	가격
GL50	접는 휴대폰	X	O	1GB	100달러
XB870	미는 휴대폰	O	O	1GB	150달러
P10	일반 휴대폰	X	X	64MB	40달러
SM60	접는 휴대폰	O	O	2GB	200달러

19. 어떤 종류의 휴대폰이 가장 저렴한가?

(A) 미는 휴대폰
(B) 일반 휴대폰
(C) 카메라 휴대폰
(D) 접는 휴대폰

20. 어느 모델이 200달러 미만으로 카메라와 MP3 플레이어를 가지는가?

(A) P10
(B) GL50
(C) SM60
(D) XB870

풀이 일반 휴대폰이 40달러로 가장 저렴하므로 19번의 정답은 (B)이다.

150달러의 가격에 카메라와 MP3 플레이어가 포함된 것은 XB870이므로 20번의 정답은 (D)이다. (C)는 200달러이므로 오답이다.

Words and Phrases slide 미끄러지다 | fold 접다 | less 더 적은, 덜한

Part D. General Reading and Retelling (p.55)

[21-22]

You are eating with a friend when he spills his soda. Suddenly, and without thinking, you jump up so you don't get any soda on your clothes. Your brain has just calculated when, where, and how fast you should move. Then it controls your muscles to do so. This information is sent from your brain to your muscles at more than 322 kilometers per hour! So it takes less than one second for you to act.

21. Which is the best title for this passage?

(A) Don't Drink Soda
(B) Our Amazing Brain
(C) Avoiding Accidents
(D) Eating with a Friend

22. Which of the following statements is NOT true?

(A) Your brain controls your muscles.
(B) Your muscles can move 322 kilometers per hour.
(C) Your brain sends information to your muscles very quickly.
(D) Your brain calculates when, where, and how fast you move.

해석 당신의 친구가 그의 탄산음료를 쏟을 때, 당신은 그와 식사를 하는 중이다. 갑자기, 그리고 아무 생각 없이, 당신은 당신의 옷에 탄산음료가 묻지 않게 하기 위해 벌떡 일어선다. 당신의 뇌는 당신이 언제, 어디서, 그리고 얼마나 빨리 움직여야 할지를 막 계산했다. 그 다음에 그것은 당신의 근육이 그렇게 움직이도록 조절한다. 이 정보는 시간당 322km 이상의 속도로 당신의 뇌에서 근육으로 보내진다! 그래서 당신이 행동하는 데에는 1초도 걸리지 않는다.

21. 이 지문에 가장 알맞은 제목은 무엇인가?

(A) 탄산음료를 마시지 마세요
(B) 우리의 놀라운 뇌
(C) 사고를 피하는 것
(D) 친구와 함께하는 식사

22. 다음 중 사실이 아닌 문장은 무엇인가?

(A) 당신의 뇌가 당신의 근육들을 조절한다.
(B) 당신의 근육들은 시간당 322km를 이동할 수 있다.
(C) 당신의 뇌는 당신의 근육들에게 매우 빨리 정보를 전달한다.
(D) 당신의 뇌는 당신이 언제, 어디서, 그리고 얼마나 빨리 움직일지 계산한다.

풀이 지문은 우리의 뇌가 명령을 내리는 과정을 설명하고 있으므로 21번의 정답은 (B)이다. 식사 도중 친구가 탄산음료를 쏟는 상황은 예시일 뿐이므로 (A)와 (D)는 오답이다.

시간당 322km 이상을 이동하는 것은 근육이 아니라 정보의 속도이므로 22번의 정답은 (B)이다.

Words and Phrases spill 흐르다, 흘리다 | suddenly 갑자기, 불현듯 | calculate 계산하다, 산출하다 | avoid 방지하다, 막다, 피하다 | muscle 근육

[23-24]
When photographers take pictures of food for advertisements, they use many tricks to make the food look delicious. For example, they use white glue instead of milk on cereal. This keeps the cereal looking fresh. Roasted chickens are sometimes stuffed with paper to make them look fat and round. Or a little bit of soap is added to milk so that the milk looks bubbly and refreshing.

23. Why are tricks used when taking pictures of food?
(A) to prepare the food for eating
(B) to prepare the food for cooking
(C) to make the food more delicious
(D) to make the food look more delicious

24. What is added to milk to make it look bubbly and refreshing?
(A) glue
(B) soap
(C) paper
(D) cereal

해석 사진 작가들이 광고를 위해 음식 사진을 찍을 때, 그들은 음식이 맛있어 보이게 하기 위해 많은 속임수를 쓴다. 예를 들어, 그들은 시리얼에 우유 대신 하얀 접착제를 사용한다. 이것은 시리얼이 신선해 보이도록 유지시켜 준다. 구운 닭은 그것들이 뚱뚱하고 동그랗게 보이도록 종이로 속이 채워지기도 한다. 또는 우유가 거품이 나고 신선해 보이도록 약간의 비누가 우유에 더해지기도 한다.

23. 음식 사진을 찍을 때 속임수가 사용되는 이유는 무엇인가?
(A) 먹을 음식을 준비하기 위해
(B) 요리에 사용할 음식을 준비하기 위해
(C) 음식을 더 맛있게 만들기 위해
(D) 음식을 더 맛있어 보이게 만들기 위해

24. 우유에 무엇을 첨가하면 거품이 나고 신선해 보이는가?
(A) 접착제
(B) 비누
(C) 종이
(D) 시리얼

풀이 사진 작가들이 음식 사진을 찍을 때, 음식을 맛있어 보이게 하기 위해 속임수를 사용한다고 했으므로 23번의 정답은 (D)이다.

우유에 거품이 나고 신선해 보이도록 하기 위해 약간의 비누를 사용한다고 했으므로 24번의 정답은 (B)이다.

Words and Phrases photographer 사진작가, 사진사 | bubbly 거품이 나는 advertisement 광고 | trick 속임수, 장난 | roasted 구운 | stuff 채워 넣다, 쑤셔 넣다

[25-26]
The word "umbrella" comes from the Latin word "umbra," and it means "shadow." Ancient people used umbrellas to shade themselves from the bright sun. The Chinese were the first to use the umbrella for rain. They covered their umbrellas with wax so no water could go through. Then, umbrellas became popular in Northern Europe in the 16th century. In 1852, Samuel Fox used steel instead of wood to make the umbrella's frame.

25. Who were the first people to use umbrellas for rain?
(A) Samuel Fox
(B) ancient people
(C) Chinese people
(D) Northern Europeans

26. What happened in the 16th century?
(A) People began to use umbrellas for shade.
(B) Steel was used to make the umbrella's frame.
(C) The umbrella became popular in Northern Europe.
(D) The umbrella was waxed so no water could leak through.

해석 "umbrella(우산)"이라는 단어는 라틴어 "umbra"에서 왔고, 이것은 "그림자"를 뜻한다. 고대인들은 밝은 태양을 피하기 위해 우산을 사용했다. 중국인은 처음으로 비를 위해 우산을 사용했다. 그들은 물이 들어가지 않도록 우산을 왁스로 덮었다. 그 후, 우산은 16세기 북유럽에서 인기를 얻었다. 1852년, Samuel Fox는 우산의 틀을 만들기 위해 나무 대신 철을 사용했다.

25. 비를 위해 우산을 사용한 첫 번째 인류는 누구인가?
(A) Samuel Fox
(B) 고대인
(C) 중국인
(D) 북유럽인

26. 16세기에 무슨 일이 일어났는가?
(A) 사람들은 그늘을 위해 우산을 쓰기 시작했다.
(B) 우산의 틀을 만드는 데에 철이 이용되었다.
(C) 우산이 북유럽에서 인기를 얻었다.
(D) 물이 새지 않도록 우산이 왁스로 덮였다.

풀이 비를 위해 우산을 사용한 첫 번째 인류는 중국인이라고 했으므로 25번의 정답은 (C)이다.

우산이 16세기 북유럽에서 인기를 얻었다고 했으므로 26번의 정답은 (C)이다.

Words and Phrases ancient 고대의, 아주 오래된 | shade 가리다, 그늘 | frame 틀, 뼈대

[27-28]

A turtle is from the family of reptiles, like snakes and lizards. But the turtle is the only reptile with a shell. The shell is made of a hard material. The hard material protects the turtle. A turtle can protect itself by pulling its head, tail, and legs into the shell. While turtles on land can protect themselves from enemies, the shape of the shell makes it easier for sea turtles to swim. Turtle shells are brown, black, or dark green. Some turtles have red, orange, or yellow spots. The spots make the shell beautiful.

27. What family is the turtle from?

(A) the family of shells
(B) the family of snakes
(C) the family of lizards
(D) the family of reptiles

28. What is NOT true about turtle shells?

(A) They are all colorful.
(B) They are used for protection.
(C) They can make swimming easier.
(D) They are made from a hard material.

해석 거북이는 뱀이나 도마뱀처럼, 파충류이다. 하지만 거북이는 껍데기를 가진 유일한 파충류이다. 그 껍데기는 단단한 재료로 만들어진다. 그 단단한 재료는 거북이를 보호한다. 거북이는 머리, 꼬리, 다리를 껍데기 속으로 당김으로써 스스로를 보호할 수 있다. 육지 거북이는 육지에서 적들로부터 자신을 보호할 수 있는 반면, 껍데기의 모양은 바다거북이 헤엄치는 것을 더욱 쉽게 만든다. 거북이의 껍데기는 갈색, 검은색, 또는 짙은 녹색이다. 어떤 거북이들은 빨간색, 주황색, 또는 노란색 점들을 가지고 있다. 그 점들은 껍데기를 아름답게 만든다.

27. 거북이는 어느 과에 속하는가?

(A) 조개과
(B) 뱀과
(C) 도마뱀과
(D) 파충류과

28. 거북이의 껍데기에 대해 사실이 아닌 것은 무엇인가?

(A) 그것들은 모두 다채롭다.
(B) 그것들은 보호를 위해 사용된다.
(C) 그것들은 수영을 더욱 쉽게 만들 수 있다.
(D) 그것들은 단단한 재료로 만들어진다.

풀이 거북이는 파충류과라고 했으므로 27번의 정답은 (D)이다.

모든 거북이가 아닌 어떤 거북이들만 다채로운 껍데기를 가지고 있으므로 28번은 (A)가 정답이다.

Words and Phrases reptile 파충류 | shell 껍데기, 껍질 | material 재료 | protect 보호하다, 지키다 | enemy 적

[29-30]

The pyramids of Egypt are truly amazing. Not only are they thousands of years old, but they are one of the largest man-made objects in the world. The largest of the pyramids, the Great Pyramid of King Khufu, is 147 meters high! That's as tall as a fifty-story building! Each stone block used to build the pyramid weighs as much as 15,000 kilograms! How these giant stones were moved is still somewhat of a mystery. Without a doubt, these pyramids are one of the man-made wonders of the world.

29. What does NOT make the pyramids truly amazing?

(A) They are located in Egypt.
(B) They are thousands of years old.
(C) People are still not sure how they were built.
(D) They are one of the largest man-made objects in the world.

30. What best describes the stones used to build the Great Pyramid of King Khufu?

(A) It is 147 meters tall.
(B) It is fifty stories high.
(C) It weighs 15,000 kilograms.
(D) It is thousands of years old.

해석 이집트의 피라미드는 정말 놀랍다. 그것들은 수천 년이 되었을 뿐만 아니라, 또한 세계에서 가장 큰 인공 물체 중 하나이다. 가장 큰 피라미드인 Khufu 왕의 피라미드는 147미터의 높이이다! 그것은 50층 건물만큼 높다! 그 피라미드를 짓는 데에 사용된 각각의 돌덩어리는 15,000kg의 무게이다! 이 거대한 돌들이 어떻게 옮겨졌는지는 여전히 상당한 수수께끼다. 의심할 여지 없이, 이러한 피라미드들은 인간이 만든 세계 불가사의 중 하나이다.

29. 피라미드를 정말 놀랍게 만드는 요소가 아닌 것은 무엇인가?

(A) 그들은 이집트에 있다.
(B) 그들은 수천 년이 되었다.
(C) 사람들은 여전히 그것이 어떻게 지어졌는지 확신하지 못한다.
(D) 그들은 세계에서 가장 큰 인공 물체 중 하나이다.

30. Khufu 왕의 피라미드를 짓는 데에 사용된 돌들을 가장 잘 묘사한 것은 무엇인가?

(A) 그것은 147미터의 높이이다.
(B) 그것은 50층 높이이다.
(C) 그것은 15,000kg의 무게이다.
(D) 그것은 수천 년이 되었다.

풀이 피라미드의 위치는 놀라운 요소가 아니므로 29번의 정답은 (A)이다.

Khufu 왕의 피라미드를 짓는 데에 사용된 각각의 돌 블록 하나는 15,000kg 무게이므로 30번의 정답은 (C)이다.

Words and Phrases truly 정말로, 진심으로 | wonder 경이, 불가사의 man-made 사람이 만든, 인공의 | object 물건, 물체 | somewhat 어느 정도, 약간, 다소

TOSEL Junior

실전3회

Section I Listening and Speaking

1 (D) 2 (B) 3 (C) 4 (C) 5 (D)
6 (A) 7 (A) 8 (D) 9 (C) 10 (B)
11 (B) 12 (A) 13 (D) 14 (B) 15 (B)
16 (D) 17 (A) 18 (D) 19 (D) 20 (C)
21 (C) 22 (A) 23 (C) 24 (D) 25 (C)
26 (A) 27 (B) 28 (C) 29 (D) 30 (B)

Section II Reading and Writing

1 (C) 2 (A) 3 (A) 4 (D) 5 (B)
6 (B) 7 (A) 8 (B) 9 (C) 10 (C)
11 (A) 12 (C) 13 (B) 14 (B) 15 (D)
16 (D) 17 (C) 18 (B) 19 (B) 20 (A)
21 (B) 22 (C) 23 (C) 24 (C) 25 (B)
26 (A) 27 (C) 28 (A) 29 (A) 30 (C)

SECTION I LISTENING AND SPEAKING

Part A. Listen and Respond (p.62)

1. Girl: Do you know the time?
Boy: ________________
(A) I know him.
(B) It's not time yet.
(C) I have some time.
(D) I don't have a watch.

해석 소녀: 너는 시간을 알고 있니?
소년: ________________
(A) 나는 그를 알고 있어.
(B) 아직 때가 아니야.
(C) 나는 시간이 조금 있어.
(D) 나는 시계가 없어.

풀이 시간을 알고 있는지 질문했으므로 시계가 없어 시간을 말해줄 수 없음을 내포한 (D)가 정답이다.

Words and Phrases watch 손목시계 | yet 아직

2. Boy: Do you like this song?
Girl: ________________
(A) It looks great.
(B) It sounds nice.
(C) It smells sweet.
(D) It tastes wonderful.

해석 소년: 너는 이 노래를 좋아하니?
소녀: ________________
(A) 보기 좋아보인다.
(B) 듣기 좋다.
(C) 달콤한 냄새가 나.
(D) 맛이 훌륭해.

풀이 이 노래를 좋아하는지 묻는 질문에 동의, 긍정을 표하는 표현인 (B)가 정답이다.

Words and Phrases sound ~처럼 들리다 | smell 냄새가 나다 | taste 맛이 나다 | wonderful 훌륭한

3. Girl: Where are we going?
Boy: ________________
(A) We can walk.
(B) We've arrived.
(C) We're going home.
(D) We'll go tomorrow.

해석 소녀: 우리 어디 가고 있는 거니?
소년: ________________
(A) 우리는 걸을 수 있어.
(B) 우리는 도착했어.
(C) 우리는 집에 가는 중이야.
(D) 우리는 내일 갈 것이다.

풀이 어디로 가는지 묻는 질문에 목적지를 말하는 (C)가 정답이다.

Words and Phrases walk 걷다 | arrive 도착하다

4. Boy: Who is the man?
Girl: ________________
(A) He is not fat.
(B) He is here now.
(C) He is my uncle.
(D) He is very happy.

해석 소년: 그 남자는 누구니?
소녀: ________________
(A) 그는 뚱뚱하지 않아.
(B) 그는 여기 있어.
(C) 그는 나의 삼촌이야.
(D) 그는 매우 행복해.

풀이 남자가 누구인지 물었으므로 그의 신분이나 관계를 표현한 (C)가 정답이다.

Words and Phrases fat 뚱뚱한 | uncle 삼촌

5. Girl: I will buy a drink.
Boy: ________________
(A) Are you cold?
(B) Are you busy?
(C) Are you angry?
(D) Are you thirsty?

해석 소녀: 나는 음료수를 살 거야.
소년: ________________

(A) 너 춥니?
(B) 너 바쁘니?
(C) 너 화났니?
(D) 너 목마르니?

풀이 음료를 살 것이라는 말에서 소녀가 목이 마른 것을 짐작할 수 있으므로 (D)가 정답이다.

Words and Phrases drink 음료 | thirsty 목이 마른

6. Boy: What kind of pie do you like?
Girl: ________________

(A) I like apple pie.
(B) This is delicious.
(C) I just want a little.
(D) One piece is enough.

해석 소년: 너는 어떤 종류의 파이를 좋아하니?
소녀: ________________
(A) 나는 사과 파이를 좋아해.
(B) 이거 맛있다.
(C) 나는 조금만 원해.
(D) 한 조각이면 충분해.

풀이 파이의 종류를 묻는 질문에 사과 파이를 좋아한다고 답했으므로 (A)가 정답이다.

Words and Phrases delicious 맛있는 | piece 조각

7. Girl: Do you want to sit down?
Boy: ________________

(A) I'm not tired.
(B) I don't agree.
(C) I don't need it.
(D) I'm not hungry.

해석 소녀: 너 앉고 싶니?
소년: ________________
(A) 나는 피곤하지 않아.
(B) 나는 동의하지 않아.
(C) 나는 그거 필요 없어.
(D) 나는 배고프지 않아.

풀이 앉고 싶은지를 물었으므로 이를 거절하는 의미를 내포한 (A)가 정답이다.

Words and Phrases tired 피곤한 | agree 동의하다

8. Boy: Do you have food?
Girl: ________________

(A) I have a book.
(B) I have a phone.
(C) I have two friends.
(D) I have some cookies.

해석 소년: 너 음식 가지고 있니?
소녀: ________________
(A) 나는 책을 가지고 있어.
(B) 나는 전화기를 가지고 있어.
(C) 나는 친구가 두 명 있어.
(D) 나는 약간의 쿠키를 갖고 있어.

풀이 음식을 가지고 있는지 물었으므로 쿠키를 가지고 있다고 답하는 (D)가 정답이다.

Words and Phrases cookie 쿠키

9. Girl: I bought some new shoes.
Boy: ________________

(A) They will go.
(B) They are mine.
(C) They look nice.
(D) I can wear mine.

해석 소녀: 나는 새 신발을 조금 샀어.
소년: ________________
(A) 그들은 갈 거야.
(B) 그것들은 내 것이야.
(C) 그거 좋아 보인다.
(D) 나는 내 것을 신을 수 있어.

풀이 새 신발들을 샀다고 말했으므로 좋아 보인다고 칭찬하는 표현인 (C)가 정답이다.

Words and Phrases mine 나의 것 | bought buy의 과거형

10. Boy: I am very sleepy.
Girl: ________________

(A) Let's go eat.
(B) You should take a nap.
(C) I don't want to play.
(D) You need more money.

해석 소년: 나는 매우 졸려.
소녀: ________________
(A) 먹으러 가자.
(B) 너는 낮잠을 좀 자야해.
(C) 나는 놀고 싶지 않아.
(D) 너는 돈이 더 필요해.

풀이 소년이 졸음이 온다고 말했으므로 낮잠을 제안하는 (B)가 정답이다.

Words and Phrases sleepy 졸음이 오는 | nap 낮잠

Part B. Listen and Retell (p.63)

11. Girl: Are you all right?
Boy: I'm fine. I just scratched my knee a little.
Girl: You should be more careful next time.
Question: What happened to the boy?

(A) He is confused.
(B) He fell down.
(C) He lost something.
(D) He broke something.

해석 소녀: 너 괜찮아?
소년: 괜찮아. 무릎만 조금 까졌어.
소녀: 다음부터 조심해.
질문: 소년에게 무슨 일이 있었는가?

(A) 그는 혼란스럽다.
(B) 그는 넘어졌다.
(C) 그는 무언가를 잃어버렸다.
(D) 그는 무언가를 깨뜨렸다.
풀이 소년은 무릎이 까졌다고 했으므로 넘어졌다는 것을 추측할 수 있다. 따라서 (B)가 정답이다.

12. Boy: Aren't you going to finish?
Girl: I can't finish it. I'm too full.
Boy: What a waste of food!
Question: What are they doing now?
(A) eating lunch
(B) watching TV
(C) playing a game
(D) doing their homework
해석 소년: 다 안 먹을거야?
소녀: 다 못 먹어. 배가 너무 불러.
소년: 음식이 너무 아깝다!
질문: 그들은 지금 무엇을 하는가?
(A) 점심을 먹고 있다
(B) 티비를 보고 있다
(C) 게임을 하고 있다
(D) 숙제를 하고 있다
풀이 소녀는 배가 너무 불러서 다 먹지 못한다고 했으므로 지금 점심을 먹고 있다는 것을 알 수 있다. 따라서 (A)가 정답이다.

13. Girl: Let's go to the schoolyard.
Boy: What do you want to do there?
Girl: I want to play basketball.
Question: Where does the girl want to go?
(A) to the park
(B) to the beach
(C) to the classroom
(D) to the schoolyard
해석 소녀: 우리 운동장 가자.
소년: 거기서 뭐 하고 싶어?
소녀: 나는 농구를 하고 싶어.
질문: 소녀는 어디에 가고 싶어 하는가?
(A) 공원에
(B) 해변가에
(C) 교실에
(D) 운동장에
풀이 소녀가 소년에게 운동장에 가고싶다고 했으므로 (D)가 정답이다.

14. Boy: Look at the sunset!
Girl: Wow! It's beautiful.
Boy: Let's take a picture.
Question: What are they looking at?
(A) a flower
(B) a sunset
(C) a picture
(D) a rainbow
해석 소년: 일몰 좀 봐!
소녀: 우와! 아름다워.
소년: 우리 사진 찍자.
질문: 그들은 무엇을 보는가?
(A) 꽃
(B) 일몰
(C) 사진
(D) 무지개
풀이 소년이 소녀에게 일몰을 보라고 말했으므로 (B)가 정답이다.

15. Girl: Come with me to buy a book.
Boy: Can my brother come with us, too?
Girl: Sure, bring him along.
Question: Who will go with them?
(A) the girl's brother
(B) the boy's brother
(C) the boy's sister
(D) the boy's friend
해석 소녀: 나랑 같이 책 사러 가자.
소년: 내 남동생도 같이 가도 돼?
소녀: 그래, 데리고 와.
질문: 누가 그들과 함께 갈 것인가?
(A) 소녀의 남동생
(B) 소년의 남동생
(C) 소년의 여동생
(D) 소년의 친구
풀이 소년이 소녀에게 남동생도 같이 책 사러 가도 되는지 묻고 있으므로 (B)가 정답이다.

16. Girl: Did you finish the book report?
Boy: I finished it two days ago.
Girl: That's fast. I finished mine yesterday.
Question: When did the boy finish his book report?
(A) today
(B) yesterday
(C) last week
(D) two days ago
해석 소녀: 독후감 다 썼어?
소년: 나는 그것을 이틀 전에 다 썼어.
소녀: 빠르다. 나는 어제 다 썼어.
질문: 소년은 독후감을 언제 다 썼는가?
(A) 오늘
(B) 어제
(C) 지난 주
(D) 이틀 전에
풀이 소년은 소녀에게 이틀 전에 독후감을 다 썼다고 말했으므로 (D)가 정답이다.

17. Boy: I have a lesson this afternoon.
Girl: Where is your lesson?
Boy: It's very close. I can walk there.
Question: How will the boy go to his lesson?
(A) He will walk.
(B) He will take a bus.
(C) He will ride his bicycle.
(D) He will take the subway.

해석 소년: 나는 오늘 오후에 교습이 있어.
소녀: 너의 교습은 어디서 하니?
소년: 무척 가까워. 거기까지 걸어갈 수 있어.
질문: 소년은 교습까지 어떻게 갈 것인가?
(A) 그는 걸어갈 것이다.
(B) 그는 버스를 탈 것이다.
(C) 그는 자전거를 탈 것이다.
(D) 그는 지하철을 탈 것이다.

풀이 소년은 교습을 가까운 곳에서 한다고 하면서 거기까지 걸어갈 수 있다고 말하고 있다. 따라서 (A)가 정답이다.

[18-19]
Girl: My favorite instrument is the trumpet. It is not a very popular instrument, but I think it sounds beautiful. I've studied how to play the trumpet for four years. Even though it looks simple, it takes a lot of practice to play the trumpet well.

18. What is the girl talking about?
(A) her favorite band
(B) her favorite music
(C) her favorite hobby
(D) her favorite instrument

19. Why does the girl like the trumpet?
(A) It looks simple.
(B) It's easy to play.
(C) It is very popular.
(D) It sounds beautiful.

해석 소녀: 내가 가장 좋아하는 악기는 트럼펫이다. 그것은 별로 인기 있는 악기는 아니지만, 아름답게 들린다. 나는 4년 동안 어떻게 트럼펫을 연주하는지 공부해 왔다. 그것은 단순해 보이지만 트럼펫을 잘 부는 데에는 연습이 많이 필요하다.

18. 소녀는 주로 무엇에 대하여 말하고 있는가?
(A) 가장 좋아하는 밴드
(B) 가장 좋아하는 음악
(C) 가장 좋아하는 취미
(D) 가장 좋아하는 악기

19. 소녀는 왜 트럼펫을 좋아하는가?
(A) 그것은 단순해 보인다.
(B) 그것은 연주하기 쉽다.
(C) 그것은 인기가 많다.
(D) 그것은 아름답게 들린다.

풀이 가장 좋아하는 악기인 트럼펫에 관해 주로 이야기하고 있으므로 18번의 정답은 (D)이다.

아름답게 들리는 점 때문에 트럼펫을 좋아한다고 했으므로 19번의 정답은 (D)이다.

Words and Phrases instrument 악기 | trumpet 트럼펫 | popular 인기 있는 | simple 간단한, 단순한 | even though 비록 ~일지라도 | practice 연습

[20-21]
Girl: Your attention please. We will close the ice rink for 20 minutes while it is cleaned. All skaters should exit the rink at this time. You may return to the rink when we finish cleaning the ice. Thank you for your cooperation.

20. Where is this announcement made?
(A) in a park
(B) in a restaurant
(C) in a skating rink
(D) in a shopping mall

21. How long will it take to clean the ice?
(A) 2 minutes
(B) 10 minutes
(C) 20 minutes
(D) half an hour

해석 소녀: 주목해 주세요. 아이스링크는 청소하는 20분 동안 폐쇄하겠습니다. 스케이트를 타는 모든 사람들은 지금 링크에서 나가셔야 합니다. 여러분들은 얼음 청소가 끝나면 링크장으로 돌아오셔도 됩니다. 협조해 주셔서 감사합니다.

20. 이 공지는 어디에서 만들어 졌는가?
(A) 공원에서
(B) 식당에서
(C) 스케이트장에서
(D) 쇼핑몰에서

21. 아이스링크를 청소하는데 얼마나 시간이 걸리겠는가?
(A) 2분
(B) 10분
(C) 20분
(D) 30분

풀이 아이스링크의 얼음 청소로 인해 스케이트를 잠시 동안 타지 못한다는 공지에 대한 내용이므로 20번의 정답은 (C)이다.

청소는 20분 동안 진행된다고 했으므로 21번의 정답은 (C)이다.

Words and Phrases attention 주의, 주목 | skater 스케이트 타는 사람 | at this time 이맘때에 | cooperation 협력, 협조 | half an hour 30분

[22-23]
Girl: Yesterday was my aunt's wedding. The weather was very nice. The flowers were beautiful and the food was delicious. There were more guests at the wedding than we expected. Everybody was happy for my aunt and her husband. Above all, my aunt was the happiest person there.

22. What is the speaker talking about?
(A) her aunt's wedding
(B) her husband's party
(C) her sister's graduation
(D) her friend's birthday party

23. What made the day most special?
(A) the nice weather
(B) the delicious food
(C) the happy wedding
(D) the beautiful flowers

해석 소녀: 어제는 내 이모의 결혼식이었다. 날씨가 매우 좋았다. 꽃도 아름다웠고 음식도 맛있었다. 결혼식에는 우리가 예상했던 것보다 더 많은 하객들이 있었다. 모두가 나의 이모와 그녀의 남편을 위해 기뻐했다. 무엇보다도, 나의 이모는 그곳에서 가장 행복한 사람이었다.

22. 소녀는 무엇에 대하여 말하고 있는가?
(A) 그녀의 이모의 결혼식
(B) 그녀의 남편의 파티
(C) 그녀의 여동생의 졸업식
(D) 그녀의 친구의 생일파티

23. 무엇이 그날을 더 특별하게 만들었는가?
(A) 맑은 날씨
(B) 맛있는 음식
(C) 행복한 결혼식
(D) 아름다운 꽃

풀이 이모의 결혼식 날의 날씨, 음식, 분위기에 관해 이야기하고 있으므로 22번의 정답은 (A)이다.

그녀의 이모가 무엇보다도 가장 행복한 사람이었다는 점을 강조하고 있으므로 23번의 정답은 (C)이다.

Words and Phrases aunt 이모 | wedding 결혼식 | expect 기대하다 | husband 남편 | above all 무엇보다도, 특히

[24-25]
Boy: Dear customers. The time is now 8:30 PM. The mall will be closing in 30 minutes. However, the food court on the 5th floor will stay open until 10:00 PM. You are welcome to enjoy some food and drink at our food court. Thank you for shopping at our mall.

24. What is this announcement for?
(A) a hospital
(B) a fun park
(C) a restaurant
(D) a shopping mall

25. What time will the food court close?
(A) at 5:00 PM
(B) at 8:30 PM
(C) at 10:00 PM
(D) in 30 minutes

해석 소년: 친애하는 고객 여러분. 지금 시간은 오후 8시 30분입니다. 쇼핑몰은 30분 후에 문을 닫을 예정입니다. 하지만, 5층 푸드코트는 10시까지 문을 열 것입니다. 저희 푸드코트에서 약간의 음식과 음료를 즐기세요. 저희 쇼핑몰에서 쇼핑해주셔서 감사합니다.

24. 안내 방송은 무엇을 위한 것인가?
(A) 병원
(B) 놀이동산
(C) 식당
(D) 쇼핑몰

25. 푸드코트는 몇 시에 문을 닫는가?
(A) 오후 5시에
(B) 오후 8시 반에
(C) 오후 10시에
(D) 30분 후에

풀이 쇼핑몰의 문 닫는을 시간과 안내사항을 말하는 것이므로 24번의 정답은 (D)이다.

쇼핑몰과 달리 푸드코트는 10시까지 열려있다고 했으므로 25번의 정답은 (C)이다.

Words and Phrases customer 고객 | mall 쇼핑 몰 | food court 푸드코트 | enjoy 즐기다

PART C. Listen and Speak (p.67)

26. Boy: Do you have time this afternoon?
Girl: Yes, I'm free. Why?
Boy: Let's practice speaking English together.
Girl: ________________
(A) I think that's a good idea.
(B) But I'm busy this afternoon.
(C) Tomorrow afternoon sounds great.
(D) I have an English class this afternoon.

해석 소년: 너 오늘 오후에 시간 있니?
소녀: 응, 시간 있어. 왜?
소년: 영어 말하는 것 함께 연습하자.
소녀: ________________

(A) 나는 그거 좋은 생각인 것 같아.
(B) 하지만 나는 오늘 오후에 바빠.
(C) 내일 오후가 좋을 것 같아.
(D) 나는 오늘 오후에 영어 수업이 있어.

풀이 소년이 영어 말하기를 함께 연습하자고 제안했으므로 제안을 받아들이는 (A)가 정답이다.

Words and Phrases afternoon 오후 | free 자유로운 | practice 연습하다

27. Girl: Why do you look so tired?
Boy: I didn't have breakfast this morning.
Girl: You should eat something now.
Boy: ________________

(A) I'm too full to eat.
(B) I'll wait till lunch.
(C) I can't wait till later.
(D) This is delicious, thanks.

해석 소녀: 너 오늘 왜 그렇게 피곤해 보이니?
소년: 나는 오늘 아침에 아침 식사를 못했어.
소녀: 너 지금 무엇이라도 먹어야겠다.
소년: ________________
(A) 나는 너무 배불러서 먹을 수가 없다.
(B) 나는 점심 식사 때까지 기다릴 것이다.
(C) 나는 나중을 기약할 수 없다.
(D) 이거 맛있다, 고마워.

풀이 아침을 거른 소년에게 소녀는 무언가 먹을 것을 권유했고 이에 점심까지 기다리겠다고 응답하는 (B)가 정답이다.

Words and Phrases tired 피곤한 | breakfast 아침식사 | lunch 점심식사 | full 가득 찬, 배부른

28. Girl: I need to buy a new notebook.
Boy: Do you have enough money?
Girl: I think I have enough.
Boy: ________________

(A) I don't need any money.
(B) A pencil is not expensive.
(C) If not, I can lend you some.
(D) I didn't bring my notebook.

해석 소녀: 나는 새 공책을 사야 해.
소년: 너는 돈을 충분히 가지고 있니?
소녀: 내 생각에 나는 충분히 가지고 있어.
소년: ________________
(A) 나는 돈이 필요하지 않아.
(B) 연필 한 자루는 비싸지 않아.
(C) 만약 없으면, 내가 빌려 줄 수 있어.
(D) 나는 내 공책을 가지고 오지 않았다.

풀이 새 공책을 살 돈이 충분히 있는 것 같다고 말하는 소녀의 말에 혹시 부족하면 빌려줄 수 있다고 답하는 (C)가 정답이다.

Words and Phrases notebook 공책 | enough 충분한 | expensive 비싼 | lend 빌려주다 | bring 가져오다

29. Boy: I had a nightmare last night.
Girl: Really? What was it about?
Boy: I don't remember it at all.
Girl: ________________

(A) It was a terrible nightmare.
(B) You have a very good memory.
(C) That sounds like a terrible dream.
(D) Most people don't remember their dreams.

해석 소년: 나는 어젯밤에 악몽을 꿨어.
소녀: 정말? 무엇에 관한 것이었니?
소년: 나는 그것을 전혀 기억하지 못하겠어.
소녀: ________________
(A) 그것은 끔찍한 악몽이었다.
(B) 너는 기억력이 아주 좋구나.
(C) 그거 아주 끔찍한 꿈처럼 들리네.
(D) 대부분의 사람들은 그들의 꿈을 기억하지 못해.

풀이 지난밤 악몽에 관해 전혀 기억하지 못한다는 소년의 말에 대부분의 사람들이 그렇다는 것을 말해주는 (D)가 정답이다.

Words and Phrases nightmare 악몽 | terrible 끔직한 | memory 기억, 기억력 | remember 기억하다

30. Boy: Is that a new watch?
Girl: Yes, I bought it two days ago.
Boy: It looks cool. I like the color.
Girl: ________________

(A) I also have a watch.
(B) Thanks, green is my favorite.
(C) I don't like wearing watches.
(D) Thanks, but it's an old watch.

해석 소녀: 그것은 새 손목시계니?
소년: 맞아, 나는 그것을 2일 전에 샀어.
소녀: 멋져 보인다. 색깔이 마음에 들어.
소년: ________________
(A) 나도 손목시계가 있어.
(B) 고마워, 초록색은 내가 가장 좋아하는 색이야.
(C) 나는 손목시계를 차는 것을 좋아하지 않아.
(D) 고마워, 하지만 그것은 오래된 시계야.

풀이 소년이 소녀의 새 손목시계 색상을 칭찬했으므로 감사 인사와 함께 시계 색상과 관련된 답을 하는 (B)가 정답이다.

Words and Phrases watch 손목시계 | cool 시원한, 멋진 | green 녹색 | wear 입고 있다, 착용하고 있다

SECTION II READING AND WRITING

Part A. Sentence Completion (p.70)

1. A: The computer is ___________.
B: I know. I will fix it.
(A) break
(B) broke
(C) broken
(D) breaked

해석 A: 그 컴퓨터는 고장 났어.
B: 알아. 내가 고칠 거야.
(A) 부수다, 고장나다
(B) 부쉈다
(C) 부서진, 고장난
(D) 틀린 표현

풀이 컴퓨터의 상태를 나타내는 보어로서 형용사가 들어가야 적합하므로 (C)가 정답이다.

Words and Phrases break 깨다, 부수다(break-broke-broken) | fix 고치다

2. A: Do you want to go?
B: I will go ___________ I have time.
(A) if
(B) for
(C) but
(D) and

해석 A: 너는 가고 싶니?
B: 나는 갈 거야 만약 내가 시간이 있으면.
(A) 만약
(B) ~위한
(C) 하지만
(D) 그리고

풀이 시간이 있으면 갈 것이라고 했으므로 가정의 의미를 가진 접속사 (A)가 정답이다.

Words and Phrases want 원하다 | if 만약, ~면

3. A: What do you usually do after dinner?
B: I ___________ in the living room.
(A) watch TV
(B) will watch TV
(C) am watching TV
(D) have watched TV

해석 A: 너는 저녁 식사 후에 주로 무엇을 하니?
B: 나는 거실에서 TV를 봐.
(A) TV를 본다
(B) TV를 볼 것이다
(C) TV를 보는 중이다
(D) TV를 봐왔다

풀이 저녁 식사 후의 일과를 묻는 내용이므로 현재 시제가 들어가야 적합하므로 (A)가 정답이다.

Words and Phrases usually 주로, 보통 | after 후에 | living room 거실

4. A: Is there some bread on the table?
B: ___________
(A) Yes, it is.
(B) No, it isn't.
(C) Yes, there are.
(D) No, there isn't.

해석 A: 식탁 위에 약간의 빵이 있니?
B: 아니, 없어.
(A) 그래, 맞아.
(B) 아니, 그렇지 않아.
(C) 그래, 있어.
(D) 아니, 없어.

풀이 빵의 존재 여부를 답해야 하므로 'there'을 사용한 (D)가 정답이다. (C)도 'there'을 사용하였으나, 'bread'는 셀 수 없는 명사로 단수 취급을 해야 하므로 오답이다.

Words and Phrases some 약간의 | bread 빵

5. A: ___________ in Seoul?
B: It is warm in spring.
(A) How the weather is
(B) How is the weather
(C) What the weather is
(D) What it is the weather

해석 A: 서울의 날씨는 어떠니?
B: 봄에는 따뜻하다.
(A) 틀린 표현
(B) 날씨는 어떠니
(C) 틀린 표현
(D) 틀린 표현

풀이 날씨가 어떠한지를 묻는 의문문으로 'How' 다음에 be 동사 'is'와 주어 'the weather'의 어순으로 와야하므로 (B)가 정답이다.

Words and Phrases weather 날씨 | warm 따뜻한 | spring 봄

Part B. Situational Writing (p.71)

6. The girl is using a ___________.
(A) cup to water the plant
(B) can to water the plant
(C) hose to clean the plant
(D) towel to clean the plant

해석 소녀가 식물에 물을 주는 데 분무기를 사용하고 있다.
(A) 식물에 물을 주는 데 컵을
(B) 식물에 물을 주는 데 분무기를
(C) 식물을 닦는 데 호스를
(D) 식물을 닦는 데 수건를

풀이 그림에서 분무기를 사용하여 식물에 물을 주고 있으므로 (B)가 정답이다.

Words and Phrases water 물을 주다 | plant 식물 | can (깡통) 분무기 | hose 호스 | towel 수건

7. The girl and boy are walking ___________.

(A) behind the dog
(B) next to the dog
(C) far from the dog
(D) in front of the dog

해석 그 소녀와 소년은 그 개 뒤에서 걷는 중이다.

(A) 그 개 뒤에서
(B) 그 개 옆에서
(C) 그 개에서 멀리
(D) 그 개 앞에서

풀이 그림에서 소녀와 소년은 개의 뒤에서 걷고 있으므로 (A)가 정답이다.

Words and Phrases behind 뒤에 | next to 옆에 | far from 멀리 | in front of 앞에

8. The boy is pushing the girl ___________.

(A) on the slide
(B) on the swing
(C) to the seesaw
(D) to the merry-go-round

해석 그 소년은 그네 위의 소녀를 밀고 있는 중이다.

(A) 미끄럼틀 위의
(B) 그네 위의
(C) 시소쪽으로
(D) 회전목마 쪽으로

풀이 그림에서 소년은 그네에 타고 있는 소녀를 밀어주고 있으므로 (B)가 정답이다.

Words and Phrases push 밀다 | slide 미끄럼틀 | swing 그네 | seesaw 시소 | merry-go-round 회전목마

9. The girl is ___________.

(A) studying at a library
(B) reading a book at a library
(C) looking for a book at a bookstore
(D) talking to her friend at bookstore

해석 그 소녀는 서점에서 책을 읽는 중이다.

(A) 도서관에서 공부하는 중이다
(B) 도서관에서 책을 읽는 중이다
(C) 서점에서 책을 찾는 중이다
(D) 서점에서 그녀의 친구와 이야기하는 중이다

풀이 그림에서 소녀는 서점에서 책을 고르고 있으므로 (C)가 정답이다.

Words and Phrases library 도서관 | look for 찾다 | bookstore 서점

10. The teacher is ___________.

(A) talking to the class
(B) taking a rest during break
(C) writing on the whiteboard
(D) checking the students' homework

해석 그 선생님은 ___________.

(A) 반 학생들에게 말하는 중이시다.
(B) 쉬는 시간에 쉬는 중이시다.
(C) 칠판에 쓰는 중이시다.
(D) 학생들의 숙제를 검사하는 중이시다.

풀이 그림에서 선생님은 칠판에 글씨를 쓰고 있으므로 (C)가 정답이다.

Words and Phrases class 반, 학급 | take a rest 쉬다 | check 확인하다, 검사하다 | whiteboard (희색) 칠판

Part C. Practical Reading and Retelling (p.74)

[11-12]

11. How much is a man's cut for a member?

(A) $7.00
(B) $8.00
(C) $9.00
(D) $10.00

12. How long is a $10.00 membership?

(A) three months
(B) six months
(C) one year
(D) two years

해석

릴리의 미용실
남자 커트: $8.00
남자 커트 와 머리 감기: $10.00
여자 커트: $12.00
여자 커트와 머리 감기: $15.00
염색: $15.00
웨이브와 컬: $20.00
회원은 커트시 $1.00 할인, 염색, 웨이브, 컬의 경우 $2.00 할인됩니다.
회원 자격 비용은 6개월에 $6.00, 1년에 $10.00, 2년에 $15.00 입니다.

11. 남자 회원의 커트 비용은 얼마인가?

(A) 7달러
(B) 8달러
(C) 9달러
(D) 10달러

12. 10달러 회원은 기간이 얼마동안 인가?

(A) 3개월
(B) 6개월
(C) 1년
(D) 2년

풀이 회원은 커트가 1달러 할인 된다고 했으므로 11번의 정답은 (A)이다.

10달러 회원은 1년 동안 할인이 된다고 했으므로 12번의 정답은 (C)이다.

Words and Phrases hair salon 미용실 | coloring 염색 | curl 곱슬, 컬 | member 회원 | membership 회원자격 | discount 할인 | fee 비용, 요금

[13-14]

13. Which teams will play on September 13?

(A) Teams A and C
(B) Teams B and D
(C) Teams A and D
(D) Teams C and B

14. When will Dan play against Jake?

(A) Saturday, September 12
(B) Saturday, September 19
(C) Sunday, September 6
(D) Sunday, September 20

해석

팀 A: Mark, Jake, Andy
팀 B: John, Sam, Kevin
팀 C: Justin, Peter, Rob
팀 D: Jack, Tom, Dan
농구 대회 일정
9월 5일 토요일 팀 A 대 팀 B
9월 6일 일요일 팀 C 대 팀 D
9월 12일 토요일 팀 A 대 팀 C
9월 13일 일요일 팀 B 대 팀 D
9월 19일 토요일 팀 A 대 팀 D
9월 20일 일요일 팀 B대 팀 C

13. 어느 팀이 9월 13일에 경기를 하는가?

(A) 팀 A 와 C
(B) 팀 B 와 D
(C) 팀 A 와 D
(D) 팀 C 와 B

14. 언제 Dan은 Jake에 맞서 시합하는가?

(A) 9월 12일 토요일
(B) 9월 19일 토요일
(C) 9월 6일 일요일
(D) 9월 20일 일요일

풀이 9월 13일에는 팀 B와 팀 D가 겨룬다고 했으므로 13번의 정답은 (B)이다.

Dan은 팀D에 속하고 Jake는 팀 A에 속하므로 팀 A와 팀 D가 시합하는 날은 9월 19일 토요일이다. 따라서 14번의 정답은 (B)이다.

Words and Phrases tournament 대회, 경기 | against ~에 맞서

[15-16]

15. What should everyone do before entering the pool?

(A) see a doctor
(B) wait for rain
(C) eat some food
(D) take a shower

16. Who must always be at the pool when people are swimming?

(A) a doctor
(B) an adult
(C) an animal
(D) a lifeguard

해석

수영장 규칙

들어가기 전에 샤워를 한다.
음식, 음료, 유리 또는 동물은 허용되지 않는다.
달리거나, 물을 튀기거나, 다이빙할 수 없다.
12세 이하 어린이는 어른과 함께 있어야 한다.
안전 요원이 근무하지 않을 때는 수영이 허용되지 않는다.
수영장 이용 시간은 오전 9시부터 오후 6시까지이다.

15. 수영장에 들어가기 전에 무엇을 해야하는가?

(A) 의사를 만난다
(B) 비를 기다린다
(C) 음식을 섭취한다
(D) 샤워를 한다

16. 사람들이 수영할 때, 누가 항상 수영장에 있어야 하는가?

(A) 의사
(B) 어른
(C) 동물
(D) 안전 요원

풀이 수영장에 들어가기 전에 샤워를 해야한다고 했으므로 15번의 정답은 (D)이다.

안전 요원이 근무 중이지 않을 때는 수영이 허용되지 않는다고 했으므로 16번의 정답은 (D)이다.

Words and Phrases swimming pool 수영장 | rule 규칙 | glass 유리 | splash (물을) 튀기다, 끼얹다 | diving 다이빙 | lifeguard 안전 요원 | on duty 근무 중

[17-18]

17. How many bagels can you get for $12.00?
(A) 6
(B) 12
(C) 13
(D) 14

18. What baked goods DOESN'T Bob's Bakery sell?
(A) buns
(B) cakes
(C) bread
(D) croissants

해석

BOB의 제과점
머 핀: 1개 1.5달러
3개에 4달러
6개 사면, 1개 무료
베이글: 1개 1.25달러
6개에 6달러
12개 묶음으로 사면, 1개 무료
도 넛: 1개 1달러
12개 묶음에 10달러
저희의 신선한 빵, 크루아상, 그리고 번빵을 먹어보세요. 저희 제빵 제품들은 모두 최고급 천연 재료로 만들어집니다.

17. 12달러로 베이글을 몇 개 살 수 있는가?
(A) 6
(B) 12
(C) 13
(D) 14

18. BOB의 빵집에서 팔지 않는 제빵류는 무엇인가?
(A) 번빵
(B) 케이크
(C) 빵
(D) 크루아상

풀이 베이글은 12개에 12달러이며 12개 구매 시 1개를 무료로 더 준다고 했으므로 17번의 정답은 (C)이다.

BOB의 제과점에서는 머핀, 베이글, 도넛 외에도 크루아상과 번빵을 팔지만 케이크는 언급된 바가 없으므로 18번의 정답은 (B)이다.

Words and Phrases bakery 빵집, 제과점 | free 무료의 | dozen 12개 묶음 | fresh 신선한 | croissant 크루아상 | bun 번빵, 둥글 납작한 빵 | bake 굽다 | finest 최상의 | natural 자연의, 천연의 | ingredient 재료

[19-20]

RADIO CONTROLLED CARS

Model	Scale	Power Type	Speed	Price
Stellar	1/10	Battery	35KPH	$110
Fiero	1/8	Gas	50KPH	$150
Rabbit	1/10	Battery	30KPH	$90
Glide	1/12	Battery	40KPH	$100

19. Which car model runs on gas?
(A) Stellar
(B) Fiero
(C) Rabbit
(D) Glide

20. How much does the slowest car cost?
(A) $90
(B) $100
(C) $110
(D) $150

해석

무선 조종 자동차

차종	크기	동력 유형	속력	가격
Stellar	1/10	배터리	시속 35킬로미터	110달러
Fiero	1/8	가스	시속 50킬로미터	150달러
Rabbit	1/10	배터리	시속 30킬로미터	90달러
Glide	1/12	배터리	시속 40킬로미터	100달러

19. 어떤 차종이 가스로 달리는가?
(A) Stellar
(B) Fiero
(C) Rabbit
(D) Glide

20. 가장 느린 차는 얼마인가?
(A) 90달러
(B) 100달러
(C) 110달러
(D) 150달러

풀이 표에서 가스 동력을 사용하는 차종은 Fiero이므로 19번의 정답은 (B)이다.

표에서 가장 느린 차는 속력이 시속 30킬로미터인 Rabbit으로 90달러이므로 20번의 정답은 (A)이다.

Words and Phrases radio-controlled 무선으로 조종되는 | kph 시간 당 킬로미터

Part D. General Reading and Retelling (p.79)

[21-22]

One of the deadliest animals on earth is the box jellyfish. Box jellyfish are found in warm oceans around the world. They are beautiful to look at because you can see through them. They are shaped like bells with long, flowing arms called tentacles. The tentacles have a very strong poison. Jellyfish use this poison to catch small fish to eat. But humans have sometimes died from the jellyfish's poison.

21. Where can box jellyfish be found?
(A) in cold water
(B) in warm oceans
(C) in rivers and lakes
(D) all around the world

22. What does a box jellyfish use to catch small fish?
(A) its mouth
(B) its strong legs
(C) its long tentacles
(D) its bell-shaped body

해석 지구상에서 가장 치명적인 동물들 중 하나가 상자 해파리이다. 상자 해파리는 전 세계에 있는 따뜻한 바다에서 발견 된다. 그들은 투명하기 때문에 보기에는 아름답다. 그들은 종 모양에 촉수라고 불리는 길고 물결 같은 팔을 가지고 있다. 촉수는 아주 강한 독을 가지고 있다. 해파리는 작은 물고기를 잡아 먹기 위해 이 독을 사용한다. 하지만 해파리의 독 때문에 인간도 때때로 죽음을 당했다.

21. 상자 해파리는 어디서 발견될 수 있는가?
(A) 차가운 물에서
(B) 따뜻한 바다에서
(C) 강이랑 호수에서
(D) 전 세계에서

22. 상자 해파리는 작은 물고기를 잡기 위해 무엇을 사용하는가?
(A) 그의 입
(B) 그의 강한 다리
(C) 그의 긴 촉수
(D) 그의 종 모양인 몸

풀이 본문은 상자 해파리가 따뜻한 바다에서 발견 된다고 했으므로 21번의 정답은 (B)이다.

상자 해파리는 촉수가 갖고 있는 독을 사용해서 작은 물고기를 먹는다고 했으므로 22번의 정답은 (C)이다.

Words and Phrases deadly 치명적인 | beautiful 아름다운 | bell 종 | flowing 물결 같은 | tentacle 촉수 | poison 독

[23-24]

Not too many people have heard about the World Pyro Olympics. It is held every year in Manila, Philippines. The word "pyro" means fire. This event is a competition for the world's biggest fireworks companies. The competition lasts for five days. Every day, two countries show off their greatest fireworks. It is an amazing thing to see! The country with the best fireworks gets to be the World Pyro Olympics Champion.

23. Why do they call it World Pyro Olympics?
(A) because it lasts for five days
(B) because it is in Manila, Philippines
(C) because it is a competition of fireworks
(D) because only the biggest companies compete

24. In total, how many countries show off their greatest fireworks?
(A) 2 countries
(B) 5 countries
(C) 10 countries
(D) 20 countries

해석 많은 사람들은 세계 파이로 올림픽에 대해 들어보지 못했다. 그것은 매년 필리핀, 마닐라에서 열린다. '파이로'라는 단어는 불이라는 뜻이다. 이 행사는 세계의 가장 큰 폭죽 회사들의 경연 대회이다. 대회는 5일 동안 지속 된다. 매일, 두 국가가 그들의 엄청난 폭죽을 자랑한다. 그것은 보기에 놀라운 것이다. 최고의 폭죽을 가진 국가가 세계 파이로 올림픽 챔피언이 된다.

23. 왜 세계 파이로 올림픽이라고 부르는가?
(A) 5일 동안 지속되기 때문에
(B) 필리핀, 마닐라에서 열리기 때문에
(C) 폭죽 대회이기 때문에
(D) 큰 회사들만 경쟁하기 때문에

24. 총 몇 개 국가가 그들의 엄청난 폭죽을 자랑하는가?
(A) 2개국
(B) 5개국
(C) 10개국
(D) 20개국

풀이 세계 파이로 올림픽에서는 폭죽 회사들이 경쟁을 한다고 했으므로 23번의 정답은 (C)이다.

대회는 5일 동안 지속되고 하루에 두 나라가 경쟁한다고 했으므로 총 10개 국가가 참여한다는 것을 알 수 있다. 따라서 24번의 정답은 (C)이다.

Words and Phrases event 행사 | competition 경쟁, 대회, 시합 | fireworks 폭죽 | amazing 놀라운 | champion 챔피온

[25-26]

Mozart was born in Salzburg, Austria, in 1756. When he was only six years old, he played music for kings and queens. By the time he was eight, Mozart wrote his first symphony. A symphony is a very long and difficult piece of music. All together, Mozart wrote about 600 pieces of music. Sadly, he died a poor man when he was 35 years old. Today, music lovers remember him as one of the greatest musicians in history.

25. What happened when Mozart was eight years old?
(A) He died very poor.
(B) He wrote a symphony.
(C) He wrote 600 pieces of music.
(D) He played for kings and queens.

26. What is NOT true about Mozart?
(A) He was born in Vienna, Austria.
(B) He died when he was 35 years old.
(C) He is one of the greatest musicians.
(D) He could write long, difficult pieces of music.

해석 모차르트는 1756년도에 오스트리아, 잘츠부르크에서 태어났다. 그가 6살 밖에 되지 않았을 때, 왕과 왕비를 위해 음악을 연주했다. 그가 8살이 됐을 때, 그의 첫 교향곡을 작곡했다. 교향곡은 매우 길고 어려운 음악이다. 다 해서, 모차르트는 약 600여 개의 음악 작품을 작곡했다. 슬프게도, 그는 35살 때 가난하게 죽었다. 오늘날, 음악을 사랑하는 사람들은 그를 역사에 있는 가장 훌륭한 음악가 중 한명으로 기억한다.

25. 모차르트가 8살 때 무슨 일이 있었는가?
(A) 그는 가난하게 죽었다.
(B) 그는 교향곡을 작곡했다.
(C) 그는 600개의 음악 작품을 작곡했다.
(D) 그는 왕과 왕비를 위해 연주했다.

26. 모차르트에 대해 사실이 아닌 것은?
(A) 그는 오스트리아, 비엔나에서 태어났다.
(B) 그는 35살 때 죽었다.
(C) 그는 훌륭한 음악가 중 한 명이다.
(D) 그는 길고 어려운 음악 작품을 작곡할 수 있었다.

풀이 모차르트는 8살 때 첫 교향곡을 작곡했다고 했으므로 25번의 정답은 (B)이다.

모차르트는 오스트리아에 있는 비엔나가 아닌 잘츠부르크에서 태어났다고 했으므로 26번은 (A)가 정답이다.

Words and Phrases symphony 교향곡, 심포니 | piece of music 음악 작품 | poor 가난한

[27-28]

Teenagers grow very quickly. Girls usually grow earlier than boys. Girls start growing quickly when they are about 12 to 13 years old. Boys grow quickly when they are about 14 to 15 years old. However, boys can grow faster. Boys can grow about 9cm a year and girls can grow about 8cm a year. The first parts of the body to grow fast are the hands and feet. That's why growing teenagers need to buy new shoes very often.

27. At what age do girls start to grow quickly?
(A) after they are 13 years old
(B) before they are 12 years old
(C) when they are 12 to 13 years old
(D) when they are 14 to 15 years old

28. What is NOT true about the way teenagers grow?
(A) Boys grow earlier than girls.
(B) The hands and feet grow first.
(C) Boys can grow faster than girls.
(D) Girls can grow about 8cm a year.

해석 십대들은 매우 빨리 자란다. 여자 아이들은 보통 남자 아이들보다 일찍 자란다. 여자 아이들은 그들이 약 12살에서 13살일 때 빠르게 성장하기 시작한다. 남자 아이들은 약 14세에서 15세가 되면 빨리 자란다. 하지만, 남자 아이들이 더 빨리 자랄 수 있다. 남자 아이들은 1년에 약 9cm, 여자 아이들은 1년에 약 8cm 성장할 수 있다. 빨리 자라는 몸의 첫 번째 부분은 손과 발이다. 그것이 성장하는 십대들이 새 신발을 매우 자주 사야 하는 이유이다.

27. 몇 살 때 여자 아이들은 빠르게 성장하는가?
(A) 13살 이후에
(B) 12살 이전에
(C) 12살에서 13살 사이에
(D) 14살에서 15살 사이에

28. 십대들의 성장에 관한 사실이 아닌 것은 무엇인가?
(A) 남자 아이들은 여자아이들보다 일찍 성장한다.
(B) 손과 발이 먼저 자란다.
(C) 남자 아이들은 여자아이들보다 빨리 성장한다.
(D) 여자 아이들은 1년에 약 8센티미터 성장한다.

풀이 여자 아이들은 약 12살에서 13살일 때 빠르게 자라기 시작한다고 했으므로 27번의 정답은 (C)이다.

남자 아이들의 성장 시기는 14살에서 15살 사이로, 여자 아이들보다 늦다고 했으므로 28번의 정답은 (A)이다.

Words and Phrases teenager 십대 | grow 자라다, 성장하다 | quickly 빠르게 | feet 발(foot의 복수)

[29-30]
The giant sequoia is one of the biggest living things on the planet. Giant sequoia trees can be found in central California. California is a state in the far west of the United States. The largest giant sequoia, called the General Sherman Tree, is 84 meters tall and has a trunk that is 11.1 meters wide. People guess that it weighs as much as 2,500 tons! Many of these giant sequoia trees are thousands of years old.

29. Where can giant sequoia trees be found?
(A) in central California
(B) in southern California
(C) in central United States
(D) in the west of California

30. How wide is the General Sherman Tree's trunk?
(A) 84 meters
(B) 2,500 tons
(C) 11.1 meters
(D) thousands of years

해석 거대한 세쿼이아는 지구상에서 가장 큰 생물 중 하나이다. 거대한 세쿼이아 나무는 중부 캘리포니아에서 볼 수 있다. 캘리포니아는 미국의 최 서부에 있는 주이다. General Sherman 나무라고 불리는 가장 큰 세쿼이아는 높이가 84미터이고 몸통 너비가 11.1미터이다. 사람들은 그것의 무게가 2,500톤이나 된다고 추측한다! 이 거대한 세쿼이아 나무 중 많은 수가 수천 년 되었다.

29. 거대한 세쿼이아는 어디에서 발견되는가?
(A) 중부 캘리포니아에서
(B) 남부 캘리포니아에서
(C) 미국 중부에서
(D) 서부 캘리포니아에서

30. General Sherman 나무의 몸통 너비는 얼마인가?
(A) 84 미터
(B) 2,500 톤
(C) 11.1 미터
(D) 수천 년

풀이 거대한 세쿼이아 나무는 중부 캘리포니아에서 볼 수 있다고 했으므로 29번의 정답은 (A)이다.

General Sherman 나무의 몸통 너비는 11.1미터가 된다고 했으므로 30번은 (C)가 정답이다.

Words and Phrases giant 거대한 | planet 지구 | central 중앙의 | state 국가, 주 | west 서쪽 | trunk 나무의 몸통 | wide 폭이 ...인 | weigh 무게가~이다

TOSEL Junior

실전4회

Section I Listening and Speaking

1 (A) 2 (B) 3 (D) 4 (C) 5 (C)
6 (C) 7 (C) 8 (C) 9 (A) 10 (C)
11 (A) 12 (C) 13 (B) 14 (D) 15 (B)
16 (D) 17 (A) 18 (B) 19 (D) 20 (C)
21 (B) 22 (D) 23 (B) 24 (B) 25 (B)
26 (B) 27 (D) 28 (B) 29 (C) 30 (B)

Section II Reading and Writing

1 (A) 2 (D) 3 (B) 4 (D) 5 (C)
6 (A) 7 (D) 8 (B) 9 (C) 10 (D)
11 (A) 12 (C) 13 (C) 14 (D) 15 (C)
16 (B) 17 (C) 18 (C) 19 (C) 20 (C)
21 (C) 22 (B) 23 (B) 24 (A) 25 (B)
26 (D) 27 (B) 28 (C) 29 (C) 30 (D)

SECTION I LISTENING AND SPEAKING

Part A. Listen and Respond (p.86)

1. Girl: How are you doing these days?
Boy: ________________
(A) Doing great.
(B) Well, too far.
(C) Sure, of course.
(D) Not that I know of.

해석 소녀: 요즘 어떻게 지내?
소년: ________________
(A) 잘 지내.
(B) 글쎄, 너무 멀어.
(C) 그럼, 당연하지.
(D) 내가 알기론 아니야.

풀이 안부를 묻는 소녀의 말에 잘 지낸다고 답하는 (A)가 정답이다.
Words and Phrases these days 요즘에는

2. Boy: How was your exam yesterday?
Girl: ________________
(A) I love cats.
(B) I messed it up.
(C) He did his best.
(D) He stood me up.

해석 소년: 어제 네 시험은 어땠어?
소녀: ________________

(A) 나는 고양이를 정말 좋아해.
(B) 나는 그것을 망쳤어.
(C) 그는 최선을 다했어.
(D) 그가 날 바람 맞혔어.

풀이 시험이 어땠냐는 소년의 질문에 망쳤다고 답하는 (B)가 정답이다.

Words and Phrases mess up 엉망으로 만들다 | stand somebody up ~를 바람맞히다

3. Girl: What is your favorite color?
Boy: ________________

(A) I have long hair.
(B) He bought a new bag.
(C) These are colored pencils.
(D) Sky blue is my favorite color.

해석 소녀: 네가 가장 좋아하는 색은 뭐야?
소년: ________________

(A) 나는 긴 머리를 가지고 있다.
(B) 그는 새로운 가방을 샀다.
(C) 이것들은 색연필이다.
(D) 하늘색이 내가 가장 좋아하는 색이야.

풀이 가장 좋아하는 색을 묻는 소녀의 질문에 하늘색이 가장 좋다고 답하는 (D)가 정답이다.

Words and Phrases sky blue 하늘색

4. Boy: This video game is awesome!
Girl: ________________

(A) Is that your hat?
(B) Where did you go?
(C) Can I play with you?
(D) Did you dye your hair?

해석 소년: 이 비디오 게임 굉장한데!
소녀: ________________

(A) 그거 네 모자야?
(B) 너 어디 다녀왔어?
(C) 내가 너랑 같이 해볼 수 있을까?
(D) 너 머리 염색했어?

풀이 게임이 대단하다며 놀라는 소년에게 같이 게임 할 수 있을지를 요청하는 (C)가 정답이다.

Words and Phrases awesome 어마어마한, 엄청난, 굉장한 | dye 염색하다

5. Girl: Where is the restroom?
Boy: ________________

(A) He needs some rest.
(B) Right after Christmas.
(C) Just around the corner.
(D) Tomorrow is my birthday.

해석 소녀: 화장실이 어디야?
소년: ________________

(A) 그는 약간의 휴식이 필요해.
(B) 크리스마스 바로 다음.
(C) 모퉁이 돌면 바로야.
(D) 내일이 내 생일이야.

풀이 화장실의 위치를 묻는 소녀에게 모퉁이를 돌면 바로 있다고 답하는 (C)가 정답이다.

Words and Phrases restroom 화장실

6. Girl: My sister has a fever of 102.
Boy: ________________

(A) They didn't show up.
(B) I got the perfect score.
(C) You must be very worried.
(D) She can do writing very well.

해석 소녀: 내 여동생 열이 102도야.
소년: ________________

(A) 그들은 나타나지 않았어.
(B) 나는 만점을 받았어.
(C) 너 많이 걱정되겠다.
(D) 그녀는 글을 정말 잘 쓸 수 있어.

풀이 여동생의 열이 높다는 소녀의 말에 걱정되겠다며 공감을 표현하는 (C)가 정답이다.

Words and Phrases fever 열 | show up 눈에 띄다 [나타나다]

7. Girl: He had one whole pizza in one sitting.
Boy: ________________

(A) I'd like lemonade.
(B) No one knows where it is.
(C) No wonder he's so chubby.
(D) I'm a little on the short side.

해석 소녀: 그는 앉은 자리에서 피자 한 판을 다 먹었어.
소년: ________________

(A) 나는 레모네이드가 좋아.
(B) 누구도 그것이 어디에 있는지 알지 못해.
(C) 그가 그렇게 통통한 건 놀랍지도 않아.
(D) 내가 좀 작은 편이야.

풀이 먹는 양이 많은 소년에 대해 이야기하는 소녀의 말에, 그가 뚱뚱한 이유를 알겠다고 말하는 (C)가 정답이다.

Words and Phrases no wonder ~는 놀랍지도 않다, 그도 그럴 것이 | chubby 통통한, 토실토실한

8. Girl: I'd like to get a scooter for my birthday.
Boy: ________________

(A) Did it snow?
(B) Were you on time?
(C) When's your birthday?
(D) Did he do his homework?

해석 소녀: 나는 내 생일에 스쿠터를 받고 싶어.
소년: ________________

(A) 눈이 왔어?
(B) 넌 제시간에 왔니?
(C) 네 생일이 언제인데?
(D) 그는 숙제를 했니?

풀이 생일에 스쿠터를 받고 싶다는 소녀의 말에 생일이 언제인지 묻는 (C)가 정답이다.

Words and Phrases scooter 스쿠터, 소형 오토바이 | on time 시간을 어기지 않고, 정각에

9. Girl: Can I get a cup of milk?
Boy: ________________
(A) Sure, here it is.
(B) Sorry, it's fully booked.
(C) I'm happy to cover for you.
(D) Fibers are good for your health.

해석 소녀: 제가 우유 한 잔 마실 수 있을까요?
소년: ________________
(A) 그럼요, 여기 있습니다.
(B) 죄송합니다, 예약이 꽉 찼어요.
(C) 제가 당신을 대신할 수 있어 기쁩니다.
(D) 섬유질은 당신의 건강에 좋아요.

풀이 우유 한 잔을 요청하는 소녀의 말에 우유를 건네 주는 (A)가 정답이다.

Words and Phrases book 예약하다 | cover for 대신하다, 보호하다 | fiber 섬유질

10. Girl: This math problem is so hard.
Boy: ________________
(A) At the library.
(B) Just a few bites.
(C) Let me take a look at it.
(D) My doctor will be so happy.

해석 소녀: 이 수학 문제 정말 어렵다.
소년: ________________
(A) 도서관에서.
(B) 몇 입만.
(C) 내가 한 번 볼게.
(D) 나의 주치의가 정말 기뻐할 거야.

풀이 수학 문제가 어렵다는 소녀의 말에 자신이 한 번 보겠다고 말하는 (C)가 정답이다.

Part B. Listen and Retell (p.87)

11. Girl: Do you have any good ideas for mom's birthday present?
Boy: Maybe we could get her a nice bag?
Girl: That's a good idea.
Question: What kind of present do they need to buy?
(A) a birthday present
(B) a goodbye present
(C) a Mother's Day present
(D)a housewarming present

해석 소녀: 엄마 생신 선물을 위한 뭐 좋은 생각이 있니?
소년: 아마 우리가 괜찮은 가방을 드릴 수 있을것 같은데?
소녀: 그거 좋은 생각이다.
질문: 그들은 어떤 종류의 선물을 사야 하는가?
(A) 생일 선물
(B) 작별 선물
(C) 어머니의 날 선물
(D) 집들이 선물

풀이 부모님의 생신 선물을 고민하고 제안하는 대화를 이어가고 있으므로 (A)가 정답이다.

Words and Phrases present 선물 | idea 발상, 생각 | goodbye 작별 | housewarming 집들이

12. M: I'd like to have a pet dog.
W: Dogs make me sneeze. I prefer cats.
M: That's funny. Cats and rabbits make me sneeze.
Question: Who sneezes when near a cat?
(A) They both do.
(B) Only the woman does.
(C) Only the man does.
(D) Neither of them does.

해석 남자: 나는 반려견이 갖고 싶어.
여자: 개들은 나를 재채기하게 해. 나는 고양이를 더 선호해.
남자: 그거 재미있네. 고양이와 토끼가 나를 재채기하게 해.
질문: 누가 고양이 가까이 있을 때 재채기를 하는가?
(A) 둘 다 그렇다.
(B) 여자만 그렇다.
(C) 남자만 그렇다.
(D) 둘다 그렇지 않다.

풀이 남자는 고양이나 토끼가 가까이 있을 때 재채기를 한다고 했으므로 (C)가 정답이다.

Words and Phrases pet dog 반려견 | sneeze 재채기, 재채기하다 | prefer 선호하다 | near 가까운, 가까이 | only 유일한 | both 둘 다의 | neither (둘 중) 어느 것도 …아니다

13. Girl: I think I'm going to order the barbeque chicken.
Boy: I was going to order the same thing.
Girl: Really? That's funny.
Question: Where are they?
(A) at a farm
(B) at a restaurant
(C) at a grocery store
(D) at a department store

해석 소녀: 나는 바베큐 치킨을 주문할 것 같아.
소년: 나도 같은 것을 주문하려고 했는데.
소녀: 정말? 그거 재미있네.
질문: 그들은 어디에 있는가?
(A) 농장에
(B) 식당에
(C) 식료품점에
(D) 백화점에

풀이 두 사람 모두 주문할 메뉴에 관해 이야기하고 있으므로 (B)가 정답이다.

Words and Phrases order 주문하다 | same 같은 | farm 농장 | grocery store 식료품점 | department store 백화점

14. Boy: Should I wear a sweater or a T-shirt?
Girl: Wear a sweater because it's cold today.
Boy: Okay, thanks.
Question: What are they doing?
(A) They are cleaning their rooms.
(B) They are washing their clothes.
(C) They are shopping for clothing.
(D) They are getting ready to go out.

해석 소년: 나 스웨터를 입을까, 티셔츠를 입을까?
소녀: 스웨터를 입어 왜냐하면 오늘 춥거든.
소년: 알았어, 고마워.
질문: 그들은 무엇을 하고 있는가?
(A) 그들은 그들의 방을 청소하고 있다.
(B) 그들은 그들의 옷을 세탁하고 있다.
(C) 그들은 옷 쇼핑을 하고 있다.
(D) 그들은 나갈 준비를 하고 있다.

풀이 소년에게 날씨가 추우니 스웨터를 입을 것을 제안하는 것에서 외출 준비를 하는 것을 짐작할 수 있으므로 (D)가 정답이다.

Words and Phrases sweater 스웨터 | clean 청소하다 | clothing 옷 | get ready 준비를 하다

15. Girl: Who are you waiting for?
Boy: My friend, Bill.
Girl: Are you going to the soccer game together?
Question: Who is the boy waiting for?
(A) his father
(B) his friend
(C) Bill's friend
(D) a soccer player

해석 소녀: 너는 누구를 기다리고 있니?
소년: 내 친구, Bill.
소녀: 축구 경기에 같이 가는 거니?
질문: 소년은 누구를 기다리고 있는가?
(A) 그의 아버지
(B) 그의 친구
(C) Bill의 친구
(D) 축구 선수

풀이 소년은 Bill이라는 자신의 친구를 기다리고 있다고 했으므로 (B)가 정답이다.

Words and Phrases wait for ~를 기다리다 | game 경기

16. Boy: Isn't your birthday next week?
Girl: No, it isn't for another two months.
Boy: Oh, right.
Question: When is the girl's birthday?
(A) this week
(B) next week
(C) next month
(D) in two months

해석 소년: 다음 주에 네 생일 아니니?
소녀: 아니야, 앞으로 두 달 동안은 아니야.
소년: 아, 그렇구나.
질문: 소녀의 생일은 언제인가?
(A) 이번 주
(B) 다음 주
(C) 다음 달
(D) 두 달 후

풀이 소녀가 자신의 생일은 앞으로 두 달 동안은 아니라고 했으므로 (D)가 정답이다.

Words and Phrases another 또 하나의, 다른

17. Girl: I heard your brother broke his leg.
Boy: Yes, he's having a hard time these days.
Girl: I hope he gets better soon.
Question: How is the boy's brother?
(A) He is hurt.
(B) He feels fine.
(C) He has a cold.
(D) He feels better.

해석 소녀: 너의 남동생이 다리가 부러졌다고 들었어.
소년: 맞아, 그는 요즘 힘든 시간을 보내고 있어.
소녀: 그가 빨리 좋아지길 바라.
질문: 소년의 남동생은 어떠한가?
(A) 그는 다쳤다.
(B) 그는 기분이 좋다.
(C) 그는 감기에 걸린 상태이다.
(D) 그는 기분이 나아졌다.

풀이 소년의 남동생은 다리가 부러져 힘든 시간을 보내고 있다고 했으므로 (A)가 정답이다.

Words and Phrases hear 듣다(hear–heard–heard) | break 부수다(break–broke–broken) | these days 요즘에는 | hope 바라다, 희망하다 | get better 좋아지다, 호전되다 | hurt 다친 | fine 좋은, 건강한

[18–19]
Boy: We are now at Central Station. You may transfer to line number 1 here. If you are getting off, please do not forget to take your things with you. Thank you. Our next stop is Maple Park. Please stand back from the doors as they close.

18. Where is this announcement being made?
(A) on a bus
(B) on a subway
(C) in a car wash
(D) on an airplane

19. What did the announcer tell people to do?
(A) close the door
(B) stand near the doors
(C) get off at the next stop
(D) take their things with them

해석 소년: 우리는 지금 Central 역에 있습니다. 여기에서 1호선으로 환승할 수 있습니다. 내릴 때는 물건을 가져가는 것을 잊지 마십시오. 감사합니다. 다음 정거장은 메이플 공원입니다. 문이 닫힐 때는 물러서 주십시오.

18. 이 공지는 어디에서 이루어지고 있는가?
(A) 버스 안에서
(B) 지하철 안에서
(C) 세차장에서
(D) 비행기 안에서

19. 아나운서는 사람들에게 무엇을 하라고 말했는가?
(A) 문을 닫으라고
(B) 문 가까이에 서있으라고
(C) 다음 역에서 내리라고
(D) 자기 소지품을 가져가라고

풀이 지금은 Central 역이고 다른 호선으로 환승할 수 있다고 했으므로 18번의 정답은 (B)이다.

내릴 때는 자신의 소지품을 가져가는 것을 잊지말라고 했으므로 19번의 정답은 (D)이다.

Words and Phrases transfer 환승하다 | get off 내리다, 하차하다 | take 가지고 가다 | stand back 물러서다

[20-21]
W: One of my favorite things to do in my free time other than listen to music is to eat. I love to cook and eat delicious food. My friends and I enjoy trying different restaurants or cooking together. To me, cooking is like painting. You need to use different colored foods to make the dish look more interesting.

20. What does the woman NOT have an interest in?
(A) eating
(B) cooking
(C) painting the dish
(D) listening to music

21. What does the woman do with her friends?
(A) go to concerts
(B) eat at restaurants
(C) cook in restaurants
(D) paint pictures of food

해석 여자: 음악을 듣는 것 외에 여가 시간에 내가 가장 좋아하는 일 중 하나는 먹는 것이다. 나는 요리하고 맛있는 음식을 먹는 것을 좋아한다. 내 친구들과 나는 다른 식당들을 시도하거나 함께 요리하는 것을 즐긴다. 나에게, 요리는 그림과 같다. 요리를 더 재미있게 보이게 하려면 다른 색깔의 음식을 사용해야 한다.

20. 여자가 흥미를 가지고 있지 않은 것은 무엇인가?
(A) 먹는 것
(B) 요리하는 것
(C) 접시를 칠하는 것
(D) 음악을 듣는 것

21. 여자는 친구들과 무엇을 하는가?
(A) 콘서트에 간다.
(B) 식당에서 식사를 한다.
(C) 식당에서 요리한다.
(D) 음식 그림을 그린다.

풀이 여자는 음악 듣는 것, 먹는 것, 요리하는 것을 좋아한다고 했으므로 20번의 정답은 (C)이다.

여자는 친구들과 식당에서 먹거나 함께 요리하는 것을 즐긴다고 했으므로 21번의 정답은 (B)이다.

Words and Phrases free time 여가 시간 | enjoy 즐기다 | cooking 요리 | painting 그림 그리기 | different 다른 | color 색을 칠하다 | dish 요리, 음식

[22-23]
Boy: One day while I was playing soccer at school, I tripped and fell. I cut my knee badly. My mother quickly came to school and took me to the hospital. The doctor put a bandage around my knee and told me to rest at home for a few days. My friends brought me flowers and cards.

22. What was the boy doing when he got hurt?
(A) running
(B) swimming
(C) playing tennis
(D) playing soccer

23. What did the boy's mother do for him?
(A) She put a bandage on him.
(B) She drove him to the hospital.
(C) She gave him flowers and a card.
(D) She picked him up off the ground.

해석 소년: 어느 날 나는 학교에서 축구를 하는 동안 발을 헛디뎌서 넘어졌다. 나는 무릎을 심하게 베였다. 내 어머니는 빨리 학교에 오셔서 나를 병원으로 데려가셨다. 의사는 내 무릎에 붕대를 감고 나에게 며칠 동안 집에서 쉬라고 했다. 내 친구들이 꽃과 카드를 가져왔다.

22. 소년은 다쳤을 때 무엇을 하고 있었는가?
(A) 달리기를 하고 있었다.
(B) 수영을 하고 있었다.
(C) 테니스를 치고 있었다.
(D) 축구를 하고 있었다.

23. 소년의 어머니는 그를 위해 무엇을 하셨는가?
(A) 그녀는 그에게 붕대를 감아주셨다.
(B) 그녀는 그를 병원으로 데려가셨다.
(C) 그녀는 그에게 꽃과 카드를 주셨다.
(D) 그녀는 그를 땅에서 들어올리셨다.

풀이 소년은 학교에서 축구를 하다가 넘어졌다고 하였으므로 22번의 정답은 (D)이다.

소년의 어머니는 소년을 병원으로 데려갔다고 했으므로 23번의 정답은 (B)이다.

Words and Phrases while ~하는 동안 | trip 발을 헛디디다 | fall 넘어지다(fall-fell-fallen) | knee 무릎 | quickly 빨리 | bandage 붕대 | rest 쉬다,

[24-25]
Girl: Attention, everyone. The time is now 9:50. Our doors will close in 10 minutes. Please go to the front desk if you would like to check out any books. Tomorrow our hours will change for the weekend. On Saturday we are open from 9:00 a.m. to 6 p.m. On Sunday our hours are from 10 a.m. to 4 p.m. Thank you.

24. What is this announcement for?
(A) a bank
(B) a library
(C) a bookstore
(D) a grocery store

25. What day is it today?
(A) Thursday
(B) Friday
(C) Saturday
(D) Sunday

해석 소녀: 모두 주목하십시오. 지금 시간은 9시 50분입니다. 10분 후에 문이 닫힐 것입니다. 책을 대출하고 싶으신 분들은 프런트로 가주세요. 내일은 주말 시간대로 바뀔 것입니다. 토요일에는 오전 9시부터 오후 6시까지 개관합니다. 일요일은 오전 10시부터 오후 4시까지입니다. 감사합니다.

24. 이 공지는 무엇에 관한 것인가?
(A) 은행
(B) 도서관
(C) 서점
(D) 식료품점

25. 오늘은 무슨 요일인가?
(A) 목요일
(B) 금요일
(C) 토요일
(D) 일요일

풀이 도서관의 운영시간에 관한 이야기이므로 24번의 정답은 (B)이다.

내일부터 주말 시간대로 바뀐다는 말로 오늘은 금요일임을 짐작할 수 있으므로 25번의 정답은 (B)이다.

Words and Phrases attention 주의, 주목 | front desk 프런트(안내 데스크) | check out 대출하다

Part C. Listen and Speak (p.91)

26. Girl: Did you ask Dad to drive you?
Boy: Yes, but he said he couldn't.
Girl: Why not?
Boy: ________________
(A) He is free.
(B) He is busy.
(C) He has a car.
(D) He will drive.

해석 소녀: 너는 아빠에게 태워달라고 했니?
소년: 응, 하지만 그는 할 수 없다고 하셨어.
소녀: 왜 안된다고 하셨어?
소년: ________________
(A) 그는 한가해.
(B) 그는 바빠.
(C) 그는 차가 있어.
(D) 그가 운전하실 거야.

풀이 소년의 아빠가 소년을 차로 태워다 줄 수 없는 이유를 묻고 있으므로 그가 바빠서라고 응답하는 (B)가 정답이다.

Words and Phrases drive 운전하다, 태워다 주다 | free 여유로운 | busy 바쁜

27. Boy: If you're feeling tired, you can go home.
Girl: Thanks. I really need to sleep!
Boy: We can finish this tomorrow morning.
Girl: ________________
(A) I will stay up late tonight.
(B) I could sleep all day long.
(C) Thanks for finishing it for me.
(D) Okay, I'll see you in the morning.

해석 소년: 네가 피곤하면, 집에 가도 돼.
소녀: 고마워. 나는 정말 자야 해!
소년: 우리는 이것을 내일 아침에 끝낼 수 있어.
소녀: ________________
(A) 나는 오늘 밤늦게까지 깨어 있을 거야.
(B) 나는 하루종일 잘 수 있어.
(C) 나를 위해 그것을 끝내줘서 고마워.
(D) 그래, 내일 아침에 보자.

풀이 소년이 하던 일은 내일 아침에 끝낼 수 있다고 했으므로, 다음 날 아침에 보자고 응답하는 (D)가 정답이다.

Words and Phrases tired 피곤한 | need 필요로 하다 | sleep 자다 | finish 끝내다.

28. Girl: I've forgotten where I put my scissors.
Boy: They're in the bathroom.
Girl: Why are they there?
Boy: ________________
(A) All my brushes are there.
(B) I needed them to cut my hair.
(C) I have no idea where they are.
(D) You borrowed them last week.

해석 소녀: 나는 내가 가위를 어디에 두었는지 잊어버렸다.
소년: 그것들은 욕실에 있어.
소녀: 그것들이 왜 거기 있지?
소년: ________________
(A) 내 모든 붓이 저기 있다.
(B) 내 머리카락을 자르기 위해 그것들이 필요했어.
(C) 그것들이 어디 있는지 전혀 모르겠다.
(D) 네가 지난주에 그것들을 빌렸었다.
풀이 가위가 왜 욕실에 있는지 묻는 질문에 대한 이유를 말하는 (B)가 정답이다.
Words and Phrases forget 잊다(forget-forgot-forgotten) | scissors 가위 | bathroom 욕실 | borrow 빌리다

29. Boy: What's your new teacher like?
Girl: She's not very interesting.
Boy: Why do you think that?
Girl: ________________
(A) I think she's very pretty.
(B) She always tells great stories.
(C) She just reads from the textbook.
(D) She's the best teacher I've ever had.
해석 소년: 너의 새 선생님은 어떤 분이시니?
소녀: 그녀는 매우 재미있지는 않으셔.
소년: 왜 그렇게 생각하니?
소녀: ________________
(A) 내 생각에 그녀는 매우 예쁘셔.
(B) 그녀는 항상 훌륭한 이야기를 해주셔.
(C) 그녀는 그냥 교과서를 읽기만 하셔.
(D) 그녀는 내가 만난 선생님 중 최고의 선생님이셔.
풀이 왜 새로운 선생님을 재미없는 분이라고 생각하는지 묻는 질문에 대한 이유를 제시하는 (C)가 정답이다.
Words and Phrases teacher 선생님 | interesting 재미있는 | always 항상 | textbook 교과서

30. Girl: Hmm. The smell of your cooking is making me hungry!
Boy: I'm glad because I've made a lot!
Girl: Oh, good! When will it be ready?
Boy: ________________
(A) I'm ready to go.
(B) In a few minutes.
(C) You smell the onion.
(D) I'm really hungry, too.
해석 소녀: 음. 네 요리 냄새가 나를 배고프게 해!
소년: 기쁜데! 왜냐하면 내가 많이 만들었거든.
소녀: 오, 좋아! 그거 언제 준비 돼?
소년: ________________
(A) 나는 갈 준비가 됐다.
(B) 몇 분 뒤에.
(C) 네가 양파 냄새를 맡아봐.
(D) 나도 정말 배고파.
풀이 요리가 언제 준비되는지 질문하였으므로 곧 몇 분 안에 완성된다고 응답하는 (B)가 정답이다.
Words and Phrases smell 냄새, 냄새가 나다, 냄새를 맡다 | glad 기쁜 | ready 준비가 된 | a few 어느 정도, 조금 | onion 양파

SECTION II READING AND WRITING

Part A. Sentence Completion (p.94)

1. A: There is __________ excuse for what you did.
B: I know. I'm so sorry.
(A) no
(B) not
(C) none
(D) nothing
해석 A: 네가 한 일에 대한 변명의 여지가 없어.
B: 알아. 정말 미안해.
(A) 없는
(B) 아니다
(C) 없음
(D) 아무것도
풀이 'excuse'라는 명사를 수식하는 수식어가 와야하므로 (A)가 정답이다.
Words and Phrases excuse 변명 | nothing 아무것도[단 하나도]

2. A: __________ one do you like – the green one or the white one?
B: I like the white one better.
(A) Why
(B) Who
(C) What
(D) Which
해석 A: 너는 어느 것을 좋아하니 – 초록색 아니면 흰색?
B: 나는 흰색을 더 좋아해.
(A) 왜
(B) 누구
(C) 무엇
(D) 어느
풀이 초록색과 흰색, 두 선택지 중 흰색을 더 좋아한다는 답변에 대한 질문이므로 제한적인 답변을 요구하는 (D)가 정답이다.
Words and Phrases green 초록색 | white 흰색 | better 더 좋은

3. A: Here is my painting, Mrs. Jackson.
B: Great! I'm very pleased with __________ work.
(A) you
(B) your
(C) yours
(D) you're
해석 A: 여기 제 그림이 있어요, Jackson씨.
B: 훌륭해! 나는 너의 작품이 매우 만족스러워.
(A) 너
(B) 너의
(C) 너의 것
(D) 너는

풀이 빈칸 뒤에 있는 명사 'work'를 수식할 수 있는 소유격 (B)가 정답이다.
Words and Phrases painting 그림 | pleased 기쁜, 만족해하는 | work 작품

4. A: Can you help me clean my room?
B: I'm afraid I have ___________ free time these days.
(A) few
(B) lots
(C) a lot
(D) little
해석 A: 너는 내 방 청소를 도와줄 수 있니?
B: 유감이지만, 요즘 자유 시간이 거의 없어.
(A) 거의 없다(가산)
(B) 많다
(C) 많다
(D) 거의 없다(불가산)
풀이 요즘 자유 시간이 거의 없어 도움을 줄 수 없다는 의미의 단어가 필요하며, 빈칸 뒤에 있는 명사구 'free time'은 셀 수 없는 명사 이므로 (D)가 정답이다.
Words and Phrases I'm afraid 유감이지만 | free time 자유시간

5. A: I'm a little worried about the cost of the gloves.
B: Don't worry. ___________ cheap.
(A) It is
(B) It has
(C) They are
(D) They have
해석 A: 나는 그 장갑의 비용이 조금 걱정된다.
B: 걱정하지마. 그것들은 저렴해.
(A) 그것은 ~이다.
(B) 그것은 ~을 가지다
(C) 그것들은 ~이다.
(D) 그들은 ~을 가지다
풀이 'gloves'가 저렴하다고 응답하는 것이므로 복수형을 받을 수 있는 'they'와 그에 알맞은 be 동사를 사용한 (C)가 정답이다.
Words and Phrases little 조금, 약간 | cost 비용 | gloves 장갑 | cheap 싼, 저렴한

Part B. Situational Writing (p.95)

6. A girl is ___________.
(A) skipping rope
(B) stepping over a line
(C) hopping over a stone
(D) jumping over some ropes
해석 그 소녀는 줄넘기를 하는 중이다.
(A) 줄넘기를 하는
(B) 선을 넘나드는
(C) 돌 위에서 깡충깡충 뛰는
(D) 줄 위에서 점프하는
풀이 그림에서 줄넘기를 하는 중이고 있으므로 (A)가 정답이다.
Words and Phrases skip rope 줄넘기하다

7. The monkey is ___________.
(A) in front of a deer
(B) next to an elephant
(C) at the back of a giraffe
(D) between a rabbit and a deer
해석 원숭이는 토끼와 사슴 사이에 있다.
(A) 사슴 앞에
(B) 코끼리 옆에
(C) 기린 뒤에
(D) 토끼와 사슴 사이에
풀이 그림에서 원숭이는 토끼와 사슴 사이에 있으므로 (D)가 정답이다.
Words and Phrases next to ~의 옆에 | in front of ~의 앞에 | at the back of ~의 뒤에 | between 사이에

8. The sharks are swimming ___________.
(A) under the boat
(B) around the boat
(C) towards each other
(D) away from the boat
해석 상어들은 보트 주위를 헤엄치는 중이다.
(A) 보트 아래를
(B) 보트 주위를
(C) 서로를 향하여
(D) 보트 멀리에서
풀이 그림에서 상어들은 보트 주의를 빙둘러 헤엄치는 중이므로 (B)가 정답이다.
Words and Phrases shark 상어 | swim 헤엄치다 | under 아래에 | around 주위에 | toward ~을 향하여 | away 떨어져

9. The teacher is ___________.
(A) doing the girl's housework for her
(B) helping the girl do her housework
(C) helping the girl with her schoolwork
(D) listening to the girl explain something
해석 선생님은 소녀의 학교 공부를 도와주는 중이다.
(A) 소녀를 위해 그녀의 집안일을 해주는 중이다.
(B) 소녀가 집안일하는 것을 도와주는 중이다.
(C) 소녀의 학교 공부를 도와주는 중이다.
(D) 소녀가 무언가 설명하는 것을 듣고 있다.
풀이 그림에서 선생님은 학생의 공부를 도와주고 있으므로 (C)가 정답이다.
Words and Phrases housework 집안일 | schoolwork 학교 공부 | explain 설명하다

10. The woman is___________.
(A) putting some cake in the refrigerator
(B) cleaning the inside of the refrigerator
(C) searching for something in the refrigerator
(D) taking out some fruit from the refrigerator
해석 그 여성은 냉장고에서 과일을 꺼내는 중이다.
(A) 냉장고에 케이크를 넣는 중이다.
(B) 냉장고의 내부를 청소 하는 중이다.
(C) 냉장고에서 무언가를 찾는 중이다.
(D) 냉장고에서 과일을 꺼내는 중이다.

풀이 그림에서 여성은 냉장고에서 과일을 꺼내고 있으므로 (D)가 정답이다.

Words and Phrases put 놓다, 넣다 | refrigerator 냉장고 | inside 내부에 | search 찾다 | take out 꺼내다, 가지고 나가다

Part C. Practical Reading and Retelling (p.98)

[11–12]

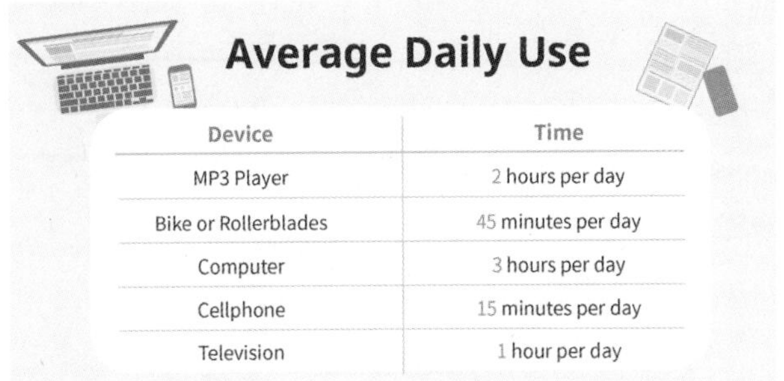

Average Daily Use

Device	Time
MP3 Player	2 hours per day
Bike or Rollerblades	45 minutes per day
Computer	3 hours per day
Cellphone	15 minutes per day
Television	1 hour per day

11. How much time is spent watching television per day?

(A) 1 hour
(B) 2 hours
(C) 3 hours
(D) 4 hours

12. Which will take one hour?

(A) computer
(B) MP3 player
(C) bike and cell phone
(D) rollerblades and television

해석

하루 평균 사용시간

장치	시간
MP3 플레이어	하루에 2시간
자전거 또는 롤러블레이드	하루에 45분
컴퓨터	하루에 3시간
휴대폰	하루에 15분
텔레비전	하루에 1시간

11. 하루에 텔레비전을 보는 시간은 얼마나 되는가?

(A) 1시간
(B) 2시간
(C) 3시간
(D) 4시간

12. 어느 활동이 1시간 걸리는가?

(A) 컴퓨터
(B) MP3 플레이어
(C) 자전거와 휴대폰
(D) 롤러 블레이드와 텔레비전

풀이 하루에 텔레비전을 보는 시간은 1시간 이므로 11번의 정답은 (A)이다.

자전거 사용 시간 45분과 휴대폰 사용 시간 15분을 합하면 1시간이되므로 12번의 정답은 (C)이다.

Words and Phrases average 평균 | daily 나날의 | use 사용 | device 장치

[13–14]

13. What time does the store close on Wednesday?

(A) at 11AM
(B) at 4PM
(C) at 6PM
(D) It does not open that day.

14. What can you NOT buy at the store?

(A) plates
(B) chairs
(C) paintings
(D) computers

해석

Victoria의 골동품
106 4번가 웨스트
빅토리아의 골동품에 오신 걸 환영합니다! 들러주시면 저희가 기꺼이 안내해 드리겠습니다. 우리는 수천 개의 멋진 물건들을 가지고 있습니다.

- 가구
- 도서
- 시계
- 보석
- 자기 도자기
- 은/은 식기류
- 화가들의 원작들

화-일 오전 11시-오후 6시,
월요일과 모든 휴일은 휴무

13. 수요일은 몇시에 문을 닫는가?

(A) 오전 11시
(B) 오후 4시
(C) 오후 6시
(D) 그날은 열지 않는다.

14. 상점에서 살 수 없는 것은 무엇인가?

(A) 접시
(B) 의자
(C) 그림
(D) 컴퓨터

풀이 화요일부터 일요일은 6시에 닫는다고 했으므로 13번의 정답은 (C)이다.

골동품 상점의 제품 목록 중 전자제품은 없으므로 14번의 정답은 (D)이다.

Words and Phrases antique 골동품 | come by 잠깐 들르다 | item 물품 | furniture 가구 | jewelry 보석 | porcelain 자기 | pottery 도자기 | silverware 은 식기류 | original 원래의, 원본

[15-16]

RESTAURANT BILL

- 1 Shrimp Appetizer $9.50
- 2 Chicken Kiev $32.80
- 2 Coca-Cola $5.00

Subtotal ------------- $47.30

- Tax 7% $3.31
- Tip $4.73

Total ------------------ $55.34

15. How much is the additional charge to the meal?

(A) $3.31
(B) $4.73
(C) $8.04
(D) $47.30

16. How much does one plate of Chicken Kiev cost?

(A) $9.50
(B) $16.40
(C) $23.65
(D) $32.80

해석

식당 영수증	
- 1 새우 전채 요리	9.50달러
- 2 치킨 키에프	32.80달러
- 2 콜라	5.00 달러
소계 ··················	47.30달러
부가세 7%	3.31달러
팁	4.73달러
합계··············	55.34달러

15. 음식 값 외에 지불한 금액은 얼마인가?

(A) 3.31달러
(B) 4.73달러
(C) 8.04달러
(D) 47.30달러

16. 치킨 키에프 한 접시의 가격은 얼마인가?

(A) 9.50달러
(B) 16.40달러
(C) 23.65달러
(D) 32.80달러

풀이 부가세 7%와 팁으로 지불한 금액을 합하면 8.04달러이므로 15번의 정답은 (C)이다.

치킨 키에프 두 접시의 가격이 32.80달러이므로 한 접시의 가격은 16.40달러이다. 그러므로 16번의 정답은 (B)이다.

Words and Phrases bill 영수증, | shrimp 새우 | appetizer 전채 요리 | subtotal 소계 | tax 세금 | tip 팁, 봉사료

[17-18]

17. Whose birthday is it?

(A) Tim's
(B) Rebecca's
(C) Tim's mother's
(D) Rebecca's sister's

18. What day is the party?

(A) Thursday
(B) Friday
(C) Saturday
(D) Sunday

해석

Tim과 Rebecca Lee가 당신을 초대하고 싶습니다.
Tim의 어머니의 80번째 생신 파티에
토요일, 5월 21일, 오후 3시
선물은 사양하겠습니다.

17. 누구의 생일인가?

(A) Tim의
(B) Rebecca의
(C) Tim의 어머니의
(D) Rebecca의 여동생의

18. 파티는 무슨 요일인가?

(A) 목요일
(B) 금요일
(C) 토요일
(D) 일요일

풀이 Tim의 어머니의 80번째 생신 파티라고 했으므로 17번의 정답은 (C)이다.

파티는 5월 21일 토요일이라고 했으므로 18번의 정답은 (C)이다.

Words and Phrases invite 초대하다 | present 선물

[19-20]

19. What time does the game start?

(A) 5 PM
(B) 6 PM
(C) 7 PM
(D) 8 PM

20. Where can you NOT buy the ticket?

(A) World Gym
(B) The Pike Cafe
(C) Charity School
(D) Jo's Sporting Goods

해석

자선 농구 경기
입장권 10달러
The Philadelphia Eagles 대 Reading Police
금요일, 5월 18일
오후 6시에 입구 열림
오후 7시에 경기 시작
입장권은 다음 장소에서 구입할 수 있습니다:
World 체육관 Vegas 학교
The Pike 카페 Jo의 스포츠 용품점

19. 경기는 몇 시에 시작하는가?

(A) 오후 5시
(B) 오후 6시
(C) 오후 7시
(D) 오후 8시

20. 당신이 입장권을 살 수 없는 곳은 어디인가?

(A) World 체육관
(B) The Pike 카페
(C) 자선 학교
(D) Jo의 스포츠 용품점

풀이 오후 6시부터 입장이 가능하고 오후 7시에 경기가 시작한다고 했으므로 19번의 정답은 (C)이다.

입장권은 World 체육관, The Pike 카페, Vegas 학교, Jo의 스포츠 용품점에서 구매 가능하다고 했으므로 20번의 정답은 (C)이다.

Words and Phrases charity 자선 단체, 자선 | available 구할 수 있는

Part D. General Reading and Retelling (p.103)

[21-22]

A delicious avocado fruit is good for you, and is one of the healthiest foods you can eat. Cut an avocado from the top to the bottom and separate the two pieces. Remove the stone with a spoon, then place the pieces cut side down and take off the skin using a knife or your fingers. Sprinkle the fruit with lemon juice and enjoy it. The taste is pleasing and feels as smooth as butter in your mouth.

21. What is the first step in preparing an avocado?

(A) Peel the skin.
(B) Remove the pit.
(C) Cut it from top to bottom.
(D) Sprinkle with lemon juice.

22. Which of the following feels like an avocado?

(A) fruit
(B) butter
(C) coconut
(D) vegetable

해석 맛있는 아보카도 과일은 당신에게 좋으며 먹을 수 있는 가장 건강에 좋은 음식 중 하나입니다. 아보카도를 위에서 아래로 자르고 두 조각을 분리합니다. 숟가락으로 씨를 제거한 다음, 잘린 조각을 아래로 놓고 칼이나 손가락으로 껍질을 제거하십시오. 과일에 레몬즙을 뿌려 드세요. 맛은 만족스럽고 입안에서 버터처럼 부드럽습니다.

21. 아보카도를 준비할 때 필요한 첫 번째 단계는 무엇인가?

(A) 껍질을 벗겨라.
(B) 씨를 제거하라.
(C) 위에서 아래로 잘라라.
(D) 레몬즙을 뿌려라.

22. 다음 중 아보카도가 가지는 느낌은 무엇인가?

(A) 과일
(B) 버터
(C) 코코넛
(D) 야채

풀이 아보카도를 먼저 위에서 아래로 잘라 분리하는 것이 첫 번째 단계이므로 21번의 정답은 (C)이다.

아보카도는 버터처럼 부드럽다고 했으므로 22번의 정답은 (B)이다.

Words and Phrases avocado 아보카도 | separate 분리하다 | remove 제거하다 | stone 씨 | place 두다 | take off 벗기다 | skin 피부, 껍질 | sprinkle 뿌리다 | pleasing 만족스러운 | smooth 부드러운 | peel 껍질을 벗기다 | pit 씨

[23-24]

The beach may look like a nice place, but there are dangers. Too much sun is bad for anyone, and babies should not be in the sun at all. Playing in the sand is fun, but look at the sand carefully for broken shells or bottles. Wear water shoes to keep the hot sand or dangers in the water from hurting your feet. Wear a sun hat to protect your eyes from the strong sun. Finally, be sure to keep a close watch on children. They may walk down the beach or go into the water alone.

23. According to the passage, which is NOT mentioned as a danger of the beach?

(A) hot sand
(B) big waves
(C) strong sun
(D) broken shells

24. Which is NOT true about the passage?

(A) You must sunbathe with babies.
(B) You should wear water shoes in the sand.
(C) You should keep a close watch on children.
(D) You must wear a sun hat to protect your eyes.

해석 해변은 멋진 곳처럼 보이지만, 위험이 있다. 너무 많은 햇빛은 누구에게나 좋지 않으며, 아기는 햇빛을 쬐지 않아야 한다. 모래에서 노는 것은 재미있지만, 모래에 깨진 껍데기나 병이 있는지 주의 깊게 살펴보라. 뜨거운 모래나 물속의 위험에 발을 다치지 않도록 아쿠아 슈즈를 신어라. 강한 태양으로부터 눈을 보호하기 위해 햇빛 차단용 모자를 착용하라. 마지막으로, 어린이를 꼭 면밀히 관찰해라. 그들은 해변을 걸어 내려가거나 혼자 물에 들어갈 수 있다.

23. 지문에 따르면, 해변의 위험 요소로 언급되지 않은 것은 무엇인가?

(A) 뜨거운 모래
(B) 큰 파도
(C) 강한 햇빛
(D) 부서진 껍데기

24. 지문에 관한 사실이 아닌 것은 무엇인가?

(A) 너는 아기와 함께 일광욕을 해야 한다.
(B) 너는 모래사장에서 아쿠아슈즈를 신어야 한다.
(C) 너는 아이들을 유심히 관찰해야 한다.
(D) 너는 눈을 보호하기 위해 햇빛 차단용 모자를 써야 한다.

풀이 위험 요소로 큰 파도에 대한 언급은 없으므로 23번의 정답은 (B)이다.

아기는 햇빛을 쬐지 않아야 한다고 했으므로 24번의 정답은 (A)이다.

Words and Phrases beach 해변 | danger 위험 | shell 껍질, 껍데기 | bottle 병| keep a close watch on 잘 지켜보다 | be sure to do something 꼭[반드시] ~을 해라

[25-26]

The highest waterfall in the world is Angel Falls in South America. It is 1,002 meters high, 19 times higher than Niagara Falls. It was discovered in 1935 by Jimmy Angel. He was flying his airplane above the waterfall. He landed his airplane on top of the mountain and found the waterfall. Soon the whole world learned about the waterfall, and it was named after the man who first saw it. Many visitors go to the waterfall each year.

25. How high is Angel Falls?

(A) 19 meters
(B) 1,002 meters
(C) 1,200 meters
(D) 1,935 meters

26. Where did Jimmy Angel land his airplane?

(A) at the airport
(B) by Niagara Falls
(C) on top of a waterfall
(D) on top of a mountain

해석 세계에서 가장 높은 폭포는 남아메리카의 Angel 폭포다. 그것은 1,002미터 높이이며, 나이아가라 폭포보다 19배 높다. 그것은 1935년에 Jimmy Angel에 의해 발견되었다. 그는 폭포 위를 비행기로 나는 중이었다. 그는 자신의 비행기를 산꼭대기에 착륙시켰고 그 폭포를 발견했다. 곧 온 세상이 폭포에 대해 알게 되었고, 그것은 그것을 처음 본 사람의 이름을 따서 명명되었다. 매년 많은 방문객이 그 폭포에 간다.

25. Angel 폭포의 높이는 얼마인가?

(A) 19미터
(B) 1,002미터
(C) 1,200미터
(D) 1,935미터

26. Jimmy Angel은 그의 비행기를 어디에 착륙시켰는가?

(A) 공항에
(B) Niagara 폭포에
(C) 폭포 꼭대기에
(D) 산꼭대기에

풀이 폭포는 그 높이가 1,002미터라고 했으므로 25번의 정답은 (B)이다.

Jimmy Angel은 산꼭대기에 비행기를 착륙시켜다고 했으므로 26번의 정답은 (D)이다.

Words and Phrases waterfall 폭포 | discover 발견하다 | land 착륙하다 | whole 전체의 | name 명명하다 | visitor 방문객

[27-28]

Clouds are made when very small water drops stick to very small pieces of dirt in the air. When the cloud meets cold air, the water falls to the ground as rain or snow. This can happen when warm air pushes cool air up the side of a mountain, and it gets colder as it rises. It can also happen when warm air moves over a colder area, like water. It rains or snows because cool air holds less water than warm air.

27. What do small water drops stick to as clouds are made?

(A) air

(B) dirt

(C) water

(D) clouds

28. What happens when the cloud meets cold air?

(A) It turns warm.

(B) The sun shines.

(C) It rains or snows.

(D) The cloud moves away.

해석 아주 작은 물방울이 공기 중의 아주 작은 먼지 조각에 달라붙으면 구름이 만들어진다. 구름이 찬 공기를 만나면, 물은 비나 눈으로 땅에 떨어진다. 이것은 따뜻한 공기가 산 쪽으로 차가운 공기를 밀어 올릴 때 발생할 수 있으며, 그것은 올라갈수록 차가워진다. 이것은 따뜻한 공기가 물과 같은 더 추운 곳으로 이동할 때도 발생할 수 있다. 시원한 공기가 따뜻한 공기보다 물을 적게 보유하기 때문에 비나 눈이 내린다.

27. 구름이 만들어질 때 작은 물방울들이 달라붙는 것은 무엇인가?

(A) 공기

(B) 먼지

(C) 물

(D) 구름

28. 구름이 차가운 공기를 만나면 어떤 일이 일어나는가?

(A) 따뜻하게 변한다.

(B) 해가 빛난다.

(C) 비나 눈이 온다.

(D) 구름이 멀어진다.

풀이 작은 물방울이 공기 중의 아주 작은 먼지 조각에 달라붙으면 구름이 만들어진다고 했으므로 27번의 정답은 (B)이다.

구름이 찬 공기를 만나면 물은 비나 눈의 형태로 땅에 떨어진다고 했으므로 28번의 정답은 (C)이다.

Words and Phrases water drop 물방울 | stick 달라붙다 | dirt 먼지 | push 밀다 | side 쪽, 측 | rise 오르다

[29-30]

Flying radio control airplanes is one of the most exciting hobbies. You must be able to follow directions, build a small airplane, and learn how to fly it with a radio remote control. Then all you have to do is find an open field. The great thing is you can have fun outside in the fresh air flying the airplane above you. The key is to just have fun and try not to let your airplane hit the ground and break. However, if you do break your plane, you can always fix it.

29. Where do people fly radio control airplanes?

(A) in a classroom

(B) inside the house

(C) outside in a field

(D) in an open market

30. What do you need to fly radio control airplanes?

(A) a radio

(B) a TV set

(C) a computer

(D) a radio remote control

해석 무선 조종 비행기를 날리는 것은 가장 흥미로운 취미 중 하나입니다. 여러분은 지시를 따를 수 있어야 하고, 소형 비행기를 만들 수 있어야 하며, 그것을 무선 리모컨으로 조종하는 법을 배워야 합니다. 그런 다음 당신이 해야 할 일은 탁 트인 들판을 찾는 것입니다. 멋진 것은 당신이 비행기를 위로 날리면서 신선한 공기 속 바깥에서 놀 수 있다는 것입니다. 핵심은 그냥 재미있게 놀면서 당신의 비행기가 땅에 부딪혀 부서지지 않도록 하는 것입니다. 그러나, 여러분이 비행기를 고장 낸다면, 당신은 언제든지 그것을 고칠 수 있습니다.

29. 사람들은 어디에서 무선 조종 비행기를 날리는가?

(A) 교실에서

(B) 집안에서

(C) 야외 들판에서

(D) 공개 시장에서

30. 무선 조종 비행기를 조종하기 위해 필요한 것은 무엇인가?

(A) 라디오

(B) TV 세트

(C) 컴퓨터

(D) 무선 리모컨

풀이 무선 조종 비행기를 날리기 위해서는 탁 트인 들판이 필요하다고 했으므로 29번의 정답은 (C)이다.

무선 리모컨으로 조종하는 방법을 익혀야 한다고 했으므로 30번의 정답은 (D)이다.

Words and Phrases radio control 무선 조종의 | direction 지시 | field 들판 | fresh 신선한 | hit 때리다, ~와 부딪치다 | fix 고치다, 수리하다

TOSEL Junior

실전5회

Section I Listening and Speaking

1 (D) 2 (C) 3 (D) 4 (B) 5 (B)
6 (A) 7 (A) 8 (D) 9 (C) 10 (D)
11 (A) 12 (A) 13 (B) 14 (A) 15 (B)
16 (A) 17 (D) 18 (B) 19 (C) 20 (C)
21 (C) 22 (B) 23 (A) 24 (A) 25 (B)
26 (C) 27 (C) 28 (B) 29 (A) 30 (B)

Section II Reading and Writing

1 (B) 2 (C) 3 (B) 4 (D) 5 (A)
6 (A) 7 (D) 8 (A) 9 (D) 10 (B)
11 (A) 12 (C) 13 (D) 14 (A) 15 (A)
16 (C) 17 (D) 18 (B) 19 (C) 20 (A)
21 (B) 22 (B) 23 (D) 24 (C) 25 (D)
26 (B) 27 (D) 28 (D) 29 (C) 30 (B)

SECTION I LISTENING AND SPEAKING

Part A. Listen and Respond (p.110)

1. Girl: Don't forget your towel.
Boy: ________________
(A) That's a good idea.
(B) Sure, take my towel.
(C) Will you need a towel?
(D) Thanks. I almost forgot.

해석 소녀: 너의 수건을 챙기는 것을 잊지 마.
소년: ________________
(A) 그거 좋은 생각이야.
(B) 물론, 내 수건 가져가.
(C) 네가 수건이 필요할까?
(D) 고마워, 나는 거의 잊어버렸어.

풀이 소녀가 수건을 가져갈 것을 상기시켜주었으므로 이에 고마움을 표현하는 (D)가 정답이다.

Words and Phrases forget 잊다 | towel 수건 | almost 거의

2. Boy: Are you going to the movies?
Girl: ________________
(A) Yes, you should.
(B) You'll really like it.
(C) No, I don't feel well.
(D) Yes, I'm staying home.

해석 소년: 너 영화 보러 갈 거니?
소녀: ________________
(A) 응, 너는 그래야 해.
(B) 너는 그것을 아주 좋아할 거야.
(C) 아니, 몸이 영 좋지 않아.
(D) 응, 나는 집에 머무를 거야.

풀이 영화를 보러 갈 것인지 물었으므로 이에 아파서 가지 못한다는 이유를 설명한 (C)가 정답이다.

Words and Phrases movie 영화 | feel 느끼다, ~감정이 들다 | stay 머무르다

3. Girl: Can I borrow your pencil?
Boy: ________________
(A) No, I don't need it.
(B) Whose pencil is it?
(C) Are you late for school?
(D) Sure, it's on the desk.

해석 소녀: 내가 네 연필을 빌릴 수 있을까?
소년: ________________
(A) 아니, 나는 그것이 필요 없어.
(B) 그것은 누구의 연필이니?
(C) 너는 학교에 늦었니?
(D) 물론, 그것은 책상 위에 있어.

풀이 연필을 빌려줄 수 있는지 물었으므로 이를 허락하는 표현인 (D)가 정답이다.

Words and Phrases borrow 빌리다 | need 필요로 하다

4. Boy: Did you hear a knock at the door?
Girl: ________________
(A) I can't hear the phone.
(B) Yes, that's my cousin.
(C) I'm too busy right now.
(D) I already closed the door.

해석 소년: 너는 문을 두드리는 소리를 들었니?
소녀: ________________
(A) 나는 전화 소리를 들을 수 없어.
(B) 그래, 그건 내 사촌이야.
(C) 나는 지금 너무 바빠.
(D) 나는 벌써 문을 닫았어.

풀이 소년이 누군가 문을 두드리는 소리를 들었냐고 물었으므로 이에 문을 두드린 사람이 누구인지를 설명하는 (B)가 정답이다.

Words and Phrases knock 두드리다 | cousin 사촌 | already 이미, 벌써

5. Girl: Don't go to the park without me.
Boy: ________________
(A) Wait for me.
(B) Well, hurry up.
(C) What's your hurry?
(D) Where are you going?

해석 소녀: 나 없이 그 공원에 가지 마.
소년: ________________

(A) 나를 기다려줘.
(B) 좋아, 서둘러.
(C) 왜 그렇게 서두르니?
(D) 너는 어디에 가는 중이니?

풀이 본인 없이 공원에 가지 말라고 했으므로 서두르라고 답하는 표현인 (B)가 정답이다.

Words and Phrases without ~없이 | hurry 서두르다, 서두름

6. Boy: I learned something interesting.
Girl: ________________
(A) Tell me about it.
(B) I agree with him.
(C) Guess what I heard.
(D) I'm right about that.

해석 소년: 나는 무언가 재미있는 것을 배웠어.
소녀: ________________
(A) 그것에 대해서 나에게 말해줘.
(B) 나는 그에 동의해.
(C) 내가 무엇을 들었는지 맞혀봐.
(D) 그건 내가 옳다.

풀이 재미있는 것을 배웠다고 말했으므로 이에 관심을 표하는 (A)가 정답이다.

7. Girl: Which bus do you take to school?
Boy: ________________
(A) I catch the eight o'clock bus.
(B) I take the bus every day.
(C) We should take the train.
(D) Taking the bus is cheaper.

해석 소녀: 너는 학교 갈 때 어느 버스를 타니?
소년: ________________
(A) 나는 8시 버스를 타.
(B) 나는 매일 버스를 타.
(C) 우리는 기차를 타야 해.
(D) 버스를 타는 것이 더 싸다.

풀이 어느 버스를 타는지 물었으므로 8시 버스라는 구체적인 답변을 한 (A)가 정답이다.

Words and Phrases catch 버스/기차를 타다 | cheaper 더 싼(cheap-cheaper-cheapest)

8. Boy: Do you know what time it is?
Girl: ________________
(A) No, I can't find it.
(B) Are you very tired?
(C) I'll wait over here.
(D) Sorry, I don't know.

해석 소년: 너는 몇 시인지 아니?
소녀: ________________
(A) 아니, 나는 그것을 찾을 수가 없어.
(B) 너는 매우 피곤하니?
(C) 나는 여기서 기다릴게.
(D) 미안해, 나는 몰라.

풀이 몇 시인지 물었으므로 이에 답을 줄 수 없음을 표현하는 (D)가 정답이다.

9. Girl: Where is your coat?
Boy: ________________
(A) I like my new coat.
(B) My coat is dark blue.
(C) I forgot where I put it.
(D) I bought you a new coat.

해석 소녀: 네 코트는 어디에 있니?
소년: ________________
(A) 나는 나의 새 코트가 좋아.
(B) 나의 코트는 어두운 파란색이야.
(C) 나는 그것을 어디에 두었는지 잊어버렸어.
(D) 나는 너에게 새 코트를 사줬어.

풀이 코트가 어디에 있는지 물었으므로 코트의 위치를 잊어버렸다고 답하는 (C)가 정답이다.

Words and Phrases coat 코트, 외투 | put 두다

10. Boy: My new CD is great.
Girl: ________________
(A) You can have it.
(B) I'll give it to you.
(C) I can't give it to you.
(D) I'd like to listen to it.

해석 소년: 내 새 CD는 훌륭해.
소녀: ________________
(A) 너는 그것을 가질 수 있어.
(B) 나는 그것을 너에게 줄게.
(C) 나는 그것을 너에게 줄 수 없어.
(D) 나는 그것을 들어보고 싶어.

풀이 새로운 CD가 훌륭하다고 말했으므로 이에 들어보고 싶다고 관심을 표현하는 (D)가 정답이다.

Words and Phrases would like to ~하고 싶다

Part B. Listen and Retell (p.111)

11. Girl: Have you seen the new theater?
Boy: I've only seen a photo of it.
Girl: It's a wonderful building.
Question: Where did the boy see the theater?
(A) in a photo
(B) in a TV ad
(C) in a painting
(D) in a drawing

해석 소녀: 너는 새로 생긴 극장을 본 적 있니?
소년: 나는 그것의 사진만 본 적 있어.
소녀: 그것은 아주 멋진 건물이야.
질문: 소년은 어디에서 극장을 보았는가?
(A) 사진에서
(B) TV 광고에서
(C) 그림에서
(D) 그림에서

풀이 소년은 새로 생긴 극장을 사진으로만 보았다고 했으므로 (A)가 정답이다.

Words and Phrases theater 극장 | painting (물감으로 그린) 그림 | drawing (색칠을 하지 않은) 그림

12. Boy: Where else could we go?
Girl: How about the museum?
Boy: Or the art gallery?
Question: What are the boy and girl doing?
(A) They are making plans.
(B) They don't like to be outside.
(C) They are eating at a restaurant.
(D) They are thinking about their futures.

해석 소년: 우리는 다른 곳 어디로 갈 수 있니?
소녀: 그 박물관은 어때?
소년: 아니면 그 미술관?
질문: 소년과 소녀는 무엇을 하고 있는가?
(A) 그들은 계획을 짜고 있는 중이다.
(B) 그들은 밖에 있는 것을 싫어한다.
(C) 그들은 식당에서 먹고 있다.
(D) 그들은 그들의 미래에 대해 생각하고 있다.

풀이 다음에 갈 곳으로 소녀는 박물관을, 소년은 미술관을 추천하고 있는 것을 통해 여행 계획을 고민하고 있음을 짐작할 수 있으므로 (A)가 정답이다.

Words and Phrases museum 박물관 | gallery 미술관

13. Girl: Do you think my painting is ugly?
Boy: No, the flowers are beautiful.
Girl: Thanks. I feel better now.
Question: Why does the girl feel better?
(A) The boy gave her flowers.
(B) The boy likes her painting.
(C) She likes the boy's painting.
(D) The boy will buy her a painting.

해석 소녀: 너는 내 그림이 못생겼다고 생각하니?
소년: 아니, 꽃들이 아름다워.
소녀: 고마워. 나는 이제 기분이 좋아졌어.
질문: 왜 소녀의 기분이 좋아졌는가?
(A) 소년이 그녀에게 꽃들을 주었다.
(B) 소년이 그녀의 그림을 좋아한다.
(C) 그녀는 소년의 그림을 좋아한다.
(D) 소년은 그녀에게 그림을 사줄 것이다.

풀이 소년이 소녀의 그림 속 꽃들이 아름답다고 말해주어 그녀의 기분이 좋아졌으므로 (B)가 정답이다.

Words and Phrases ugly 못생긴 | painting (물감으로 그린) 그림

14. Boy: Let's walk to the village.
Girl: How long will that take?
Boy: It'll only take twenty minutes.
Question: Where are they going?
(A) to the village
(B) to the video shop
(C) to the parking lot
(D) to the supermarket

해석 소년: 마을까지 걸어가자.
소녀: 그건 얼마나 걸릴까?
소년: 그건 20분 밖에 걸리지 않아.
질문: 그들은 어디에 가는 중인가?
(A) 마을로
(B) 비디오 가게로
(C) 주차장으로
(D) 슈퍼마켓으로

풀이 마을까지 가는데 걸어서 걸리는 시간에 관해 이야기하고 있으므로 (A)가 정답이다.

Words and Phrases village 마을 | take (얼마의 시간이)걸리다 | video shop 비디오 가게 | parking lot 주차장 | supermarket 슈퍼마켓

15. Girl: I'm going to visit my friend for the weekend.
Boy: That'll be fun for you.
Girl: I'm really looking forward to it.
Question: Who will the girl visit?
(A) her uncle
(B) her friend
(C) her teacher
(D) her grandparents

해석 소녀: 나는 주말에 내 친구를 방문할 거야.
소년: 그거 너에게 재미있겠네.
소녀: 나는 그것을 정말 기대하고 있어.
질문: 소녀는 누구를 방문할 것인가?
(A) 그녀의 삼촌
(B) 그녀의 친구
(C) 그녀의 선생님
(D) 그녀의 조부모님

풀이 소녀는 주말에 그녀의 친구를 방문하는 것을 기대하고 있으므로 (B)가 정답이다.

Words and Phrases weekend 주말 | look forward to ~을 기대하다 | visit 방문하다, 방문

16. Boy: Is it dangerous to swim here?
Girl: No. It's very safe.
Boy: That's good. I'm not a great swimmer.
Question: What is the problem?
(A) The boy doesn't swim very well.
(B) The boy is worried about the girl.
(C) The swimming place is dangerous.
(D) The boy doesn't know how to swim.

해석 소년: 여기서 수영하는 것은 위험할까?
소녀: 아니, 매우 안전해.
소년: 다행이다. 나는 수영을 잘할 줄 아는 사람이 아니야.
질문: 무엇이 문제인가?
(A) 소년은 수영을 아주 잘 하지 못한다.
(B) 소년은 소녀를 걱정하고 있다.
(C) 그 수영 장소는 위험하다.
(D) 소년은 수영을 할 줄 모른다.

풀이 소년은 수영을 잘하지 못해서 수영 장소가 위험한지 걱정하고 있으므로 (A)가 정답이다.

Words and Phrases dangerous 위험한 | safe 안전한 | swimmer 수영을 할 줄 아는 사람, 수영을 하고 있는 사람

17. Girl: How much do you weigh?
Boy: About 40 kilos.
Girl: Then you're heavier than me.
Question: What is true?
(A) They weigh the same.
(B) The boy weighs less than the girl.
(C) The girl weighs less than her sister.
(D) The boy weighs more than the girl.

해석 소녀: 너는 몸무게가 어떻게 되니?
소년: 약 40킬로야.
소녀: 그럼 너는 나보다 무겁네.
질문: 무엇이 사실인가?
(A) 그들은 몸무게가 같다.
(B) 소년은 소녀보다 몸무게가 적게 나간다.
(C) 소녀는 그녀의 여동생보다 몸무게가 적게 나간다.
(D) 소년은 소녀보다 몸무게가 많이 나간다.

풀이 소녀는 몸무게가 40킬로그램인 소년이 자신보다 몸무게가 많이 나간다고 했으므로 (D)가 정답이다.

Words and Phrases weigh 무게가 ~이다

[18-19]
Boy: Science class was fun today. Our teacher asked us to build a strong bridge. I made my bridge out of wooden sticks and glued them together. I tested my bridge to see how strong it was. When I put 6 kilos on the bridge, it didn't break. My bridge finally broke when I put 10 kilos on it.

18. What was the bridge made of?
(A) spaghetti
(B) sticks
(C) paper
(D) glue

19. How much weight made the bridge break?
(A) three kilos
(B) six kilos
(C) ten kilos
(D) twelve kilos

해석 소년: 오늘 과학 수업은 즐거웠다. 우리 선생님이 우리한테 강한 다리를 만들라고 하셨다. 나는 나무 막대기로 다리를 만들었고 그들을 접착제로 붙였다. 내 다리가 얼마나 강한지 시험해봤다. 다리 위에 6킬로를 놨을 때, 부서지지 않았다. 10킬로를 놨을 때 드디어 부서졌다.

18. 다리를 무엇으로 만들어졌는가?
(A) 스파게티
(B) 막대기
(C) 종이
(D) 접착제

19. 얼마 만큼의 무게가 다리를 부서지게 했는가?
(A) 3킬로
(B) 6킬로
(C) 10킬로
(D) 12킬로

풀이 소년은 나무 막대기로 다리를 만들었다고 했으므로 18번의 정답은 (B)이다. 다리 위에 10킬로를 놨을 때 부서졌다고 했으므로 19번의 정답은 (C)이다.

Words and Phrases class 수업 | strong 강한 | wooden sticks 나무 막대기 | glue 접착제 | break 부서지다

[20-21]
Girl: It is now 4:30. We would like to remind our visitors that the museum will close in half an hour and reopen at nine a.m. tomorrow. Our gift shop will remain open until six p.m. We hope you have enjoyed your visit to the museum today.

20. When will the gift shop close?
(A) at four-thirty
(B) at five o'clock
(C) at six o'clock
(D) at nine o'clock

21. What is this talk about?
(A) location of the gift shop
(B) directions to the museum
(C) operating hours of the museum
(D) special exhibits in the museum

해석 소녀: 지금은 오후 4시 반입니다. 방문객분들에게 30분 후에 박물관이 닫을 거라는 것과 내일 오전 9시에 다시 연다는 것을 알려드립니다. 저희 기념품샵은 오후 6시까지 열려 있을 예정입니다. 오늘 박물관 방문을 즐기셨길 바랍니다.

20. 기념품샵은 몇시에 닫는가?
(A) 4시 반
(B) 5시
(C) 6시
(D) 9시

21. 이 이야기의 목적이 무엇인가?
(A) 기념품샵의 위치
(B) 박물관 가는 길
(C) 박물관 운영 시간
(D) 박물관에 있는 특별한 전시

풀이 기념품샵은 6시까지 연다고 했으므로 20번의 정답은 (C)이다.

방문객들에게 박물관 운영시간을 알려주고 있으므로 21번의 정답은 (C)이다.

Words and Phrases visitor 방문객 | museum 박물관 | half an hour 30분 | gift shop 기념품샵 | enjoy 즐기다

[22-23]

Boy: It took my family an hour to drive to my grandparents' house. The traffic was very busy. We had to wait behind a bus for a long time. We also waited while a fire truck and an ambulance passed us. When we finally arrived, my grandparents were glad to see us.

22. What is the speaker mainly talking about?

(A) watching a fire
(B) driving in traffic
(C) playing in the street
(D) a visit from his grandparents

23. How did his grandparents feel?

(A) glad
(B) tired
(C) afraid
(D) worried

해석 소년: 우리 가족은 조부모님 댁까지 차 타고 한 시간이나 걸렸다. 교통이 무척 복잡했다. 우리는 버스 뒤에서 오래 기다려야 했다. 또한 소방차와 구급차가 지나갈 때까지 기다려야 했다. 우리가 마침내 도착했을 때, 조부모님은 우리를 만나서 기뻐하셨다.

22. 화자는 무엇에 대해 말하고 있는가?

(A) 불을 보는 것
(B) 교통 속에서 운전하는 것
(C) 거리에서 노는 것
(D) 조부모님이 방문하는 것

23. 조부모님은 어떤 감정이었는가?

(A) 기쁜
(B) 피곤한
(C) 두려운
(D) 걱정되는

풀이 화자는 교통 속에서 운전하는 것에 대해 이야기 하고 있으므로 22번의 정답은 (B)이다.

조부모님이 화자와 화자의 가족을 만났을 때 기뻤다고 말했으므로 23번의 정답은 (A)이다.

Words and Phrases traffic 교통 | fire truck 소방차 | ambulance 구급차 | pass 지나가다 | finally 마침내 | arrive 도착하다 | glad 기쁜

[24-25]

Girl: Giving a speech in front of your class can be scary. It's a good idea to know your speech well. Practice it as much as you can. When you're giving your speech, take your time. Don't speak too quickly and remember to look up at the class. You'll be fine.

24. What is the speaker mainly talking about?

(A) how to give a speech
(B) how to write a speech
(C) how to take better notes
(D) how to improve pronunciation

25. What should you remember?

(A) to speak quickly
(B) to look at the class
(C) to practice only a little
(D) to look at your paper often

해석 소녀: 반 친구들 앞에서 연설을 하는 것은 무서울 수 있다. 자신의 스피치를 잘 아는 것이 좋다. 그것을 연습할 수 있을 만큼 해라. 연설을 할 때, 여유를 가져라. 너무 빠르게 말하지 말고 반 친구들을 쳐다보는 것을 기억해라. 괜찮을 것이다.

24. 화자는 무엇에 대해 이야기하고 있는가?

(A) 연설을 하는 방법
(B) 연설을 쓰는 방법
(C) 메모를 잘하는 방법
(D) 발음을 개선하는 방법

25. 무엇을 기억해야 하는가?

(A) 빨리 말하는 것
(B) 반 친구들을 쳐다보는 것
(C) 조금만 연습하는 것
(D) 종이를 자주 보는 것

풀이 여자는 연설을 하는 방법에 대해 말하고 있으므로 24번의 정답은 (A)이다.

반 친구들을 쳐다보는 것을 기억하라고 했으므로 25번의 정답은 (B)이다.

Words and Phrases speech 연설 | practice 연습하다 | quickly 빠르게 | look up 쳐다보다 | remember 기억하다

PART C. Listen and Speak (p.115)

26. Boy: I'd like to go out for a hamburger.
Girl: Me too. Let's go.
Boy: I'm going to have fries, too.
Girl: ________________

(A) I'll go with you.
(B) That's not right.
(C) That sounds good.
(D) When did you go?

해석 소녀: 나는 햄버거를 먹으러 가고 싶다.
소년: 나도 그래. 가자.
소녀: 나는 감자튀김도 먹을 거야.
소년: ________________
(A) 나도 너랑 같이 갈게.
(B) 그것은 옳지 않아.
(C) 그거 좋은데.
(D) 너는 언제 갔었니?
풀이 소년이 햄버거와 함께 감자튀김도 먹을 것이라고 했으므로, 이에 긍정을 표현하는 (C)가 정답이다.
Words and Phrases fries 감자튀김

27. Boy: I think we're lost.
Girl: We should ask someone for help.
Boy: Who should we ask?
Girl: ________________
(A) Okay, let's wait.
(B) I'll help you look.
(C) Let's ask that man.
(D) We won't ask anyone.
해석 소년: 내 생각에 우리는 길을 잃었어.
소녀: 우리는 누군가에 도움을 요청해야 해.
소년: 우리는 누구에게 요청해야 할까?
소녀: ________________
(A) 그래, 기다리자.
(B) 내가 보는 것을 도와줄게.
(C) 저 남자에게 요청하자.
(D) 우리는 아무에게도 요청하지 않을 거야.
풀이 누구에게 도움을 요청해야 할지 질문했으므로 저 남자에게 요청하자고 제안하는 (C)가 정답이다.
Words and Phrases lost 길을 잃은 | look 찾다, 찾아보다 | anyone 누구, 아무

28. Boy: Let's buy some comic books.
Girl: I don't have enough money.
Boy: That's okay, I'll pay for them.
Girl: ________________
(A) Why? What's wrong with them?
(B) Thanks. That's really nice of you.
(C) Thanks. You can pay me back later.
(D) This time you can borrow my money.
해석 소년: 만화책 좀 사자.
소녀: 나는 돈이 충분하지 않아.
소년: 괜찮아, 내가 낼게.
소녀: ________________
(A) 왜? 그들에게 무슨 문제가 있니?
(B) 고마워. 너는 정말 친절하구나.
(C) 고마워. 넌 나에게 나중에 갚아도 돼.
(D) 이번에 너는 내 돈을 빌려도 돼.
풀이 소녀는 돈이 충분하지 않다고 했고, 이에 소년은 대신 지불해주겠다고 했으므로 고마운 마음을 표현하는 (B)가 정답이다.
Words and Phrases comic book 만화책 | pay 지불하다 | pay somebody back ~에게 갚다 | borrow 빌리다

29. Girl: Did you buy your mom a birthday gift?
Boy: Not yet. I don't know what to get her.
Girl: I think she would like flowers.
Boy: ________________
(A) I didn't think of flowers.
(B) I don't want any flowers.
(C) When are you having a party?
(D) Your mom's flowers are beautiful.
해석 소녀: 너는 엄마 생신 선물을 샀니?
소년: 아니 아직. 나는 그녀에게 무엇을 드려야 할 지 모르겠어.
소녀: 내 생각에 그녀는 꽃을 좋아하실 것 같아.
소년: ________________
(A) 난 꽃은 생각 못 했어.
(B) 나는 어떤 꽃도 원하지 않아.
(C) 너는 언제 파티를 할 예정이니?
(D) 너의 엄마의 꽃은 아름다워.
풀이 소년은 엄마의 생신 선물로 무엇을 드려야 할지 모르겠다고 했고, 소녀는 그녀가 꽃을 좋아하실 것 같다고 말했으므로 그런 생각은 하지 못했다고 응답하는 (A)가 정답이다.
Words and Phrases yet 아직

30. Girl: Wow! It's really hot today.
Boy: We have to cool off.
Girl: Let's go to the swimming pool.
Boy: ________________
(A) Is it hot enough?
(B) That's a great idea.
(C) I just love a surprise.
(D) Okay, what's your plan?
해석 소녀: 와! 오늘 정말 덥구나.
소년: 우리는 더위를 식혀야 해.
소녀: 우리 수영장에 가자.
소년: ________________
(A) 충분히 뜨겁니?
(B) 그거 좋은 생각이야.
(C) 나는 그냥 서프라이즈를 좋아해.
(D) 그래, 너의 계획은 뭐니?
풀이 소녀가 수영장에 가자고 했으므로 이에 동의하는 (B)가 정답이다.
Words and Phrases cool off 식히다 | surprise 뜻밖의 일, 놀라움

SECTION II READING AND WRITING

Part A. Sentence Completion (p.118)

1. A: Where is ___________?
B: Sorry, we ate all of it after dinner.
(A) I baked the cake
(B) the cake I baked
(C) the cake baked
(D) baked the cake

해석 A: 내가 구운 케이크는 어디 있어?
B: 미안해, 우리가 저녁식사 후에 전부 먹었어.
(A) 나는 케이크를 구웠다
(B) 내가 구운 케이크
(C) 구운 케이크
(D) 케이크를 구웠다

풀이 명사(구)가 들어가야 할 자리이므로 (B)가 정답이다. 일반적으로 분사가 단독으로 명사를 수식할 경우 분사는 명사 앞에 위치해야 하므로 (C)는 오답이다.

Words and Phrases bake 굽다, 구워지다

2. A: ___________ I go to the dentist today?
B: Of course. It's time for a checkup.
(A) Am
(B) Have
(C) Must
(D) Would

해석 A: 오는 꼭 치과에 가야 해?
B: 물론이지. 검진 받을 때야.
(A) 이다
(B) 가지다
(C) ~해야 하다
(D) ~할 것이다

풀이 조동사를 사용하여 의문문을 만들어야 하며, 치과에 가야한다는 의무의 의미를 담고 있으므로 (C)가 정답이다.

Words and Phrases dentist 치과, 치과의사 | checkup 검진

3. A: Did you see ___________ found the bag?
B: Yes, and I thanked him.
(A) when
(B) who
(C) what
(D) whom

해석 A: 누가 그 가방을 찾았는지 너는 봤니?
B: 응, 그리고 내가 그에게 고맙다고 했어.
(A) 언제
(B) 누가
(C) 무엇이
(D) 누구를

풀이 가방을 찾아 준 사람이 누구인지 보았다고 대답했으므로 누구인지를 묻는 (B)가 정답이다.

Words and Phrases thank 감사하다, 고마워하다

4. A: ___________ very dark outside.
B: Don't worry. My dad will drive you to your house.
(A) It get
(B) It was
(C) It going
(D) It's getting

해석 A: 바깥이 매우 어두워지는 중이다.
B: 걱정마. 나의 아빠가 너를 집에 태워다 주실 거야.
(A) 틀린 표현
(B) ~였다
(C) 틀린 표현
(D) (어떤 상태가) 되다

풀이 바깥이 점점 더 어두워지는 진행의 상태를 나타내므로 (D)가 정답이다.

Words and Phrases drive 태워다 주다

5. A: What will you do tonight?
B: I will go out for dinner ___________ I finish early.
(A) if
(B) for
(C) but
(D) and

해석 A: 너는 오늘 밤에 무엇을 할 거니?
B: 일찍 끝나면 저녁 먹으러 나갈 거야.
(A) (만약) ...면
(B) (왜냐하면) ...니까
(C) 그러나, 하지만
(D) 그리고

풀이 조건을 나타내는 접속사 (A)가 정답이다.

Part B. Situational Writing (p.119)

6. They are ___________.
(A) fishing
(B) watering
(C) feeding fish
(D) taking a walk

해석 그들은 낚시를 하고 있다.
(A) 낚시를 하고
(B) 물을 주고
(C) 물고기에게 먹이를 주고
(D) 산책을 하고

풀이 그림에서 그들은 낚시를 하고 있으므로 (A)가 정답이다.

Words and Phrases feed 먹이를 주다 | water 물을 주다

7. The cat has ___________.
(A) taken the cup
(B) drunk the milk
(C) broken the cup
(D) spilled the milk

해석 고양이는 우유를 쏟았다.

(A) 컵을 가져갔다

(B) 우유를 마셨다

(C) 컵을 깨트렸다

(D) 우유를 쏟았다

풀이 그림에서 고양이가 우유를 쏟았으므로 (D)가 정답이다.

Words and Phrases spill 쏟다

8. My shirt is too __________ for me.

(A) tight

(B) loose

(C) thick

(D) wide

해석 내 셔츠는 나에게 너무 꽉 낀다.

(A) 꽉 조이는

(B) 헐렁한

(C) 두꺼운

(D) 넓은

풀이 그림에서 소년은 딱 맞는 셔츠를 입고 있으므로 (A)가 정답이다.

Words and Phrases tight (옷이) 꽉 조이는 | loose 헐렁한, 느슨한 | thick 굵은, 두꺼운

9. She is looking into the __________.

(A) screen

(B) window

(C) closet

(D) mirror

해석 그녀는 거울을 들여다 보고 있다.

(A) 화면

(B) 창문

(C) 벽장

(D) 거울

풀이 그림에서 소녀는 거울을 보고 서 있으므로 (D)가 정답이다.

Words and Phrases closet 벽장

10. The boy is __________ the girl.

(A) behind

(B) next to

(C) in front of

(D) far away from

해석 그 소년은 소녀의 옆에 있다.

(A) 뒤에

(B) 옆에

(C) 앞에

(D) 멀리

풀이 그림에서 소년은 소녀의 옆에 있으므로 (B)가 정답이다.

Words and Phrases next to 옆에 | behind 뒤에

Part C. Practical Reading and Retelling (p.122)

[11-12]

OCEAN BEACH
CHILDREN'S ANIMATION FILM FESTIVAL
August 5-7

Feature Films (Sun Theater)		Classic Films (Star Theater)	
UP!	3:00 p.m	CINDERELLA	3:00 p.m
BOLT	4:30 p.m	101 DALMATIANS	5:00 p.m
MADAGASCAR	6:00 p.m	LION KING	6:30 p.m
TALE of DESPEREAUX	7:30 p.m	FINDING NEMO	8:00 p.m
WALL-E Late feature	9:00 p.m		

TICKET PRICES: Feature Films: $6.00 Classic Films: $4.00

11. Where are the feature films being shown?

(A) at Sun Theater

(B) at Star Theater

(C) at Beach Theater

(D) at Classic Theater

12. How much does it cost when you see UP and LION KING?

(A) 6 dollars

(B) 8 dollars

(C) 10 dollars

(D) 12 dollars

해석

OCEAN 해변

아이들의 만화 영화 축제

8월 5일-7일

장편 영화(Sun 극장)		고전 영화(Star 극장)	
Up!	3:00 p.m.	CINDERELLA	3:00 p.m.
BOLT	4:30 p.m	101 달마시안	5:00 p.m.
MADAGASCAR	6:00 p.m.	LION KING	6:30 p.m
DESPEREAUX의 이야기	7:30 p.m.	NEMO를 찾아서	8:00 p.m.
Wall-E 늦은 상영	9:00 p.m.		
표 가격: 장편 영화: 6달러 고전 영화: 4달러			

11. 장편 영화는 어디에서 상영 되는가?

(A) Sun 극장

(B) Star 극장

(C) Beach 극장

(D) Classic 극장

12. UP과 LION KING을 보려면 얼마를 시불해아 하는가?

(A) 6 달러

(B) 8 달러

(C) 10 달러

(D) 12 달러

풀이 장편 영화는 Sun 극장에서 상영된다고 했으므로 11번의 정답은 (A)이다.

장편 영화인 'UP'은 6달러이고 고전 영화인 'LION KING'은 4달러이므로 둘을 다 볼 경우 합이 10달러이므로 12번의 정답은 (C)이다.

Words and Phrases animation 만화 | feature film 장편 영화 | theater 극장 | classic film 고전 영화

[13-14]

13. How long has the restaurant been open?

(A) three years
(B) four years
(C) twenty years
(D) twenty-seven years

14. When can you have the two-for-one special?

(A) on Sunday
(B) on Monday
(C) on Wednesday
(D) on Friday

해석

The Pancake Mill 식당	
27주년 기념!	
아침-점심-파이 가게	
영업 시간 오전 6시부터 3시까지	
특선 1인분 가격으로 2인분을	
햄과 치즈 오믈렛	6달러
팬케이크 (소시지나 햄 중 고르시면 같이 나옵니다.)	5달러
딸기 팬케이크	4달러
1인분 가격으로 2인분을 제공하는 특선 메뉴는 일요일에만 가능합니다.	
월요일 점심 특선 5.99달러	
수요일 BBQ 점심-무제한 뷔페 5.99달러	

13. 이 식당은 얼마나 오랜 기간 영업해왔는가?

(A) 3년
(B) 4년
(C) 20년
(D) 27년

14. 1인분 가격으로 2인분을 제공하는 날은 언제인가?

(A) 일요일
(B) 월요일
(C) 수요일
(D) 금요일

풀이 광고에서 식당은 27주년을 기념한다고 했으므로 13번의 정답은 (D)이다.

1인분 가격으로 2인분을 제공하는 특선은 일요일에 가능하다고 했으므로 14번의 정답은 (A)이다.

Words and Phrases mill 방앗간 | celebrate 축하하다 | special 특별 상품 | all-you-can-eat 양껏 먹을 수 있는, 뷔페식의

[15-16]

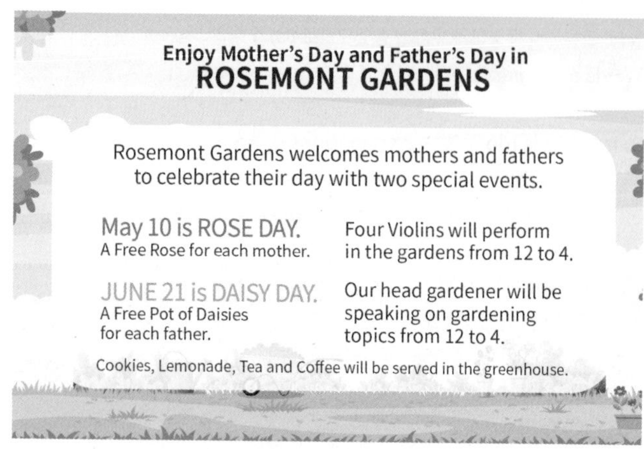

15. What will only mothers receive on May 10?

(A) a rose
(B) a daisy
(C) a violin
(D) a cookie

16. Where will visitors have tea?

(A) in the kitchen
(B) in the restaurant
(C) in the greenhouse
(D) in the rose garden

해석

어머니의 날과 아버지의 날을 즐기세요
ROSEMONT 정원에서
Rosemont 정원은 두 가지 특별 행사와 함께 그들의 날을 축하하기 위해 어머니들과 아버지들을 환영합니다.
5월 10일은 장미의 날. 각각의 어머니에게 무료 장미 한 송이.
4개의 바이올린이 12시부터 4시까지 정원에서 연주를 할 것입니다.

6월 21일은 데이지의 날. 각각의 아버지에게 무료 데이지 화분 하나.
우리의 부장 정원사가 12시부터 4시까지 정원 가꾸기 주제에 대해 말할 것입니다.
쿠키, 레모네이드, 차와 커피가 온실에서 제공될 것입니다.

15. 5월 10일에 어머니들은 무엇을 받는가?

(A) 장미
(B) 데이지
(C) 바이올린
(D) 쿠키

16. 방문자들은 어디에서 차를 마실 수 있는가?

(A) 부엌에서
(B) 식당에서
(C) 온실에서
(D) 장미 정원에서

풀이 5월 10일에는 어머니들에게 무료 장미를 한 송이씩 준다고 했으므로 15번의 정답은 (A)이다.

쿠키, 레모네이드, 차와 커피는 온실에서 제공된다고 했으므로 16번의 정답은 (C)이다.

Words and Phrases celebrate 축하하다 | perform 행하다, 공연하다 | pot 화분 | gardener 정원사 | gardening 정원 가꾸기 | serve 제공하다 | greenhouse 온실

[17-18]

UNIVERSITY SPORTS CAMPS
Boys and Girls Between 9 and 14 Years of Age

VOLLEYBALL	BASKETBALL	SOCCER
Girls Aug. 17-21 $120	Girls July 13-17 $125	Girls / Boys Aug. 24-27 $100
Girls / Boys Aug. 24-27 $120	Boys Aug. 10-14 $125	

Times: All school camps run from 9 AM to noon.

17. How much does it cost for the girls' basketball camp?
(A) one hundred dollars
(B) two hundred dollars
(C) one hundred and twenty dollars
(D) one hundred and twenty-five dollars

18. When do boys have basketball camp?
(A) July 13-17
(B) August 10-14
(C) August 17-21
(D) August 24-27

해석

대학교 스포츠 캠프
9세에서 14세 남자와 여자

배구 여자 8월 17-21일 120달러
남자/여자 8월 24-27일 120달러
농구 여자 7월 13-17일 125달러
남자 8월 10-14일 125달러
축구 남자/여자 8월 24-27일 100달러

시간: 모든 학교 캠프는 오전 9시에서 정오까지 운영됩니다.

17. '여자 농구 캠프' 비용은 얼마인가?
(A) 백 달러
(B) 이백 달러
(C) 백이십 달러
(D) 백이십오 달러

18. 남자들은 언제 농구 캠프를 하는가?
(A) 7월 13-17일
(B) 8월 10-14일
(C) 8월 17-21일
(D) 8월 24-27일

풀이 여자 농구 캠프 비용은 125달러라고 했으므로 17번의 정답은 (D)이다.

남자 농구 캠프 일정은 8월 10일부터 14일이라고 했으므로 18번의 정답은 (B)이다.

Words and Phrases university 대학교 | volleyball 배구

[19-20]

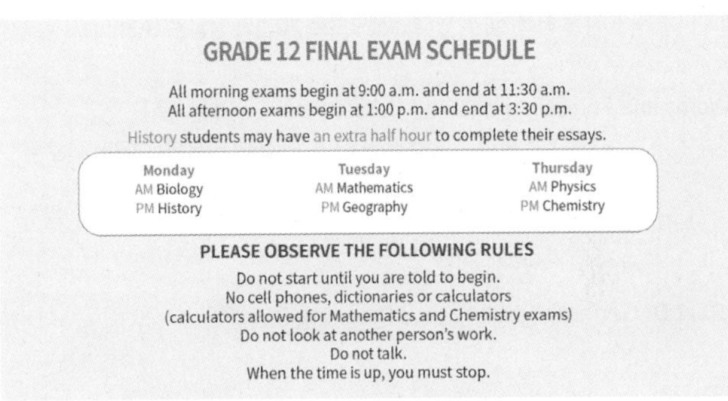
GRADE 12 FINAL EXAM SCHEDULE

All morning exams begin at 9:00 a.m. and end at 11:30 a.m.
All afternoon exams begin at 1:00 p.m. and end at 3:30 p.m.
History students may have an extra half hour to complete their essays.

Monday	Tuesday	Thursday
AM Biology	AM Mathematics	AM Physics
PM History	PM Geography	PM Chemistry

PLEASE OBSERVE THE FOLLOWING RULES
Do not start until you are told to begin.
No cell phones, dictionaries or calculators
(calculators allowed for Mathematics and Chemistry exams)
Do not look at another person's work.
Do not talk.
When the time is up, you must stop.

19. Which of the following exams permits a calculator?
(A) Biology
(B) Physics
(C) Chemistry
(D) Geography

20. Which exam has a four o'clock finish time?
(A) History
(B) Physics
(C) Chemistry
(D) Geography

해석

12학년 기말 시험 일정
모든 아침 시험은 오전 9시에 시작하고 오전 11시 30분에 끝납니다.
모든 오후 시험은 오후 1시에 시작하고 3시 30분에 끝납니다.
역사학 학생들은 에세이를 완성하도록 추가 30분을 더 가질 수 있습니다.
월요일 오전 생물 화요일 오전 수학 목요일 오전 물리학
오후 역사 오후 지리 오후 화학

다음 규칙에 따라주세요.
시작하라고 말하기 전까지 시작하지 마시오.
휴대폰, 사전, 계산기를 사용하지 마시오.
(계산기는 수학과 화학 시험에서 허용됩니다.)
다른 사람의 시험지를 보지 마십시오.
떠들지 마시오.
시간이 다 되면, 멈추어야 합니다.

19. 어느 시험이 계산기를 허용하는가?
(A) 생물학
(B) 물리학
(C) 화학
(D) 지리학

20. 어느 시험이 4시에 끝나는가?
(A) 역사
(B) 물리학
(C) 화학
(D) 지리학

풀이 계산기는 수학과 화학 시험에서 허용된다고 했으므로 19번의 정답은 (C)이다.

오후 시험은 3시 30분에 끝나지만, 역사학 학생들은 에세이를 완성하도록 추가 30분을 더 가질 수 있다고 했으므로 20번의 정답은 (A)이다.

Words and Phrases grade 학년 | essay 에세이, 과제물, 글 | observe 준수하다 | following 다음의, 다음에 나오는 | calculator 계산기

Part D. General Reading and Retelling (p.127)

[21-22]
At one time crocodile farms were popular in Australia. Visitors came to see saltwater crocodiles being caught because these crocodiles are so dangerous. They can grow up to 6.2 meters and weigh 1.5 tons. The shows were exciting for the visitors. In one show, a man put his head inside the open mouth of a crocodile. Today, most of the farms have closed. People began to think that dangerous crocodile shows were not such a good idea after all.

21. What is the best title for the passage?
(A) Tips on Feeding Crocodiles
(B) Last of the Crocodile Farms
(C) The Dangers of Saltwater Crocodiles
(D) Australia's Most Interesting Crocodiles

22. What happened to the crocodile farms?
(A) They became safer.
(B) They became less popular.
(C) They became more popular.
(D) They became more dangerous.

해석 한때 악어 농장은 호주에서 인기가 있었다. 방문객들은 바다악어들이 잡히는 것을 보려고 왔는데 그 이유는 이 악어들이 매우 위험하기 때문이다. 그들은 6.2미터까지 자랄 수 있고 1.5톤까지 나갈 수 있다. 쇼는 방문객들에게 흥미진진했다. 한 쇼에서, 한 남자가 악어의 벌린 입으로 머리를 집어넣었다. 오늘날, 대부분의 농장들은 문을 닫았다. 사람들은 위험한 악어 쇼는 결국 그렇게 좋은 생각이 아니었다고 생각하기 시작했다.

21. 다음 글에 가장 적절한 제목은 무엇인가?
(A) 악어에게 먹이를 주는 요령
(B) 악어 농장의 마지막
(C) 바다악어의 위험성
(D) 호주의 가장 흥미로운 악어들

22. 악어 농장들에 무슨 일이 있었는가?
(A) 그들은 더 안전해졌다.
(B) 그들은 인기가 떨어졌다.
(C) 그들은 더 인기가 많아졌다.
(D) 그들은 더 위험해졌다.

풀이 호주 악어 농장들의 마지막을 다루고 있으므로 21번의 정답은 (B)이다.

한때 방문객들에게 인기있었던 악어 농장은 오늘날 문을 닫았다고 했으므로 22번의 정답은 (B)이다.

Words and Phrases crocodile 악어 | saltwater 바다의 | after all 결국에는

[23-24]
Taste is one of the five senses, and there are four tastes that people have. The first taste is sweet. Try putting sugar or honey on your tongue. The second taste is salty. Try licking a little salt. The third taste is sour, the taste of a lemon, and the fourth taste is bitter. Bite into an olive or taste coffee. Taste is not the same as flavor. Flavor is the smell of a food with its taste.

23. Which of these has a sour taste?
(A) salt
(B) olives
(C) coffee
(D) lemons

24. What is flavor?
(A) the taste of a food
(B) the look of a food
(C) the taste and smell of a food
(D) the look and smell of a food

해석 맛은 오감 중 하나이고, 사람들이 가진 미각에는 네 가지가 있다. 첫 번째 맛은 단맛이다. 여러분의 혀에 설탕이나 꿀을 올려보라. 두 번째 맛은 짠맛이다. 소금을 조금 핥아 보아라. 세 번째 맛은 신맛, 레몬 맛이며, 그리고 네 번째 맛은 쓴맛이다. 올리브를 깨물거나 커피를 맛 보라. 맛은 풍미와 같지 않다. 풍미는 음식의 맛과 향기다.

23. 어느 것이 신맛이 나는가?
(A) 소금
(B) 올리브
(C) 커피
(D) 레몬

24. 풍미는 무엇인가?
(A) 음식의 맛
(B) 음식의 모양
(C) 음식의 맛과 향기
(D) 음식의 모양과 향기

풀이 신맛은 레몬 맛과 같다고 하였으므로 23번의 정답은 (D)이다.

풍미는 맛과 같지 않으며, 오히려 음식의 맛과 향기라고 했으므로 24번의 정답은 (C)이다.

[25-26]

One of the most well-known and popular games in the world is chess. Chess began over 1,600 years ago in India. It is a game that requires a lot of thinking about how the other player will move his or her game pieces. For many years scientists even tried to create a chess-playing computer. In 1997, Deep Blue became the first computer to win a chess game. It beat the world champion chess player, Garry Kasparov.

25. When did people start playing chess?

(A) in 1997
(B) 600 years ago
(C) 1,000 years ago
(D) 1,600 years ago

26. What is the name of the computer that won a chess game?

(A) India
(B) Deep Blue
(C) Blue Chess
(D) Garry Kasparov

해석 세계에서 가장 유명하고 인기 있는 게임 중 하나는 체스이다. 체스는 1,600년 전에 인도에서 시작되었다. 다른 플레이어가 자신의 게임 조각을 어떻게 움직일지에 대한 많은 생각을 요구하는 게임이다. 수년 동안 과학자들은 심지어 체스를 하는 컴퓨터를 만들려고 했다. 1997년에, Deep Blue는 체스 게임에서 우승한 최초의 컴퓨터가 되었다. 그것은 세계 챔피언 체스 선수인 Garry Kasparov를 이겼다.

25. 사람들은 언제부터 체스 게임을 하기 시작했는가?

(A) 1997년
(B) 600년 전
(C) 1,000년 전
(D) 1,600년 전

26. 체스 게임에서 우승한 컴퓨터의 이름은 무엇인가?

(A) India
(B) Deep Blue
(C) Blue Chess
(D) Garry Kasparov

풀이 체스는 1,600년 전 인도에서 시작되었다고 했으므로 25번의 정답은 (D)이다.

체스 게임에서 우승한 최초의 컴퓨터의 이름은 'Deep Blue'라고 했으므로 26번의 정답은 (B)이다.

Words and Phrases well-known 잘 알려진 | require 요구하다 | thinking 생각 | piece 조각 | create 창조하다 | beat 이기다

[27-28]

The most beautiful villages in Mexico are called the "Magical Villages." One of these villages is Tapalpa. The country around this village has high mountains, beautiful waterfalls and a green jungle. The houses and buildings in the village are some of the oldest in Mexico. The food is wonderful, and every week there are colorful festivals to enjoy. A trip to the magical village of Tapalpa is a surprise for many travelers to Mexico.

27. What is Tapalpa?

(A) a high mountain in Mexico
(B) the oldest village in Mexico
(C) a beautiful waterfall in Mexico
(D) one of Mexico's magical villages

28. How do many visitors feel when they first see Tapalpa?

(A) bored
(B) afraid
(C) magical
(D) surprised

해석 멕시코에서 가장 아름다운 마을들을 "마법의 마을들"이라고 한다. 이 마을들 중 하나는 Tapalpa다. 이 마을 주변 지역에는 높은 산, 아름다운 폭포 그리고 녹색 정글이 있다. 마을 내의 주택과 건물은 멕시코에서 가장 오래된 것들 중 일부이다. 음식은 훌륭하고, 매주 즐길 수 있는 다채로운 축제가 있다. 마법의 마을인 Tapalpa로의 여행은 멕시코를 여행하는 많은 여행객에게 놀라운 일이다.

27. Tapalpa는 무엇인가?

(A) 멕시코의 높은 산
(B) 멕시코의 가장 오래된 마을
(C) 멕시코의 아름다운 폭포
(D) 멕시코의 마법의 마을들 중 하나

28. 많은 방문객들은 Tapalpa를 처음 보았을 때 어떤 감정을 느끼는가?

(A) 지루함
(B) 두려움
(C) 마법
(D) 놀라움

풀이 멕시코에서 가장 아름다운 마을을 "마법의 마을들"이라고 하는데 이 마을들 중 하나가 Tapalpa라고 했으므로 27번의 정답은 (D)이다.

이 지역을 방문하는 많은 여행자들은 놀라움을 느낀다고 했으므로 28번의 정답은 (D)이다.

Words and Phrases village 마을 | country 지역, 고장 | jungle 정글 | traveler 여행자

[29-30]
Cleaning one's teeth is something people have done for a very long time. Long ago, people chewed on small sticks to clean their teeth. As the years passed, the sticks became bigger until they were the size of a pencil. One end was chewed until it became soft and like a brush. The first true toothbrush was made by the Chinese, who used animal hairs for the brush. This toothbrush was introduced to the rest of the world by travelers to China.

29. How did people clean their teeth before toothbrushes?
(A) They used pencils.
(B) They chewed on leaves.
(C) They chewed on small sticks.
(D) They chewed on animal hair.

30. Who introduced the toothbrush to the rest of the world?
(A) traveling doctors
(B) travelers to China
(C) Chinese dentists
(D) Chinese travelers

해석 이를 닦는 것은 사람들이 아주 오랫동안 해온 일이다. 오래전에, 사람들은 이를 닦기 위해 작은 막대기를 씹었다. 세월이 지날수록, 막대기는 연필 크기가 될 때까지 커졌다. 한쪽 끝은 그것이 부드러워지고 붓처럼 될 때까지 씹혔다. 최초의 진정한 칫솔은 솔을 위해 동물 털을 사용했던 중국인에 의해 만들어졌다. 이 칫솔은 중국을 여행하는 여행자들에 의해 전 세계에 소개되었다.

29. 사람들은 칫솔 이전에 어떻게 이를 닦았는가?
(A) 그들은 연필을 사용했다.
(B) 그들은 나뭇잎을 씹었다.
(C) 그들은 작은 막대기를 씹었다.
(D) 그들은 동물 털을 씹었다.

30. 누가 칫솔을 전 세계에 소개했는가?
(A) 여행하는 의사들
(B) 중국을 간 여행자들
(C) 중국 치과의사들
(D) 중국인 여행자들

풀이 오래전에 사람들은 작은 막대기를 씹어서 이를 닦았다고 했으므로 29번의 정답은 (C)이다.

중국으로 여행 온 사람들이 전 세계에 칫솔을 소개하였다고 했으므로 30번의 정답은 (B)이다.

Words and Phrases chew 씹다 | stick 막대기, 나뭇가지 | pass 지나가다, 흐르다 | toothbrush 칫솔 | hair 털 | introduce 소개하다 | rest 나머지, 다른 사람들